EMPLOYEE
REPORTS

EMPLOYEE REPORTS

*How to
communicate
financial information
to employees*

ANTHONY HILTON

Foreword by
Sir Ronald Leach, GBE, FCA

WOODHEAD-FAULKNER

Woodhead-Faulkner Ltd
8 Market Passage
Cambridge CB2 3PF

First published 1978

© Anthony Hilton 1978

ISBN 0 85941 057 9

Design: Ron Jones

Production: Book Production Consultants

Typesetting: Amos Typesetters, Hockley, Essex

Printed in Great Britain by Lowe & Brydone Printers Ltd, Thetford, Norfolk

FOREWORD

by Sir Ronald Leach, GBE, FCA
Past President, The Institute of Chartered Accountants in England and Wales

I recently took part in a small international conference, the subject of which was the position and responsibility of directors and the desirable constitution of boards. This conference included leading businessmen, trade union leaders and professors from several nations. After three days a surprisingly unanimous view emerged. Although under existing English law directors are deemed to be responsible only to shareholders, it was considered that this practice could no longer be looked on as acceptable under modern conditions. The view was taken that directors may now be considered to have responsibility to at least two groups, namely shareholders and those working in the business.

It follows that reporting by directors must be to a much wider audience than shareholders. This view was supported by a report issued to a working party of the Accounting Standards Committee in August 1975 entitled *The Corporate Report*. It also emerges strongly from the White Paper on the Conduct of Company Directors.

Although there it is probably generally accepted that employees should receive financial information (and the White Paper says that the annual report and accounts must be sent to all exployees) there are many different views as regards implementation and Mr Anthony Hilton's book contains, I believe, the most complete analysis and review of these problems which has so far emerged.

Since I was so closely interested in the produc-

tion of accounting standards consequent upon the formation of the Accounting Standards Committee in January 1970, it is right to comment that the accountancy profession has the task of deciding how financial transactions should be recorded and reported. It may seem academic to speculate as to what information should be given to employees and in what form, unless the basic principles of ascertaining profit are determined. This problem has been accentuated by the unfortunate debate on how the effects of inflation on company results should be recorded. Unless the accountancy profession can decide this with a reasonable measure of unanimity, how can one expect employees to place reliance on the information put before them? Unless account is taken of the effect of inflation on business results, a great many people can be deceived and form inaccurate opinions. However, I am hopeful that with the publication of the recent interim recommendation by the Accounting Standards Committee, definite progress will now be made on this issue.

It is trite to say that good communications are essential to good industrial relations. It is nevertheless true and I believe that the communication of generally acceptable financial and related data to all those concerned with businesses must make a substantial contribution.

I am sure that all those concerned with company reporting will find Mr Hilton's book fascinating and compulsive reading.

PREFACE

This book was written to help people. It was not written to lay down a prescribed formula for communicating with employees, nor to provide a model employee report, where all the management has to do is fill in the figures in the blank spaces. Rather, it was designed to stimulate management to think about the problems of employee communication, in the context of writing financial reports for their employees.

The idea of the book is to provide a focus for the debates which are continually raging within firms about how much information to give to employees, which employees should be given it, how the communication should be carried out and who in the management team should have the prime responsibility for doing it.

In the belief that the best way to see how much you can achieve in your own company is to look at what other firms are doing, and have achieved, it draws heavily on examples. Some of these come in for criticism, and I am sure that many of my criticisms will in turn attract criticisms from readers which will probably be equally, if not more, valid. The point is that, inevitably in such a new and sensitive area, personal taste plays a major part in deciding what is a good or not-so-good report. There are as yet no hard and fast rules in the business – and indeed it will be a sad day for the innovative and enterprising companies when there are. For among the most encouraging aspects of the study of employee accounts are the vigour and imagination which has gone into their preparation.

Communicating financial information to people who have no experience of dealing with company accounts is not going to be easy – but then few exercises which are really worthwhile ever are.

May I say that I hope that in spite of the difficulties, those charged with the task of drafting a report to employees will find something in this book which will make their task easier, and that they will have as much pleasure in writing an employee report as I have obtained from surveying their efforts.

A.V.H.

ACKNOWLEDGEMENTS

This book could not have been written without the goodwill and help of the very many companies which were willing to enter their employee reports for the competition organised by *Accountancy Age* and who thereby provided the raw material for comment and criticism, first in the magazine and later in this book. It is their book as much as it is mine.

In addition, many individuals gave unstintingly of their time and advice, of whom only a handful can be mentioned here. But I owe a particular debt to Leo Cavendish, Stanley Gale, Cass Robertson and Michael Branden, all of whom played a major part in helping me understand the range and depth of the reporting problem. I need hardly say that the misconceptions and mistakes which may remain are entirely my responsibility.

Finally, my thanks to Cathy Carr, who not only succeeded in transforming a near-illegible manuscript into copy suitable for the publishers, but contrived to remain cheerful while she did it.

CONTENTS

LIST OF ILLUSTRATIONS
(The illustrations are between pp 50 and 51)

LIST OF TABLES

PART ONE

THE CONCEPT OF THE EMPLOYEE REPORT

CHAPTER ONE

THE TREND IN DISCLOSURE LEGISLATION AND THE EVOLUTION OF THE EMPLOYEE REPORT

When Adam Smith was a boy it was possible to see the world as a series of nation states and to talk of international specialisation or self-sufficiency as alternatives, so that a country could, if it so desired, have nothing to do with its neighbours. That world, if it ever existed, is long gone now. The modern business universe is a miracle of integration, a marvel of modern communication so much taken for granted that it is only when something goes wrong that people really notice it is there.

And yet, amid this evident interdependence with other nations, the British in particular retain an odd, almost naïve, insularity in some of the most important areas of business life, and in particular in the area which is close to the heart of this book, namely employee participation and communications. We all of us tend, when considering the communications problem, to think purely in terms of our four company walls, and at a pinch the walls of Whitehall. But what this chapter will show is that this world is too small, and that no matter what we do in Britain over the next few years we shall still lag far behind what is happening, and has already happened, elsewhere in Europe.

The purpose of this opening chapter is to put the development of disclosure of information to employees in its legal and social context in the United Kingdom and to show how each bit of legislation added more to the obligations of employers. Then, the UK scene complete, we shall move across the Channel for a whirlwind tour of Europe to show how what seems terribly advanced here is really rather old hat by many Continental countries' standards. And yet it is by those Continental standards that we shall be judged, because the EEC harmonisation programme for company law will drag us up to the best of European practice; it will not pull the Europeans back down to our level in the sphere of industrial relations.

The problem of the conventional report

In an ideal world an employee would be able to pick up the annual report of his company and see immediately how his firm was doing. Any worries he might have could be instantly dismissed. He would see there and understand why his overtime had been cut back, or why the company was streamlining its product range.

In practice, it does not work like that. Even shareholders do not understand the shareholders' report, nor, if research is to be believed, do they read very much of it, preferring either blissful ignorance or (and not much better) to cull their information from the press.

The employee fares even worse, because much of the information in the shareholders' report is not relevant to him, being prescribed as it is in the United Kingdom by the Companies Acts or the Stock Exchange.

The improvements in disclosure standards in the past few years, with the parallel and vast proliferation of footnotes, add further strains and stresses to the report and accounts, to the extent that today there is considerable doubt whether the financial report achieves any meaningful communication with anybody. Even the accountants — who make their living out of producing such documents — have recognised there is a problem, although they cannot yet come up with the solution. So it is worth, right at the beginning, getting rid of the notion that the shareholders' report is any good at all for employees. But employee reports in themselves are not an easy option.

The trend in legislation on disclosure

Although it was hard to see it in any single Act, the trend of legislation in the late 1960s and early 1970s was in the direction of greater disclosure, and these trends came together in the Industrial Relations Code of Practice. This was born of the Industrial Relations Act 1971 and was one of the few sections to survive in its successor, the Trade Union and Labour Relations Act 1974.

The Code is significant because, not only does it call on employers to provide to employees the same information they give to shareholders —

something which few today would take exception to — but it states that this should be provided in the most convenient form. Many employers will consider their annual report the most convenient form, but on cost grounds alone there is a case for producing a shortened, more relevant version — an employee report.

However, the Code is not specifically concerned with reporting information to employees. It has as its aims the establishment and maintenance of stable negotiating institutions between management and employees and to promote consultation and communication at all levels. But it tries, too, to provide practical guidance to employers on what they could and should disclose and in Section 54 specifically refers to the need for management to give information to employees. Obviously, this could be done by word of mouth. But it makes a lot more sense to do it in writing — and back it up with verbal statements if you want to.

This Code is voluntary — although management will be unwise to ignore it. But there have been a great many changes in recent years in social and company law which management has no choice but to note. The pity of what has been done is that the law has had to be brought in to achieve what many companies were happy to do anyway.

Legislation is emotive. It puts people's backs up, even when it makes them do what they would have done in any case. But the significance of this law is in the way it reflects social attitudes and puts in context the quasi-legal beginnings of employee reports.

As we have just said, the fact that such reports should be coming to the fore now is a result of many conflicting legal and social pressures, and it is the force of these pressures which makes one believe that the employee report is here to stay. But it is interesting to note how rapid the progress has been. Just after the 1967 Companies Act, in fact in 1968, the Donovan Commission, which was an inquiry into trade unions and labour relations, could still be taken seriously as a major study, although it made no mention of the need for regular disclosure of financial information to employees. The following year, in the Labour Government's ill-fated Industrial Relations Bill, and in the Conservatives' scarcely more successful Act two years later, statutory disclosure clauses were included for the first time. Perhaps there was no evidence even then of any great commitment towards disclosure — but the Act was closely modelled on United States legislation, and there the disclosure of information is closely regulated by statute and case law.

By the mid 1970s, legislation was coming on stream, including the inept and much criticised Industry Act. But, contrary to popular belief, the bulk of British industry is not affected by the disclosure provisions of the Industry Act, the prime purpose of which was to set up the National Enterprise Board and create a framework for planning agreements between large industrial sectors and government. The firms affected are a handful of the largest of those engaged in the manufacturing sector.

The Industry Act is controversial, first in the nature of the information which companies can be made to supply to the Minister and which, in turn, may be passed on to trade unions, and second in the fines the company faces if it does not comply. That, at least, is the theory. But in practice the Act has been something of a dead letter. Even if it were not, it would benefit less the rank-and-file employee than the official union machine.

Meanwhile, separate strands were developing to cater more directly for employee needs. In 1972 came the first public mutterings that information might be provided as a right to employees. First the Commission on Industrial Relations produced draft guidelines on disclosure of information and suggested strongly that employees should receive at least what was sent to shareholders. The TUC in a separate venture that same year outlined key areas where it felt its members had a right to more information. The areas included sales, turnover, profits, the value of the company, and, significantly, plans for investment and expansion. (All of these are discussed in detail in Chapter 6, which shows that many companies today publish willingly almost everything the TUC was then asking for.)

The Health and Safety at Work Act, the next important piece of legislation, extended the legal obligations on employers to disclose information, but again the law went little further in its requirements than what many companies were already providing. It was, in many ways, a codification of the best practice in industry, and what it specifically required was that employers have, and publish, a safety policy which states that policy's principles, who is responsible for it and how it will be implemented. Devoting a page to safety in an employee report usually more than meets the requirements.

Other legislation came in the most unlikely forms — for example, the Finance Act of 1970 stipulated that if you want to run a tax-exempt pension fund then you have to tell the employees on whose behalf it is operating and what are its terms and benefits. The Social Security Act of 1975, continuing this theme, demanded that employers who wished to contract out of the new state pension scheme had to justify their decision with hard facts, backed up by consultation with the employees or their union representatives. Neither provision has any great significance in itself. But each piece of legislation seems to add another similar innovation. Put them together and you have a formidable package.

Most of what we have said so far, however, is concerned with the general question of disclosure of information to employees in specific areas and about specific subjects. It is not at this stage concerned with employee reports, and indeed it is conceptually quite a leap from the piecemeal and unco-ordinated disclosure requirements laid down by law to an integrated information programme designed purely for the employee, which is the employee report.

The first real reference to employee reports — in which they were named as such — was in the Tony Benn-inspired document *The Company and the Community*, which was a discussion paper produced by the Labour Party shortly after it came to power in 1974 advocating among many things that all companies should develop regular programmes of reporting to employees. Nothing came of the document.

Instead, to the alarm of the Left, the idea was seized on with vigour by the Conservative Party, notably Michael Heseltine, MP for Henley and one-time Minister for Industry in the Heath Government. What Benn had advocated initially was that all employees in companies with a workforce of over 500 either got the full report and accounts which companies had no obligation to give them, or should be provided with an acceptable variation. The CBI, initially, threw up its hands in horror — basically because of Benn's reputation on the "loony Left" — but following the Heseltine initiative, which was a circular letter to companies urging them to get the financial message across to the employees, there was a rapid changing of attitudes. Now it was the Left's turn to react, on the basis that anything the CBI and Heseltine thought was a good idea must have been a dreadful mistake. So although Benn's Green Paper eventually came to nothing, at least not directly, some similar thinking lay behind the next major item of legislation produced by the Labour Government — the Employment Protection Act — and this, unlike many of the other measures, really did make an impact.

The Employment Protection Act of 1975 was the real turning point — the moment when the information trickle became a flood. It achieved this by laying down the most stringent conditions to be followed before anybody could be made redundant, and, in contrast to the Industry Act, this affects every firm where there is a recognised trade union. So it casts its net much wider.

The root of its disclosure requirement is a demand that employers must tell unions what they need to know for collective bargaining purposes. The ill-fated 1971 Industrial Relations Act showed how Whitehall likes to take its industrial relations ideas from the Americans (and then wonders why they don't work here) and there are elements of American practice in this Act. In the United States, for example, the provision of information is specifically aimed to assist collective bargaining so that the unions are not negotiating in the dark but can bargain "in good faith", so enabling the market economy to function with maximum efficiency. The same thinking lies behind the teeth of the Employment Protection Act, where, if employers refuse to co-operate, they may ultimately have to deal with the Advisory Conciliation and Arbitration Service (ACAS), which basically will keep pestering them until a solution is found.

Given that the information to be disclosed is to assist in collective bargaining and the subjects to be bargained about not only vary between companies but are evolving fast; then this increasing sophistication means that both sides are going to need some high-quality information. Thus, while in the period shortly after the Act few if any firms were prepared to release performance indicators, investment plans and profit forecasts, it is inevitable that in a few years' time they will have to, because it is this form of information which is of most use. It is worth noting that the onus is on the union to ask for the information it wants. Therefore it is a relatively simple task for it to push back the frontiers of disclosure.

Disclosure and worker participation

So let us pause at this point to gather the two main threads. The first obvious point is that there will have to be much more formalised disclosure between the boards of companies and the unions. Union officials, for example, will shortly be entitled to have a voice in the formulation of pension fund policies — something which, up to now, has always been thought of as an exclusive prerogative of management.

Disclosure to employees is attractive because there is a lot of information which has to be put across by law and it can be used as the vehicle for this. It is attractive because it ties in with the mood of the times, which is to assist the employee to identify with the business, and to feel that his aims are best served by the success of the business.

And it is attractive, most of all, because it is symbolic. Management wants to be seen to be responding to the pressures of the time; it wants to be seen to be alert and aware. What better way of providing tangible proof of its willingness to respond than by producing an employee report. It is quick, it is cheap, it is new and it is seen by everyone. In short, it is a marvellous gimmick. But that is precisely the danger — that it does become simply a gimmick. This is one of the things which must be avoided from the outset, and the best way to achieve that objective is not to make false or over-ambitious claims for employee reports.

An employee report is only a part — and indeed a small part — of an employee communications programme. By itself it will probably not do much for employee/management relations, so it is important not to expect too much from it, particularly in the short term. But even if it isn't going to transform the industrial landscape overnight, it is still worth doing, worth putting thought into, and worth spending money on.

We must also consider Bullock. Without going into the pros and cons of the $2x + y$ formula for worker representation on the board, the point which has not been lost on anyone is that some form of worker participation will certainly evolve. And if this participation is to be channelled into productive ends — if it is to be the vehicle to release the latent energy of the employees at large — then it is going to have to be fuelled by a constant and ever more relevant flow of information. The alternative — participation without knowledge — is a formula for frustration and disaster. It seems, therefore, just a short time until the manager adds a new item to his monthly budget along with allocations for wages, rent, rates, advertising and PR — a separate and distinct allocation for expenditure on employee communications.

Few companies have this at the moment. Most lump it in either with public relations or with personnel costs, but they will not be able to get away with this much longer. For employee communications is a branch of management in its own right — as important as purchasing or selling or production — and at long last it is beginning to be recognised as such.

Then there is the employee report itself. It is immediately attractive perhaps for the wrong reasons, but reasons which are valid none the less.

Employee reporting in Europe

In the actual number of employee reports produced, the United Kingdom probably leads the world. However, in setting a social and industrial climate in which participation can be fostered, we seem well behind Europe. But even if early moves in this direction have been disappointing, the Continental experience suggests that there will have to be further attempts as we try to catch up with the advanced European countries.

A major objective of the European Economic Community is the harmonisation of European company law, and it is an objective which is causing great difficulty. Inevitably, however, the harmonisation which does take place will have repercussions on the information flow to employees.

The EEC harmonisation programme works by producing directives which deal with a specific aspect of company law. These are then thrashed around, drafted and redrafted until representatives of the member countries agree to the compromise. The final directive then goes forward to the Council of Ministers and if adopted goes to each of the countries for ratification and incorporation in their domestic laws. It is a long and tedious process.

Two of these directives will affect reporting. The "Fourth Directive" basically lays down the form and content of annual accounts. In this it leans heavily towards the Franco-German approach with all that this means in terms of strict rules for layout and valuations. It is a complete contrast to the more discretionary approach of the Americans and British, who like to produce what they think is a "true and fair" picture based on their judgement. However, the Fourth Directive, while it will alter the appearance of UK accounts, will not, in fact, require any fundamental changes in the information to be disclosed as opposed to the way that information is to be presented. Most of what is to be asked for is already covered one way or another in British accounts.

But do not let this relatively mild directive make you complacent. The advance of worker participation is the subject of a further "Fifth Directive". It will no doubt be adulterated in the course of negotiations and horse-trading, but even so, participation is much further advanced in other EEC countries and this is reflected in the Fifth Directive which proposes that all large companies should be run by a two-tier board. Where the company has more than 500 employees, then the employees would fill one-third of the seats on the upper tier — the supervisory board. Bullock has some powerful allies across the Channel.

The main point is that as the workers would be directors, the employees would have access to absolutely all the information about their company which was available. This makes rather a nonsense of worries of breaches of confidentiality caused by employee reports, and it is a timely reminder of how fast things are moving.

Also in the pipeline is an as yet unnumbered directive which will deal with information to go into prospectuses. This should have only an oblique effect on the employee. But it, and the others, underline the pace of change. The fact that it may take several years to flow through does not in any way diminish its inevitability. And it does reinforce the argument that companies should voluntarily do today what they are going to be forced to do tomorrow. At least they then have a chance to change in an orderly fashion, and get some credit for it.

But the EEC, advanced though its thinking is in some respects, is committed to unanimity, and to moving forward by agreement. Thus its proposals will always be a compromise, and appear distinctly old-fashioned when set against the *avant-garde* approach of other European countries. West Germany for instance, with a corporate structure imposed by the Allies after World War Two, now has an industrial relations system which is the envy of its neighbours. One consequence is that it has one of the most legalistic approaches in Europe to the dissemination of information. For example, under the Works Constitution Act of 1972 strict rules are laid down about what must be disclosed not just to works councils, but to individual employees in firms of more than 1000 people. In addition, the "co-determination clauses" require that one-third of the supervisory board in such companies must comprise employee representatives. So it is not difficult to see where the EEC is getting its ideas from.

But what, in practice, does the German company have to disclose? The following extract from the Act is instructive, because it shows that, apart from the one safeguard that they need not disclose trade and business secrets, there is little that the board can keep to themselves. For example, they must divulge manpower statistics, manpower planning, the logic behind the company wage structure, the absolute levels of wages and salaries and key performance indicators on costs, revenues, profits and the order book. In addition, the company has to be specific on its future plans

and general economic prospects. Thus the relevant section of the Act reads:

"The employer shall inform the finance committee in full and in good time of the financial affairs of the company and supply the relevant documentation in so far as there is no risk of disclosing the trade or business secrets of the company, and demonstrate the implications for manpower planning.

"The following, *inter alia,* are financial matters covered by this provision:
1. the economic and financial situation of the company;
2. the production and marketing situation;
3. the production and investment programmes;
4. rationalisation plans;
5. production techniques and work methods, especially the introduction of new work methods;
6. the reduction of operations in or closure of establishments or parts of establishments;
7. the transfer of establishments or parts of establishments;
8. the amalgamation of establishments;
9. changes in the organisation or objectives of establishments; and
10. any other circumstances and projects that may materially affect the interests of the employees of the company."

In addition, the German system gives responsibility and a fair degree of power to the works councils and trade unions to make sure that the spirit of the Act is followed. Each production unit has its own works council and if it feels it is being obstructed and not getting the information to which it is entitled, it can appeal to the local labour court. This can actually imprison as well as fine offenders, but it uses these powers only in exceptional circumstances, preferring instead to work through conciliation and arbitration.

Works councils in Germany also have the responsibility to educate their membership, the employees, which they normally do by running programmes of education in company affairs, through publications and at special meetings. The councils deal with education at the plant level whilst the trade union operates at a national level with responsibility to provide information on national, economic and social questions.

Next to West Germany in terms of economic power comes France. There is no direct legislation on disclosure as such but there are two Acts which have direct bearing on the provision of information — one passed just after the war to lay down the formula for works councils and a second passed in 1970 which provided for a national minimum wage, and which laid down the framework for corporate wage bargaining. In addition there is a voluntary agreement within the UIMM — a major employers' organisation which seeks to bring about an orderly expansion of education and information flow within the member companies.

French industrial society however has been in a state of flux, with power first slowly switching from the local works councils to the national unions which brought an increase in collective bargaining, moving back again with the recent growth of plant bargaining. The growth of information programmes has been equally disjointed and, much more than in Britain, has run foul of politically based opposition from the unions.

But where France really has made progress is in the field of social accounting — a technique which seeks to measure the social responsibility of business, and which is clearly a giant step on from the traditional realms of accounting thought. *The Corporate Report*, the discussion paper prepared by the UK-based Accounting Standards Committee, which investigated the scope and aims of financial statements, made the following comments on social accounting:

"Through legislation, society is imposing duties on business enterprises to comply with anti-pollution, safety and health and other socially beneficial requirements. Legislation of this type seems likely to increase in the future.

"Such regulations impose new costs, formerly borne by the community generally, on individual enterprises. There is good reason therefore for requesting such compulsory expenditure to be reported. Equally good arguments can be put forward for disclosing expenditure of this nature undertaken voluntarily.

"It is tempting to propose that entities disclose information which will show their impact on, and their endeavours to protect society, its amenities and environment. In our opinion such a proposal would be impractical at the present time since the necessary generally agreed measurement techniques are not available.

"We believe that social accounting (the reporting of those costs and benefits, which may or may not be quantifiable in money terms, arising from economic activities and substantially borne or received by the community at large or particular groups not holding a direct relationship with the reporting entity) will be an area of growing concern to the accounting profession and one in

which it has an opportunity to help develop practical reporting techniques."

Taking a lead, to a small extent, from *The Corporate Report*, and still more from the United States, where the Department of Health, Education and Welfare produced a searching document *Towards a Social Report*, the French have made positive steps in this direction in the shape of the Sudreau Report on company law reform. The US document pointed to the impact of corporate behaviour on health, social mobility, the environment, crime and education without setting any particular standards on how these should be measured. Sudreau recommends, on the other hand, that companies draw up an annual social balance sheet based on indicators of its social situation and working conditions. They are therefore less comprehensive than the US ideas.

Coupled with the social balance sheet, Sudreau calls for an annual employment report which draws heavily on existing practice in the Netherlands as required there under the labour legislation. This will contain information on pay, working hours, staff structure, job advancement, the social environment and the social contribution — all phrases which could mean companies tell a great deal of virtually nothing, depending on how they interpret them. Unfortunately not many reports are available in English. However, the Roussel Uclaf engineering group, which with 10,000 employees is a large firm by any standards, has actually translated its report into English. In eight A4-size pages it covers topics such as numbers and geographical distribution (worldwide) of staff, staff turnover and absenteeism, job security, pay and profit-sharing, working environment and safety, involvement of employees in group development and inter-staff communication.

Before leaving the topic of social accounting it is worth noting that it is destined to become increasingly popular. There has been some notable work in West Germany, the Netherlands and the Scandinavian countries, though proposals there are still a long way from becoming law, and there have been interesting if politically naïve efforts in Britain from organisations like Social Audit — financed by the Rowntree Trust — and Counter-Information Services. But to get grass roots support for social accounting a much greater level of awareness in the community at large is needed about how companies work. At the moment, as we see every day in the streets around us, in the places where we work, on television and in the newspapers, this awareness does not exist.

The move to educate employees is emerging in some countries as a counterweight to the deficiencies of the traditional published accounts. While the level of disclosure in the Netherlands, the United States and Britain is quite high, countries like Italy provide notoriously little real information in the statutory accounts. Even West Germany and France sometimes seem deficient in this respect. But it is one of the smaller nations which has made the greatest progress. Belgium has had, since 1974, detailed rules for supplying information to works councils and these have, as a specific object of policy, to enable the employee to understand better the way in which the company operates. Belgian practice also has some interesting hints on when this information should be provided and has moved a long way from the idea of a once-a-year report. But as it is specifically concerned with works councils the problems are slightly different.

What the Belgians have done is categorise the information that firms have to supply into four different time periods. The first information is termed basic, and is just that. It is to be conveyed to each works council member within two months of his election and covers such information as the constitution of the firm; its competitive position in the market; its financial structure; production and productivity levels; the budget; calculations of costs; staff expenditures; the research programme; cash received from the government; future prospects; plans and an organisational chart. This information, though regarded as basic, obviously goes a lot further than the average employee report in the United Kingdom. But there is much more. In the next category, described as "periodic" information, which means that it is supplied roughly once a quarter, management has to provide up to date trading information — changes in orders, sales, markets and production levels, adjustments in costs, prices, stocks and productivity, and any fluctuations in employment levels. In addition it has to produce the current management budget and a statement of short term management objectives. Then on an annual basis, in contrast to the management information, the works council is provided with a financial review which analyses the company's financial stability and the availability of cash; how well it has performed against the targets set at the beginning of the year and what the future holds in terms of profitability and prospects.

A company could find an excuse to avoid the Act. But it appears with the passage of time that companies are becoming more and more at ease with the system and proving much less willing to invoke confidentiality unless they have really deep-seated fears about the results of giving too much away. There is also the problem for the management that the works councils have the right of appeal to the Ministry of Economic Affairs, where they can try to have the waiver overturned. This acts as a deterrent to management's over-zealous use of the confidentiality clauses.

In Italy, as has been mentioned, they don't believe in disclosing much to anybody, not even (or perhaps especially) to the taxman, and it is no real surprise to find there are no rules on the disclosure of information to employees. There are, however, various voluntary agreements which taken together provide a framework for the exchange of information on trade union rights, redundancies and economic trends. In general, however, the employees are still identified firmly with the company and there is no separate system of reporting to them.

The Netherlands, as you might expect from our earlier comment, is further down the line. The Works Council Act of 1971 gave the Councils statutory rights to information. It is the purpose of the law to give the works councils a detailed insight into the level of profitability of the company — before the profits are distributed — and to see how well the different parts of the company are performing. In general, however, the information provided does not go further than that which you would expect in the annual report of a British public company.

The industrial climate in the Netherlands is quite different from the rest of Europe in the degree of central control of the economy — particularly the control of wages, since 1945 — and it is much harder for the employer to use confidentiality as an excuse for keeping quiet. He can legally withhold personal details about his own income or wealth, but not much else.

In the Scandinavian countries, Denmark, Norway and Sweden, all of which at one time or another have been held up as a model, the problem is slightly different. All three have worker representation on the board either directly, as in Denmark, or on the supervisory board, or via the "corporate assembly", in Norway, and on an experimental basis on the board, in Sweden. So there is basically no problem about access to information. But again there is little of direct relevance to Britain in that, in general, the companies are small and there is still, in spite of the board representation, continued difficulty in getting the employees involved with the financial side of the business.

In Sweden the unions and employers also have an agreement to set up joint audit committees which will prepare and review information about companies — which will then be available for distribution — and in cases of dispute the union may appoint its own "workers' auditors". The Government, meanwhile, has launched a major educational programme to make employees and school children aware of finance and industrial organisation (though this has met opposition) and has also made it compulsory for companies to open their books to unions.

What this analysis does show is that the communications systems which are developing are firmly rooted in the legal and social framework of the country concerned and they are unlikely therefore to transplant easily. But it also suggests that the employee in Britain, France or Germany tends to be worried about the same problems, and appears to want similar information. The form in which he is given information may be different but there will be substantial similarities in the content.

But if companies are swamped with what has happened so far they had better learn fast to tread water, for the tide of legislation is not going to stop now. There seems little doubt that Britain will follow the thinking in Europe. Indeed, as early as 1974, there were signs that this was happening, when a Labour Party policy group produced suggestions for legislation which would require a two-tier board of which half the members of the supervisory board would be appointed by trade unions — and these employee representatives would have been entitled to call for information. The Bullock proposals published in 1977 call for even more direct worker involvement on the actual main board of the company, and the TUC had earlier proposed that companies of more than 200 people should have a two-tier board with half the supervisory board consisting of representatives of employees.

Inevitably therefore, the demand for information is here, and here to stay. There can be no more telling reason for producing a report for employees.

CHAPTER TWO

CORPORATE REPORT VERSUS EMPLOYEE REPORT

The annual report of the British public company is one of the most informative documents produced by any business organisation anywhere in the world. Even in comparison with the United States, which prides itself on its Securities Law and feels that it sets the ultimate standard in company reporting, the typical UK report stands up well. Nor has its development stopped. Indeed, quite the opposite has happened over the past decade so that each year now brings a further disclosure requirement and a further tranche of information for the reader of the accounts.

But what this chapter will do is first show the efforts being made to extend the scope of annual reports, and then discuss the direction of their evolution in the future, so that by the end of the chapter it should be apparent that no amount of evolution in the traditional report will be enough for it to satisfy the demands and the conflicting interests of those who want to find out what is going on. The annual report is a worthy document but it is now being asked to do too much.

Back in the early 1970s a well-known retailer hit trouble and decided to spell out to the employees what its problems were. But for some reason, what it told the employees did not quite tally with what it had been, and was, telling the Stock Exchange. The differences were spotted by the Press which picked up the discrepancy and demanded some explanation as to which story was true. The damage to the credibility and standing of the company's management was acute.

You can take that cautionary tale several ways. You could claim the company would have had no problems at all if it had told the employees nothing. But what about the rumours, to say nothing of the social pressure and legal responsibilities of our time? A second possible moral from the case is that you should not report separately to employees at all. They should merely be given the annual report and left to struggle through it, just like the shareholders. This way there is no risk of the two sets of information being

in conflict. Then there is the third way, which is to produce an employee report which is honest, hard-hitting and relevant to its audience. Showing how to do this is the purpose of this book.

But why bother? A lot of companies want to stick with the one annual company report in spite of its limitations. Why is it that they are prepared to dig in their heels?

Arguments in favour of a single company report

The most powerful argument for sticking with the company report and it alone is that no-one accuses you of being patronising and gimmicky and of peddling propaganda — all of which are the usual charges levelled at employee reports. But there is great irony in this, for the typical corporate report is frequently prepared by a public relations expert, and even if it is not, it is rare indeed to see one which is not patronising, gimmicky and peddling propaganda. A vast number of chairman's statements are patronising — they gloss over problems and fail to explain decisions because they feel the shareholder is not interested, won't understand and only cares about his dividend. They are gimmicky — all those glossy pictures of new machines and products — loaded with visual impact but really telling you very little about the company. And on the propaganda side it is rare indeed to read a report which has no political overtones, which totally resists the opportunity to take a sideswipe at government or opposition. Such swipes may indeed be justified, but they are propaganda none the less.

An obvious example of this comes in the accounts of Sheffield steelmaker Samuel Osborn, which has published a corporate code of conduct in its annual report for some time. This statement tackles the question of what responsibilities a company has beyond those it owes under the law to shareholders. "Whilst a company has a duty to its shareholders and others who provide capital for the company," it says, "it also accepts a duty to its employees, customers and suppliers. The company must also have regard to the public interest, both locally and nationally."

Osborn does not appear to think that these goals are incompatible with maximum profitability. The code of conduct continues: "In pursuing the maximum profit from the operations of the company, employees must so arrange prices, wages, salaries and supplies, so that the concepts in this code are observed."

Fane Vernon, chairman of Midlands engineers Ash and Lacy, opens his annual report with this statement of the objectives of the company:

"The prime objective of our company is to earn the maximum possible profits per share. High profits help to achieve
– maximum job security for our employees
– pride and satisfaction in our work and in our company
– better opportunities for promotion at all levels
– increasing dividends for our shareholders
– money for reinvestment
– the confidence of our suppliers and financial backers
– customer satisfaction and loyalty

"We seek to achieve all these desirable objectives by making the best use of all our resources and by securing the total commitment of each employee to the success of his or her company or unit."

That is old-fashioned capitalism and it has the virtues of clarity and consistency, whatever you may think about its appropriateness in the second half of the twentieth century. Note that it does not assume any conflict between high profit and the interests of suppliers and employees. In a free market system everyone, according to this theory, benefits from higher profits.

Adapting this sort of approach does impose strains. The shareholder may or may not accept the philosophy inherent in the report but if he doesn't like it he can always sell the shares. The employee does not really have such a simple choice, partly because the relevance of the philosophy to him is less clear-cut, and more importantly because he is unlikely to leave his employment because he disagrees with the philosophy of the chairman. But the point is that the same document does not really meet the needs of these two distinct users. And trying to distort it to meet different needs creates continued problems.

But some companies will put up with these difficulties because they believe passionately that a separate report has the definite inference that it is designed for a person of lesser intelligence. One

can sympathise with their concern, but really in this circumstance, it is misplaced. First, the argument confuses intelligence with knowledge. One should never underestimate the intelligence of the employee, but it is just as important never to overestimate his knowledge. What this means, in effect, is that the average employee will not fail to understand the normal annual statement because he lacks intelligence. He will fail to understand because he lacks the knowledge even of the most basic rudiments of how the financial world operates. Nor is he alone in that. No-one expects a shop steward to read a balance sheet, even although it is the key to his future, the statement of risk which shows whether the company is likely to stay in business for the next twelve months.

A man on the shopfloor who can work out a yankee on the afternoon racing at York could equally well turn his mind to a balance sheet. But a lot of experience has gone into those betting calculations, and he can see the point of them. He cannot, at the moment, see the point of understanding financial statements. Such inauspicious beginnings do not bode well for the attitude of the shopfloor, and particularly the shopfloor member in the firing line, the shop steward, to employee accounts, or the traditional report. It should not really be a surprise that when presented with financial information from management he rejects it.

Therefore, the separate report is simplified because it needs to start from first principles to establish a foundation on which to build. While it is obviously desirable for all employees to aspire to understanding the published accounts, it is not going to happen in this generation — not unless our educational system in the schools is transformed and the report itself altered beyond belief.

Another often stated protest is that if there is only one recognised source of facts on a company, then finding out about that company is relatively easy — the information is either in that source or it is not available, so you know where you are. But the more the number of sources multiply and the more companies have to produce different sets of information for different groups on a segmented and piecemeal basis then the harder it is in some ways to form a picture of the company. The argument, therefore, for one report is that you avoid these discrepancies and these dangers. But it is not a realistic argument for these times, for even if the employee does not get his report, companies are still going to have to provide multiple information to the shareholder, the Inland Revenue, and the Price Commission, to name but three. Thus the advocates of the one report are really ignoring reality. At the root of their argument is the fear that because communication is difficult, because it causes problems and because it may backfire, then they don't want to do it. It's the old argument that the way to get ahead is never to take a risk because that way you never get caught out. As a philosophy it may have, depressingly, the attraction of success, but it is not the management approach which solves problems. You can avoid trouble for a long time and delay the day of reckoning for longer still, but you will get caught out in the end. The secret therefore is to communicate and when you do it, to do it well. You won't avoid problems, but you might just solve them.

Another argument in favour of using the company report to provide information to employees is more subtle. It is an argument put forward very strongly by Peter Prior of H. P. Bulmer, the cider manufacturers, and a man who embodies much of what is best in defining management in terms of leadership, rather than in terms of control. It is wrong in principle to prepare a special report for employees he says, adding, "At present we certainly err on the side of passing on more information than is really necessary to the shareholders, since auditors, often pedantic rather than practical, encourage directors in the average company report to cover detail with excessive zeal. But there is little evidence to indicate that the average shareholder is more intelligent or more discerning than the average worker."

If participation means anything, says Prior, it means an end to "them and us". If it is to be successful it has to identify that common interest between shareholder and employee in the prosperity and growth of the company. The annual report, as a document going to both employee and shareholder, would be a very powerful symbol of this common interest. An employee report on the other hand, as a simplified, less comprehensive document, would go quite the other way. It would serve to emphasise the gulf, especially if — as is often the case — the employee report is a tatty shadow of the glossy product that goes to shareholders.

Prior believes it is better to provide the employee with the full report accompanied by an informal exposition taking up certain important features of the figures in a simple way. This, he says, should also be sent to the shareholders. His views find an echo with P. J. Munyard, group financial controller of Braham Millar. He makes the point forcibly that he does not like the term "employee accounts", because it is "unnecessarily patronising. It is based on the assumption that none of our employees would understand the normal accounts and therefore a simple form needs to be devised."

But Prior's argument seems to be one about semantics rather than principle. He, like Munyard, refuses to underestimate the intelligence of the employee. But he also admits that there is a problem in that the annual report today does not communicate information effectively — either to employees or to its primary audience, the shareholders. So Prior accepts that something needs to be done, and using his company newspaper he in fact produces a simplified version of the report. The only real difference is that Prior feels this is just as vital for the shareholder as it is for the employee, and he makes sure the shareholder gets it. The weakness of Prior's argument in the present business climate is that we are not producing the kind of company report which is up to the job which he wants it to perform. The company report produced today barely communicates with shareholders, and if it were to convey information to both shareholder and employee it would need to be considerably modified.

There is a lot to be said for companies sending these reports to their shareholders as a matter of course. Braham Millar does, so that the recipient, shareholder or employee, "can decide for himself which he wants to read." Other companies do likewise, because it is the simplest and most effective way of ensuring that the employees are told nothing which the shareholders do not know. It is not always possible — particularly in large organisations which produce many reports, each with its own local flavour — but if both groups can get the same report then not only will many shareholders find it more useful but it might even prevent the creation of a further divide between the two.

Recommendations of the Accounting Standards Committee report

This is where the accounting profession, to its great credit, produced a most thoughtful document. Called *The Corporate Report*, it was produced by a working party chaired by Derek Boothman, an unusual accountant in that he combined both business and professional practice to great success. He therefore brought to the job a wide experience, and the results of this came through in his committee's work. *The Corporate Report* broke new ground in several major areas. Perhaps most important, it recognised that the company had a responsibility to report to people other than the shareholders. "In our view", it said, "the fundamental objective of corporate reports is to communicate economic measurements of, and information about, the resources and performance of the reporting entity useful to those having reasonable rights to such information." This obviously recognises interests which go far beyond those of the shareholder, and it suggests responsibility for management and directors which go far beyond the traditional stewardship function.

But which people, other than the shareholders, have these rights? The report spells them out and if the list shows nothing else, it proves how much of an issue the accountability of companies in society has now become. The users of annual reports — those who, in the words of the committee, have "reasonable rights to information concerning the reporting entity" — include the following:

the equity investor group
the loan creditor group
the employee group
the analyst–adviser group
the business contact group
the government
the public

In other words, the authors of *The Corporate Report* think that virtually every section of society has a specific or a general interest in the company's performance, and have a right to find out or be told how it has performed. What they are saying is, in fact, tacitly recognised in the political and business life of the United Kingdom today. But it is still a surprise to hear it coming from accountants — even *avant-garde* accountants. Clearly they feel the truths they preach to be, if not self-evident, at least clearly established as part of the conventional wisdom.

But to support this wide accountability of industry, the report makes the following claim — which is, in fact, the premise on which the whole argument rests. It says first, "Our basic approach has been that corporate reports should seek to satisfy, as far as possible, the information needs of users." So far, so good. But it then adds, "We believe there is an implicit responsibility to report incumbent on every economic entity whose size or format renders it significant. This responsibility arises from the custodial role played in the community by economic entities." In other words, because companies draw from the community scarce economic resources, they have a responsibility to explain and justify to that community how these resources have been used. It is because of this basic assumption, which is again totally in

keeping with the spirit of the times, that the authors can identify and isolate such a wide ranging collection of interest groups who are potential users of accounts.

Having isolated those to whom the company had a responsibility to report, the document then went on to demonstrate the kind of information it felt should be communicated. In doing this it introduced several new concepts and brought out whole new areas of corporate responsibility. Simply listing the headings as we can only do here may not do justice to the richness and variety of the individual topics, but it at least impresses with its volume. According to the committee, reports of the future might include information which will help the reader:

evaluate the performance of the business;
assess the effectiveness of the company in fulfilling its objectives. These objectives may have been set, not just by management but by its members, its owners or by society itself. (Compliance with the obligations of stewardship is necessary but by no means sufficient for this section.)
evaluate managerial performance, efficiency and objectives including employment, investment and profit distribution plans;
ascertain the experience and background of company directors and officials. This should include details of other directorships and official positions;
assess the economic stability and vulnerability of the reporting business;
assess the liquidity of the business, its present and future requirements for additional fixed and working capital and its ability to raise long-term and short-term finance;
assess the capacity of the entity to make future reallocations of its resources, for either economic or social purposes or for both;
estimate the future prospects of the entity, including its capacity to pay dividends, remuneration and other cash outflows and predicting future levels of investment, production and employment;
assess the performance, position and prospects of individual establishments and companies within a group;
evaluate the economic function and performance of the entity in relation to society and the national interest and the social costs and benefits attributable to the entity;
attest to compliance with taxation regulations, company law, contractual and other legal oblig-

ations and requirements (particularly when independently verified);

ascertain the nature of the entity's business and products;

make economic comparisons, either for the given entity over a period of time or with other entities;

estimate the value of users' own or other users' present or prospective interests in or claims on the entity.

ascertain the ownership and control of the entity

To put across this information in a way which would not totally swamp the reader, the authors suggested six new additional statements which should be included in all annual reports. Between them the six would supply the bulk of the information required. It is worth quoting this section in full. It says:

"We recommend that, where appropriate, corporate reports contain the following statements in addition to those now current:

a. A statement of value added, showing how the benefits of the efforts of an enterprise are shared between employees, providers of capital, the state and reinvestment. This statement will assist users to evaluate the economic performance of the entity.

b. An employment report, showing the size and composition of the workforce relying on the enterprise for its livelihood, the work contribution of employees and the benefits earned. This report will assist users in assessing the performance of the entity, evaluating its economic function and performance in relation to society, assessing its capacity to make reallocations of resources and evaluating managerial performance, efficiency and objectives.

c. A statement of money exchanges with government, showing the financial relationships between the enterprises and the state. This statement will assist users to assess the economic function of the entity in relation to society.

d. A statement of transactions in foreign currency showing the direct cash dealings of the reporting entity between this country and abroad. This statement will assist users to judge the economic functions and performance of the entity in relation to society and the national interest. It may also provide information of assistance in assessing the stability and vulnerability of the reporting

entity and in estimating its capacity to make future cash payments.

e. A statement of future prospects, showing likely future profit, employment and investment levels. This statement will assist users to evaluate the prospects of the entity and to assess managerial performance.

f. A statement of corporate objectives showing management policy and medium term strategic targets. This statement will assist users to evaluate managerial performance, efficiency and objectives."

It goes on to say that "It is impractical to suggest that the needs of all users could be entirely met by a general purpose report." What this amounts to, of course, is an open request for reports on the lines of employee accounts, which will give specialised information to specific groups. Indeed, the report says later "We strongly support the production of simplified versions and special interest extracts of corporate reports."

All this is, of course, a vast amount to absorb at any one time, and the authors of *The Corporate Report* were not naïve enough to assume that all which they thought of as of value would happen overnight. But they have already made a significant degree of progress in getting their ideas accepted, and one company, Blackwood Hodge, went so far as to model its report on the committee's suggestions. The reader wishing to see how this looked in practice can see some of the key pages reproduced here as extracts from the annual accounts of 1975 [Fig. 1].

The Blackwood Hodge example is instructive because here was a company which did, in fact, try, using the best ideas available at the time, to produce the "all-purpose" report — designed to satisfy all interest groups. By and large however, the board was disappointed with the response which greeted their initiative — for they found that the wider audience for which the report was designed failed to materialise. It was as if the preconceptions about the annual report, and the entrenched ideas about what it should contain, were so deep-rooted that they ruled out the possibility of attracting a wider audience. Those who were used to reading annual reports — mainly the analysts, the press and a few shareholders — responded warmly to the new-look accounts. But the employees, who were obviously the major new group the board hoped to attract, were not enthusiastic.

What this would suggest, if not prove, is that a company report cannot be all things to all men.

The Corporate Report did in fact recognise this danger — it saw that one report would be too bulky — and it suggested that special reports might be prepared for the different interest groups. This, not surprisingly, found little favour with the accountants at large, because they felt that a proliferation of small reports would inevitably serve to undermine the traditional big one — the annual report to shareholders — in the production of which the accountancy profession has a major influence. Without wishing to make too much of the point it is possible that the resistance to this proposal among accountants owed more to the fact that they saw their traditional influence being undermined, rather than that they basically doubted the merits of the proposal itself.

Certainly, there are no such doubts in the mind of Derek Boothman. To his mind the employee report is the most significant embodiment so far of the principles he was trying to outline.

It is certainly true that *The Corporate Report* is an ideal starting point for anyone seeking to produce employee accounts. The themes and concepts promoted by it have formed the basis of many companies' early efforts in communicating with their employees.

We have seen, then, that one annual report cannot be all things to all men, but there are still arguments for and against, so we can expect to have annual reports around — and improving — for a long time yet. Change and the ability to adapt to change are the life blood of any organisation, and one of the longer term objectives of employee reports should be to increase employee understanding and thereby make employees more willing to accept and co-operate in change. It is important therefore that management shows itself prepared to change too.

CHAPTER THREE

WHY COMPANIES PRODUCE EMPLOYEE REPORTS

Theoretical reasons

Academics looking at the question of why companies have produced employee reports have isolated four reasons, and the purpose of this chapter is to match their theory against what companies say happens in practice.

What are the supposed reasons?

First, imitation. "Everyone else is doing it, so our company ought not to be left behind."

Second, propaganda. The company pays a lot in tax, or is being slowly throttled by mistaken government policies, and it is high time the employees (and the public at large) were made to realise what is going on.

Third, public relations — the approach which tries to say, "Aren't you lucky to be working for such a great company as this?"

And, finally, education. There is partly a genuine desire to make employees more fully aware of the underlying problems of business life and partly the feeling that if employees are educated in the facts they will be less hostile to management.

But this does not altogether tie in with the reasons companies gave when they were surveyed by Middlesex Polytechnic lecturer Paul Norkett in 1976. He found three main reasons listed by companies:

To stifle rumours	13%
To improve public relations	31%
To improve industrial relations	44%

In the same survey, incidentally, Norkett also asked companies what they most feared from disclosure of information, and their answers are again interesting. This is what they were most worried about:

Excessive cost	5.4%
Information leaking to competitors	17.3%
Information being misunderstood	67.3%

So much for the theory. To find out what happened in practice we asked companies which had actually gone through the process why they decided to try, and what they think they and the employees got out of it.

Reasons given by the companies

Obviously, many of the companies made the same or closely allied points, and so their comments are abridged in order to concentrate on what had not been covered elsewhere.

The financial accountant of Revertex, B. C. Hozier, said : "Basically, the company felt that the Annual Report which for some years had been distributed to all employees was becoming rather complex and there was a need to set out figures in a more reasonable fashion for employees. Though there has been little feedback from the employees, those who have been asked have commented that they are of more use than the full accounts and more understandable."

The Johnson Group, a cleaning and dyeing chain, has, according to their financial controller D. E. Bolton, "a strong tradition of close working relations. Unfortunately, as we are essentially retailers, there is no concentration of employees as they are fragmented over nearly 800 trading outlets. We were conscious that we had not laid down any lines of communication with these employees on financial matters and felt this essential to foster their identification with the Group's prosperity." Johnsons was one of the few companies interviewed which, having produced one report, did not repeat the exercise on the same scale the following year, not because it did not want to, nor because it was disheartened by the disappointing feedback: it got hit by a takeover bid just at the crucial year-end period when the report was due to be prepared.

This fragmented kind of business obviously has peculiar difficulties when it tries to communicate with its employees. But when it does make the effort the results are encouraging, as the next example — the only other shop-based industry in the sample — shows.

Gordon Ralph is financial controller of the Ladbroke Group, the gaming organisation with 12,000 employees spread around the country, many in small, isolated betting shops. The company produced its report, he says, "to give these employees a better understanding of the constituent parts that make up the total Ladbroke Group". He put most emphasis on the method of distribution, and the need to tell employees what the report was for. Copies of the employee report were handed to each employee by the local manager, who briefly explained its purpose. Concludes Ralph, "We consider that the relationship between management and employees was improved as a result of this exercise and we intend to issue further reports."

Turner Manufacturing, a Midland-based engineering company with some 2,000 employees, had "a desire to communicate with the workforce and, if possible, to allay some of the suspicion which they seem to hold on accounting matters", says its company secretary, P. J. Horrel. "In particular we wished to show [the employees] the requirements of acceptable profitability to provide the funds for investment in new plant and therefore the future safeguarding of their employment. We also wished to dispel the feeling that they were working wholly and exclusively for the benefit of shareholders."

Horrel's company is quite small and much of what is in the report has already been passed on at regular briefing meetings of management and employees. Nevertheless, the written statement was felt to be needed as a useful additional way of pushing home the message. The written report was useful, too, because Turners wanted to draw to the employees' attention the amount of tax paid by company and employee. "We have endeavoured to show how much the Government takes from both employee and company by way of income tax and corporation tax whilst, at the same time, giving the Government credit for leaving the deferred tax within the company", Horrel said.

Turner Manufacturing has had a "fairly minimal feedback", though this is more or less what is expected. The management feels, however, that the report has very much the tacit approval of the workforce and it has quite clearly done no harm and probably some undefined good.

These so far are public companies but private companies often need to report just as much as public firms do. The next two provide good examples.

Coubro and Scrutton is a firm with £10 million turnover and 1100 employees — a private family group, with the philosophy that "the wellbeing of its staff is second only to the need to achieve a fair return on capital employed." Legislation and the need to communicate as a result of new laws played a big part in the company's thinking. In 1975 a pension and life assurance scheme and in 1976 a "prolonged disability" scheme were introduced for employees. "Both the latter schemes brought with them the need to communicate with employees telling them in an intelligible manner what we were trying to do" says the company. "With the Social Security Pensions Act 1975, we have tried to reduce the tortuous terminology of legislators and bureaucrats to something almost digestible." Once it was decided to produce a simplified version of the accounts, Coubro and Scrutton's board chose six key points it wanted to highlight. First, being part of a group meant greater job security. Second, the growth of the group since 1972. Third, the large part of total sales revenue taken by wages and pension contributions. Fourth, money retained for new investment exceeded dividends paid to shareholders by more than six times. Fifth, the investment planned for the coming year, and finally, the group's contribution to UK exports. "We felt that essential facts should be laid out clearly in this first issue without attempting detailed explanations or self-justification. Therefore, we did not try to explain the effects of inflation. This will be attempted in the second issue", they said.

Reaction to the report has been good. Employees were pleased that someone had taken the time to explain to them what was happening, and that their own efforts were, by implication, being recognised and appreciated and positive requests for further information followed, with the composition of the shareholdings being a favourite query.

Courage, the brewers, developed its *Money Special* in 1974, and since then has rapidly extended its communication programme with audio-visual presentations to employees by main board and top local management. The company claims that "its reports have achieved their objective in alerting the workforce to the company's trading situation and creating a greater awareness of the company's desire to communicate to all concerned about these matters." Courage is now a subsidiary of the giant Imperial Group but the report to employees, though it mentions the parent, effectively treats Courage as if it were an independent company.

Yorkshire-based chemical concern Hickson and Welch was an early entry into the field, with a most glossy production. But after two years it dropped this in favour of a tabloid newspaper format "to improve readership". The earlier reports were akin to the shareholders' reports with pictures, pie charts, graphs and so on. But, says Group accountant G. Ringwood, who prepared the report along with his managing director, "these earlier reports designed to explain accounts and the profit analysis to a layman in easy terms were, in fact, not read by the mass of recipients." So the Group changed course and produced a much cheaper, and much quicker to prepare, tabloid which gave "the salient figures for the Group, a short detailed comment on the performance of each major subsidiary and comment by the Group managing director and chairman on certain policies and prospects. Feedback has notably improved, and the new report is much more popular, with its intended audience" says Ringwood.

Hickson and Welch backed their report up with three 90-minute explanatory sessions during working hours to which all employees were invited. The response was oddly weighted, reported the Group accountant. No shopfloor people came as the unions made it clear that they would do the interpreting. Very few female staff and scarcely no-one under 21 came, but about 70% of the remainder of the staff attended.

McCorquodale, the printing group, is one of those companies which once every six months is subject to takeover rumours. The effect of this on the workforce is unsettling and one can detect a justifiable tetchiness in its reasons for producing a report to employees. In the words of its Group treasurer, "a lot of comment is made from time to time by the press, the rumour mongers and uninformed persons, so we felt it right and proper that at the same time as the shareholders received their copy of the report and accounts we would send a simplified statement to employees." McCorquodale has little formal communication between management and employees although there is "informal communication at plant level" the treasurer explained. "There has been absolutely no feedback whatsoever from employees concerning these statements and the company has taken the attitude that no news is good news. We are sure that if the employees resented such circularisation then we would have known but an employer seldom gets praise from employees. It is very difficult to assess whether industrial relations have been improved by issuing this report but it is certain that they have not been worsened."

Smiths Industries, the electronic component giant, is another old hand at this new game. It defines its objectives in the words of the chief accountant, M. Wenzerul, as trying to produce "a document which portrayed the important facts of the financial performance of the company during the year in a manner which, by attention to content and design, would be more readily assimilated by the non-professional investor and the employees." Note the introduction of the "non-professional investor". Smiths is suggesting that the ordinary shareholder gets much more out of these simplified reports than he does from the annual statement. And Smiths feels it is making progress. Very few copies of the report are left lying about, and the statistics in the report often provide the basis of questions and discussions at employee councils.

Also in the electrical business, though on a much smaller scale, is M.K. Electric, which in its second year of such reports decided to introduce the concept of inflation accounting "especially" said finance director, E. Race, "because the company had increased its profitability under the historic cost convention." It was a major requirement of the report to put over the inflation message, that paper profits did not necessarily spell prosperity. M.K. Electric reported that the grapevine had approved the production of the report though there was no official feedback. "One can only hope," said the finance director, "that employees appreciated the non-statutory gesture so helping relations to be better than they would have been had a report not been issued."

There is a pattern in several of these responses concerning the role and attitude of the trade unions. It seems clear, even from such a small sample, that union hostility, or even a simple lack of co-operation, can greatly reduce the impact and effectiveness of the employee report. One can suggest, even at this early stage, that if the union distrusts the employee report, then some at least of this distrust will be passed on to the employees at large. The next company is therefore particularly interesting because it tackled the problem head-on.

Part of the Mardon Packaging Group, Mardon Son and Hall is based in Bristol. The scene is set by finance director, A. R. Knight, who sees the employees' report as part of an open style of management. "We believe that employees are interested in many other things than financial information" he says, "and in particular, they are interested in matters that affect their security of employment. We try to keep them informed of changes in the structure of the business while these changes are still being discussed by the management." This is achieved in four ways: talks with the unions, articles in the house magazine, briefing groups conducted along the lines suggested by the Industrial Society and by explanations of the corporate plan, delivered by the managing director. "In other words," he concludes, "we believe that communication is very much an ongoing exercise and the employees' annual report is just a part of this."

The major problem Mardon found was the "suspicion and scepticism" of the employees, so the company launched a four-point programme to try to combat this. First, it ran courses for the employees using outside experts. The outsiders were thought necessary to avoid the criticism that it was management indoctrination. Second, the finance director attended the courses, and when employees requested information, he did what he could to supply it. Third, while the accounts were being prepared, shop stewards were allowed to spend two weeks in the offices seeing how it was done. Fourth, finance and financial affairs are introduced from time to time into the firm's schedule of briefing groups. Whether or not this will be enough to defeat the sceptics remains to be seen. But meanwhile the company deserves an accolade for seeing the problem and trying to do something about it.

Macarthy Pharmaceuticals is a diverse organisation employing some 3000 people in the United Kingdom in over 100 depots and 60 shops. While over 100 people may work in a depot, the retail end of the business comprises chemists with perhaps two or three staff — many of them part-time. The firm has no strong employee representation, nor a central works council, and certainly experienced no pressure from the employees to produce such a report. "Motivation for the company secretary to suggest the production of such a report came from an awareness of other companies' efforts in this direction and his own personal conviction that a greater degree of staff participation was inevitable in the years ahead," reports Macarthys' Mr Blond. The employees' report was therefore just one of the necessary steps on this path. With commendable candour, he says that the major hurdle the company secretary faced in the production of the report was in getting the board to agree that the exercise was necessary in the first place. Perhaps because of this scepticism the company made an effort afterwards to find out what the employees thought of it and 200 questionnaires were sent out at random of which 60% were returned. The results showed by far the greatest interest was in the history of the group, followed, though not closely, by a desire for much greater information about the employees' particu-

lar location, and the performance of his own section. A significant number also thought that the report was extravagant.

To round off the section let us conclude with the comments from two of the most convinced advocates of employee reports, Tarmac, the construction group, and Eldridge Pope, the brewers.

Tarmac described their experience in this way:

"Tarmac have, for several years, presented a summary of annual results in the employees' newspaper *Tarmac World*. The material was normally treated separately from the main body of the newspaper, which is in tabloid style, and generally took the form of a separate supplement.

"In 1975, Tarmac felt that the newspaper was not the appropriate means of communicating company results to employees, feeling that a more formal approach was necessary and one which would be identified totally with management and with the Annual Report to shareholders.

"We believe that there are a vast number of misconceptions about the business of communicating financial information to employees which do little to help the cause of greater involvement of the workforce in the company's affairs. Workforces vary enormously between companies and in Tarmac's case the potential audience for the Report for Employees covers a wide range of age, experience, education and commitment to the company. In addition, as with many other large organisations, there was the problem of convincing some members of management that to just 'tell the workers about the Annual Report and Accounts' was not good enough.

"We have the benefit of two high quality professional contributions to help our studies and decision making. Firstly, we employed a specialist agency to help with the decisions that were made about content, style and presentation. Secondly, we have had the benefit of a survey of employee attitudes to the company, to its communication of information and to jobs within the company. These two contributions were of considerable assistance and the independent specialist research particularly acted as an important catalyst towards increasing management awareness of the need for a separate Employee Report.

"The actual distribution of the reports was a matter on which there was considerable debate. Many managers were happy for the report to go to all staff employees, but initially there was considerable doubt as to the usefulness or wisdom of sending it to all the weekly paid employees. In the event, the report (some 22,000 copies) was posted to all staff employees at their home addresses and distributed in bulk to all our sites for weekly paid employees.

"In addition to the monthly newspaper, *Tarmac World,* information is generally conveyed to employees through Notice Boards and Press Announcements. The Annual Report for Employees is the only formal communication between Tarmac Ltd and all employees of the Group at the present time. Notwithstanding the size of the Group, Tarmac has a considerable advantage with the vast majority of its employees working in very small units and this being so, the Group endeavours to obtain maximum benefit from the close day-to-day contact which can exist between the workforces at the individual operating units and their local management."

Eldridge Pope also comes across strongly as a company which knows what it wants to do:

"Briefly we wanted something which was simple, readable and preferably home produced — and incidentally it is very definitely home produced, being devised by our own staff and printed on our own press.

"The report itself results from an evolutionary process which revolves round the idea that the accounts should not stand on their own, but should form part of an Employees' AGM. The Meeting was already taking place before the first set of accounts was prepared and at these Meetings a brief synopsis of the company's performance was given using bar charts, graphs and so on.

"Following through the thinking it seemed logical and desirable that in the same way as shareholders have a set of accounts to discuss at their AGM, the employees should have their own report. It was felt that this should be as simple in form and content as possible and should be (and be seen by employees to be) the product of the company itself and not farmed out to a designer who would then produce a costly 'glossy.' Our major problem is time. Those who are primarily involved with producing the Report have also to cope with our statutory annual accounts and since the interval between the shareholders' and employees' AGM is normally not more than one month there is very little time for design work and plate making. The accounts are intended as a means to an end and not an end in themselves. They are primarily designed for discussion at the employees' AGM. This meeting

consists of a brief address of welcome (usually by the chairman); a brief review (5–10 mins) by the managing director (this is designed to sum up the year's activities and to map out any salient features or changes in the current year); there then follows a feature of about half an hour. Usually in the past this has been used to explain the company's financial performance. It also included an address by John Garnett of the Industrial Society and this year a presentation on marketing within the company. Finally, the meeting winds up with a question and answer session of half to three quarters of an hour.

"Although the brewery is not closed down everyone who is not in a key position is free to attend and the fact that the meeting is always packed, quite apart from the number and quality of questions, indicates that the exercise is very well worthwhile.

"This year we have added to the text a brief address of welcome and a few words from the managing director on the final page. This is to cater for those who for one reason or another are not able to get to the meeting. The longer passage is very specifically located on the last page in order to encourage the reader when he opens the accounts to read on and not be put off by indigestible chunks of text."

Conclusions

What can we learn from those companies which have actually taken the plunge? First, companies gave a wide variety of reasons for doing a report but all derived from the desire to improve communication with the employee, and to increase his understanding of how the business operated; some companies defined their reasons only in vague terms, others had a crisp, clearly defined objective. Many companies had only minimal feedback, though the report was never thought to have done any harm. The correlation between those companies which started with clearly defined objectives, and those companies which felt they had got something through to the employees is too obvious to be dismissed easily.

Having taken the plunge companies have to keep going, for, as Turner Manufacturing suggested, any effort to back out in future would arouse suspicion among the employees. This is a widely held view — not confined just to those few who have tried to back out, and who should therefore know — but it is also encouraging because it does imply that the employees have taken notice of the reports and the mere fact that they would miss them if they were not there is surely progress of a kind. After years of silence, and the need to overcome near-total ignorance, most companies are taking the view that they are in for a long haul. So the second lesson is that you do not take on an exercise like this lightly. Once you start it, it will be virtually impossible to stop without doing damage to your industrial relations.

The sheer variety of people involved in the production of reports also emerges clearly. In some cases it is the accountant, in others the personnel manager, in a third it is the managing director. This again is important, for no one factor has been responsible for more bad reports than the disastrous combination of a hung committee and a poor PR man. Whoever is in charge needs to have the authority to push through what they want, for such reports quickly become compromised if too many people get involved.

The fourth lesson is that there is no one golden format for communicating financial information. Some companies have improved their response by switching from conventional reports to tabloid newspapers. Others are convinced that they made a breakthrough when they went from tabloid to A4. At this stage, therefore, we only need to note that the choice of presentation is vitally important. This will be returned to and dealt with at some length in Chapter 12.

The most effective response was found in companies where the report was integrated into a wider communications programme, and particularly where it was used as the basis for a presentation by management. There are problems here of course, because one of the obvious developments for employee reports is that they appear more than simply once a year — Norcros, for example, is already producing interim statements — and the strain on management if each has to be verbally presented will be acute. So reports must be able to survive on their own merits, but should also be wholly integrated when possible into the rest of the communications programme.

Finally, what emerged was the realisation that the report has repercussions far beyond the workforce. It is a major public relations exercise for the company if the employee receives it at home or takes it there, for it will be read by his family and it will be compared with those received by friends in other companies or used by personnel officers in recruitment. This has never happened with annual accounts, but it will inevitably happen with reports to employees. So it is worth spending time on the job to make sure that when it is done it is done properly.

CHAPTER FOUR

A REVIEW OF CURRENT PRACTICE

Some general characteristics

It is tempting to look at the vastly growing number of employee reports and conclude that so many companies are making such great efforts that everything must be splendid. But the reality is different. The authors of employee reports have still not found the winning formula to make the report accepted by and useful to the employee. Too many reports are produced as gimmicks. Too few actually pay off in genuine results.

In the current state of the art, reports have three general characteristics. First, there is no real problem of disclosure — companies are very open. Second, the flow of information is almost always one-way, from management to employee. Third, all reports have "political" overtones in terms of company (not national) politics.

Taking content first: it is becoming increasingly clear that the CBI, the TUC, the accountancy bodies and the Advisory Conciliation and Arbitration Service are talking roughly the same language when they discuss what needs to be disclosed. (Sceptics should turn to Chapters 5–7, where this is explained in greater detail.) The range of subjects covered in employee reports is now so large that no matter what you want to produce you should probably be able to find a precedent for it somewhere, but some appear far more than any others, and these were identified by Middlesex Polytechnic's Paul Norkett in the research study mentioned in Chapter 3. He looked at 159 different sets of accounts and in spite of their inherent diversity he isolated the following four items:

92% of reports had an income statement
87% of reports had a balance sheet
29% of reports had fund flow statements
18% of reports had value-added statements

The surprise in this list is the low rating given to value-added statements which have received considerable support in the press and the accountancy profession. But the most likely explanation for the low rating is that many of the reports Norkett used related to 1975, which was before the campaign for such treatments ground into top gear. Norkett concluded that in general most employee accounts were no more than a simplified presentation of financial data already published elsewhere. All contained information relating to costs, revenues and assets and liabilities. But no accounts gave financial or cost information which would not normally be given or could not be calculated from the published accounts — provided these conformed with Stock Exchange and Companies Act requirements. He also found that some 43% of the reports in his sample gave employment figures ranging from flat totals for the numbers employed to elaborate tables covering length of service, productivity, absenteeism and pensions. Two other popular features were general information about the company — its products, activities, social matters — and organisational details.

On the basis of his survey Norkett concluded, perhaps rather harshly, that there was no evidence that employees were being provided with information in excess of statutory requirements. Such additional information as did appear was confined mainly to labour statistics or organisational details, and indeed the financial content of employee reports was much less than would normally be expected from the published accounts. But this outwardly comprehensive list of contents, which seems to cover all the options, is in fact not enough; in too many ways it is irrelevant to the needs and desires of the employee. The employee, above all, wants reassurance — he wants to know that his job is safe, that the orders are still coming in and that he has reasonable prospects for a pay increase. But he gets the opposite. He gets a mass of data which he can't comprehend because it is totally outside his experience. So he becomes confused and uncertain. Next, he wants local information — he wants to know about his world, his factory, his workmates, his product. But again he gets the opposite. He gets information about a group, the existence of which has probably been a mystery to him, and if it includes a family tree, he probably feels even more isolated by seeing his own unit's insignificance in the overall scheme of things. Thirdly, he wants information about the future. And he gets the opposite. He gets information about the past, often not even the immediate past, and sometimes not even new information, if the Press have got there first. Obviously, if employee accounts are to be improved, there has to be a radical rethink of their content.

The second general feature of employee reports is that they generally confine themselves to passing information one way — there is no provision for encouraging the employee to pass information back. Lord McCarthy, one of the foremost experts in industrial relations and communication in the United Kingdom, regards this as a basic weakness. His view, crudely summarised, is that the only way to communicate, the only way actually to get through to the shopfloor employee, is to go to him with a problem and ask for help in trying to solve it — to say, for example, that the company had three alternative approaches to a new product launch and which way did the employees feel would be the most effective and efficient? That, of course, is a good deal further down the road than many companies are now but it does underline the point about merely giving out information — which will inevitably then be tainted, in the employees' eyes, with the stain of management propaganda — and using information as a means of solving problems, and actively encouraging response. Almost no employee reports have the information which actively encourages response. They do not, for example, explain a management problem — a decision which has to be taken — and ask for suggestions. But they ought to try. For even if no suggestions are forthcoming, it might bring home to some, at least, of the employees the kind of problems management has to grapple with. At the moment the feedback is minimal, and this can only be because either the content is wrong, or, deep down, the employee is simply not interested.

The third point is that employee reports are political — they are a further verse in the long-running saga of British industrial life. What we are seeing in a lot of companies at the moment is a not totally genuine effort at communication but something which management thinks is tactically expedient. They supply data, which is not the same thing as supplying information. You can tell the firms who are not totally committed; they are the ones with muddled internal organisation — a refusal to give the job to one man and let him get on with it. They are the ones who provide the wrong content, which bears little relation either to the desires of the employees or even to the personality of the company. Above all, they are the ones where the job is rushed — tagged on the end of the annual report as an afterthought. The whole project, in short, reeks of a lack of planning, and the employees probably conclude, if they take any notice at all, that the management is trying to snatch a bit of credit for disclosing information it is shortly going to have to release anyway. Where the effort is genuine, where there is a real attempt to communicate with the employees, the exercise is, if anything, even more political. Because then the management is trying to by-pass the union and re-establish direct links with the employees. And in such circumstances it is almost inevitable, however regrettable, that the union will see the development as a threat. Unions, it is always worth remembering, have a different approach to the disclosure of information by management. While management tends to see it as an educative process, unions are much more likely to consider it as military intelligence — gathering information about the enemy which can then be used to advantage in the next round of collective bargaining. They will go on having this view of information, by and large, until the flow becomes a two-way flow, and they, and the employees, are expected to give something in return. And as we have just said, we are still a long way from that.

Moving from general to specific observations about employee reports, it is possible to isolate three specific approaches to their preparation. These are (*a*) the shareholder approach, (*b*) the demand approach and (*c*) the business planning approach, and it is worth examining the characteristics of each of these in turn.

The "shareholder" approach to preparation

This approach is based on the belief that:

(*a*) shareholders and employees should both be aware of the financial realities of the business — as seen by management;

(*b*) no group should get information which is denied to the other people;

(*c*) management has obligations to inform employees about the financial state of the business in which they spend their working lives.

The purpose of the report is to promote financial understanding and to spread financial literacy, so that a better educated workforce will ultimately become more co-operative in the factory and more aware of the place of business in the community. Management is recognising that the employee has a right to financial knowledge and is making an effort to put this in a form it thinks the employee will find easier to absorb. In practice this means that almost all employee accounts are reworked versions of the shareholder report. The Cavenham report is an example [Fig. 2]. The balance sheet is a key element in this approach as it is the statement of risk. An employee who can understand the balance sheet can assess the chances of his firm staying in business. The profit and loss account also has to be included. Employees may accept the need for profit, but they still have to be made aware of how small profits are in relation to the rest of the business.

Other items generally included under such a treatment include value added statements — particularly now these are tending to replace profit and loss accounts, and a sources and application of funds statement — often used to highlight the inadequacy of retained profit to finance the company's activities and to emphasise the gap that must be filled by bank borrowing or share issues. Next, the effects of inflation. Inflation accounting rarely appears in employee reports but there is a considerable literature on inflation itself as is seen in Chapter 14. It derives from the previous statements which show why profits were needed and where the cash has gone, and is often linked with a statement on investment.

The above general category contains a vast range of reports, some good, some bad. But it does have a tendency to include more than its statistically justified share of bad ones. There are various reasons for this. One is that, because the only raw material available is the annual report to shareholders and because no additional material is allowed, it means the media man has a field day. His job can be as simple and as hard as using only the words used in the annual report — or rather extracts from it — and representing these words in a more easily digested and visibly appealing form. Understandably, it is a daunting task and is probably why the design disasters and visual excesses of presentation tend to happen under this approach. It is hard for them not to get carried away, given some of the material they have to work on.

The final characteristic of such reports is their vagueness — no-one is really quite sure why they are doing them other than that they have the best of intentions.

The "demand" approach to preparation

The next distinct approach to employee reporting is the demand approach, which works on the principle that you ask the employee what he wants, and then, as far as possible, you give it to him. The demand approach is essentially responsive and is based on the belief that the purpose of an employee report is to provide information because it will improve the human relations aspects of the organisation. The assumption is that by sharing information, by demonstrating that management cares, there will be improvements in morale, a greater sense of common purpose and less distrust of management. In some senses the demand view of the provision of information has already been overtaken by events, notably by legislative provisions embodied in the Industry Act and the Employee Protection Act.

The types of behaviour that are relevant to morale and which should be affected by reporting financial results to employees are:

(a) sickness/absenteeism rates;
(b) commitment to work, on the shopfloor;
(c) accident rates;
(d) a higher level of trust, particularly in relation to change;
(e) avoidance/reduction in disputes.

Frequently management assumes paternalistically that it knows and understands what people want to know. However, many companies draw upon the wealth of published research which can provide general guidance on the subject. In some cases companies will commission specific research among their employees to determine their information needs. Having established this they formulate the draft messages and try them out on the employee to see if the main messages get across, if they are understood, and if they are in tune with what the reader wants. The other alternative is to bring the employee or his representative in right at the beginning and build up the report from there. How they are consulted will usually affect the content. Where paternalistic judgement has been employed information will tend to follow the shareholders' report. Where employees have been consulted through formal channels then ACAS type information will be supplied. Where employees themselves have been asked, "reasons why" will predominate and will lead towards the explanation of business objectives. There will also be a leaning towards local information, and some kind of forecasts.

This approach has great attractions, and will be dealt with at length later — the attractions being that it accords with the picture that many managements have (justifiably) about themselves —

that they are open and have no desire to keep anything from the employees. What happens when this approach is applied is that there is a great deal of employee-based information, reflecting, of course, the perspectives of the employee, and there will be a demand for trends — profits over five years — rather than for single figures, so things can be put in perspective.

The "demand approach" school has a degree of commonsense on its side in that the point of the document is to convey a message to employees, and it will fail miserably if it is not acceptable to them. Union involvement at the planning stage is one sure way to make it acceptable. Indeed, there are many who say that no matter what course you adopt you have to have the employee representative or union in right from the beginning. If he is not involved, then he will fight the report, and if he fights the report, much of what you set out to achieve will have been sacrificed. Record Ridgway adopted this approach, when the finance director sat down with six shop stewards and over a period of weeks worked out with them what information could be given to them. To consider the merits and weaknesses of this approach it is necessary to see what resulted. The Record Ridgway report as agreed was three pages long (which were made up to four with the addition of a statement from the chairman on page 1). Page 2 of the report [Fig. 3] had a statement of home and overseas sales and profits for the years since the group was created, expanding on the graphs which had already appeared on page 1. Directly underneath that, which took half a page, were two pie charts illustrating the markets in which the group sold, one for the current year, the other for the year previously. The pie gave a value in £s for the United Kingdom, America, the Middle and Far East, Europe, Africa and Australasia. The third item was a statement of assets and liabilities. Assets listed were land, buildings and machinery; money owed by customers; stocks and work in progress and investments. Liabilities were money owed to suppliers, taxation owed to government, money borrowed from the bank and outside shareholders' interests. This was presented in straightforward tabular form. The next page began "The best way of showing profit in its proper perspective is to show the wealth which the company and its employees have created by their efforts and how each has been rewarded for that effort. This is shown by the value added statement." That was followed by a statement showing how much had been spent on new plant and equipment (including leased goods) for the previ-

ous four years. It split this between land and buildings and equipment, and it also — in a separate column — adjusted the figures for inflation using specific capital goods indices. (It showed, incidentally, a precipitous decline in the real rate of investment.)

Then the final page was devoted to employee statistics — the number employed round the world, the number of days lost through absence, accidents and sickness, and local and national disputes, the average hours worked by employees throughout the different factories, and overseas. Then came the age distribution of the employees and their length of service, labour turnover and expenditure on training and the total employee costs — wages plus pension — at home and overseas.

This information was supplemented in the chairman's statement by a general forecast of where the group was hoping to improve its market share, encouraging noises about the order book, and an indication that the group was going to increase its capital spending, without being specific. Theo Dengel, finance director of Record Ridgway, had this to say of the report:

"The need to communicate what is happening in the company is obvious, and C. and J. Hampton, the main company prior to the 1972 merger which created Record Ridgway, had been pioneers in the 1950s in establishing an annual presentation to employees. When I joined the group in 1974 it was necessary completely to reconstruct all accounting systems to create adequate monthly management reports; this was followed by a revamping of the annual report, and it seemed logical to satisfy the demand by shop stewards for more information. The publication of *The Corporate Report* was well timed and it was used as a model. I formed a study group with about six senior shop stewards where over a period of weeks we discussed what information was of use to them and what we could provide, bearing in mind stock exchange requirements and the need to watch commercial interests. The shop stewards consulted their union officials and eventually we produced a blank draft. This was put to the full shop stewards' committee for their reaction and approval. One of their main requirements was 'no gimmicks, we want plain facts we can understand' [a stipulation, he says, which accounts for the rather plain presentation]. This year we have tried to improve presentation and introduced the effect of inflation accounting. The initial reaction has been one of suspicion."

Dengel reports that reaction from the shopfloor

to the report was mixed. Some thought it a waste of money, others said it was important to have the information. The people who had been with the company a long time were more appreciative and wanted the reports to continue and to be expanded — opposite views were expressed where the sense of belonging had not yet developed. It was too early to assess whether there had been any marked effect on industrial relations — but it had focused attention on the need for a better communications policy.

This kind of report is clearly successful to some degree but there are three problems which can't be avoided. The first is what you do next year to maintain the employee's interest. You will have given him the bulk of the information in year one, and therefore year two, barring disasters, is going to be dull in comparison. That problem could perhaps be overcome. The next one however cannot. It is that the approach is based on the false assumption that people who are totally ignorant of finance know what it is that they want to know. But how can they really be expected to hit on all the right questions? Actually, given the difficulties, it is surprising how many do come up with the right questions. But there are some problems that never get touched upon — the effect of high interest rates, of sagging productivity levels, of overseas investment, all of which are things on which management may want to comment, to show that job security does not just happen but is something which has to be worked for. Thirdly, what happens when the employee asks for straightforward profit figures, in the future? Do you give them the historic profits, do you adjust them for inflation or do you give them both and leave it to them to take their pick? Whichever you choose you are going to be engulfed in a tide of scepticism. So the demand approach is obviously no easy way out, and this leads us to the third treatment, the business planning approach.

The "business planning" approach to preparation

This approach, largely developed by one-time McKinsey man Mike Branden in his time at Charles Barker Metra, is explained by him as follows:

"The business planning approach is based on the belief that the main purpose of an employee report is to contribute to the improvement of industrial performance. The assumption is that the employee report will feed employees' understanding of how their business operates and their knowledge of the current situation, and that this will, in turn, enable them to adapt their behaviour in ways that will improve performance. The types of behaviour that are relevant to performance, and that are likely to be influenced by an employee report because they should be based on a sound knowledge of the company's financial situation, are:

pay bargaining;
implementation of major changes;
new technology;
new work organisation;
avoidance of disputes.

"The first step is to define those business objectives whose achievement may depend on employees' behaviour. It may be possible to find definitions of such objectives written down formally in a business plan. More often, however, it will be necessary to interview key managers, and perhaps even set up a meeting for all of them to attend in order to sort out priorities and inconsistencies. The next step is to define specific reasons why employees should co-operate in the achievement of the selected objectives. This means assessing employees' major concerns, usually job security and pay, and then figuring out the logical connections between employees' concerns and the business objectives. For example, a pay bargaining objective can be linked to job security by pointing out that job security depends on sales volume, sales volume depends on competitive pricing and competitive pricing depends on cost inflation and profit margins. If profit margins cannot be squeezed, then job security will depend on controlling cost inflation, and wage inflation in particular. The next step is to define the factual information that must be presented to employees if they are to be able to assess the nature and the extent of the benefits they will obtain in return for co-operation. Thus, in the example quoted above, it will be necessary to provide information on volume trends, evidence that supports the contention that competitive pricing is essential to maintaining volume, and the profit and loss account presented in a way that it enables employees to perceive the relative importance of preserving profit margins and controlling cost inflation. The next step is to develop a coherent report structure that will convey the required information with logic and clarity in both the ordering and the presentation of individual terms. Thus, in the example quoted above, it will be logical to start with a presentation of volume trends leading into a discussion of competition and market shares, trends in prices, and the profit and loss account. The presentation of the profit and loss account itself should highlight the points made about cost inflation and margins.

"The content of employee reports developed through using this approach will cover the whole span of management functions. There will be sections on marketing and sales, and more detailed information will be given on cost breakdowns, and also on the application of funds, for example, on the different categories of investment spending. Some information conventionally included in shareholders' reports will be left out:

information on overseas production activities; the balance sheet (although trends in working capital requirements may well be discussed, this is more in the manner of the sources and application of funds statement than in the manner of the balance sheet).

"A typical table of contents might therefore be:

market trends
the structure of prices, including profit margins
changes that will boost the wage/profit cake."

The objections to this approach are two, both of which Branden recognised. The first is that it really does push the management side very hard, and it quite abandons the idea that information is or should be presented objectively. On the contrary, the business planning approach requires that you select the information you put in quite ruthlessly to suit your own ends. This is still a bit too much for most managements to swallow; they are not yet ready for it. The other weakness of this approach is that it perhaps overstates the power of employee reports in being accepted by employees and therefore being useful as a management tool.

But the case still exists even if it is overstated and this, indeed, is the lesson of this chapter. Employee reports may not have the impact which management intended or expected, but they will have some impact, and it is important therefore that management thinks clearly about what it is trying to do before it embarks on the project. This is the value of the three approaches to employee accounts as currently presented. For if a management can choose the approach which most matches its style and intentions then it can set about the project with its objectives more clearly fixed. Getting the objectives right is the vital first step in any programme of communication.

PART TWO

TOWARDS A MODEL REPORT

CHAPTER FIVE

THE CBI RECOMMENDATIONS ON DISCLOSURE

The main problem faced in writing an employee report is to know what to put in and what to leave out. The only way to solve this problem is to develop a theme, which is what this and succeeding chapters will attempt to do. They will take an existing body of opinion, in this chapter the CBI recommendations for a disclosure policy and in subsequent chapters those of the TUC and the accountancy profession, and show how these thoughts can be adapted for an employee report.

The CBI proposals had their origins in June 1975 in a booklet entitled *The Provision of Information to Employees*. It was largely based on current practice in a number of companies, but again covered the whole field of disclosure, not simply employee reports — with the result that many things it suggested were what management might say in confidence to a briefing group or consultative committee, but would be unlikely to commit to print.

However, the CBI also stressed the need for companies to provide employees with "as much information as is relevant to their needs and wishes and which will assist them to identify with their company paying due regard to constraints arising out of competitive requirements and confidentiality." The CBI's list of things to be disclosed has subsequently been criticised as being too pie-in-the-sky and, as we shall see, it does create the feeling that there is everything in there but the kitchen sink. But even with this weakness its intentions are good, and there is something to be borne in mind by all managements in its reminder of the inherent dangers of a too restrictive policy on information disclosure, nominally in the interests of protecting the company's position from competitors but in fact through lack of conviction of the need for it. It says "Companies should bear in mind whether the consequences of failing to provide information might not be more damaging in industrial relations terms than the dangers of such information becoming common knowledge." When you strip away the polite language it is a tough statement.

So the first step is to list the CBI's proposals so that everybody is clear what these involve. They divide into two sections — information about the company as a whole, and information relevant to employment. (The asterisks denote information which the authors of the recommendations thought might be sensitive and might have to be kept confidential.)

Information about the company as a whole

1. *Organisation of the company*
   Company activities
   Organisation of the company in relation to its subsidiaries or holding company (if any)
   Names of directors
   Information on shareholdings
   Unit structure
   Management structure up to and including directors
   Product range
   General company objectives and policies
2. *Finance*
   Turnover
   Profits
   Dividends
   Losses
   Liabilities
   Total fixed assets
   Details of directors' remuneration and emoluments
   Details of chairman's remuneration and emoluments
   Total wages and salary bill
   Total labour costs as a percentage of operating costs*
   Administration costs as a percentage of total costs*
   Costs of materials*
3. *Competitive situation and productivity*
   Export performance
   Details of main national and international competitors

31

Competitive possibilities
Orders, production and marketing situation
Production schedules*
Work levels and standard performance levels*
Labour costs per unit of output*
Savings arising from increased productivity

4. *Plans and prospects*
Mergers and takeovers*
Investment and expansion*
Closures*
Changes in location*
Research and development*
Product changes*

Information relevant to employment

1. *Manpower*
Average numbers employed
Numbers employed by sex, grade, occupation, departments etc
Labour turnover, redundancies and dismissals
Absenteeism
Redeployment, training and retraining
Days lost through disputes

2. *Industrial relations*
Grievance procedures
Safety rules, policies and programmes
Health and welfare matters
Disciplinary and dismissal procedures
Trade unions
Recruitment and promotion policies and methods
Induction programmes
Working rules
Social matters

3. *Pay and conditions*
Rates of pay
Notice periods
Hours of work
Holidays
Sick pay
Pension schemes
Results of negotiations affecting pay and conditions
Principles and structures of payment systems
Job evaluation systems
Holiday schedule arrangements
Profit sharing, stock option and saving schemes
Life assurance schemes
Average earnings

4. *Information relevant to the immediate work situation*
Comparative departmental production figures
Comparative achievement of targets
Changes in the working environment
New appointments and changes in personnel

Any general changes affecting individuals in a working group

The proposed treatment is to take the suggestions a section at a time, and illustrate how companies have actually followed the recommendations in their own reports, without their necessarily knowing they were doing so. There is no motive in the selection of the reports used to illustrate the particular sections, other than that they are to hand, and in many cases it is known that they were not intentionally following any published guidelines but were merely including information which they thought was interesting and relevant. And what this chapter shows is that however outrageous any suggested disclosure may seem, there is a good chance that some company, somewhere in the country, has done it.

The company's organisation

Much of the required information on this is already published in the annual report — particularly on the subsidiary companies of a group and its activities. But to help the reader to work out changes of command structure and responsibilities, and how companies interlock, a chart is a much better choice than a list. It is much easier to follow than a straight list of companies, particularly if names of directors are integrated into the organisation chart, as in the production management example of Staffordshire Potteries reproduced here [Fig. 4]. Information on shareholdings is crucially important, too, and is frequently sought after by employees, largely because they feel there may be some mystery involved, and it is information which is legally available to all. In large companies employers should take the opportunity to show employees that through their pension funds and insurance policies they own a fair chunk of their own business. And in private companies, where the option may not exist, it is equally important, indeed probably more important, to show where the shares are and what the dividend is. If you do not, the employee will, without doubt, greatly overestimate the shareholders' reward. Many companies do this already, and one of the best in content, and reproduced here [Fig. 5], was published by Norcros. Note how it emphasises the partnership between employee and shareholder; on another page (not illustrated) it explains how you buy a share and how the price fluctuates. It gives a very comprehensive breakdown of the actual shareholdings and it lists the names of big institutions, some of which at least should ring a bell with the employees. Indeed, its only shortcoming is that it did not explain how the dividends institutions receive come back to the employee via higher pension and insurance payouts.

On now to the next suggestion, which was that the unit structure and the management structure up to board level should be spelt out. Staffordshire Potteries is one of the few companies to devote space to explaining who does what in production management. Very impressive it is too, and it went down well with the employees. People like to know who they are working for — who their boss's boss is — and how many steps there are up the ladder between them and the big bosses in the board-room. It helps them identify if they know where they fit into the organisation. Hence the suggestion of the CBI that the unit and management structure up to and including directors should be disclosed. No doubt they would endorse the Staffordshire Potteries chart reproduced in Fig. 4 — and one not reproduced here, which linked production to the board.

The CBI also suggested that product ranges should be mentioned. But this could be integrated as in the above example, with the production diagram. It is well known that you sell local newspapers by putting in as many names and photographs of local people as you can reasonably squeeze into the pages. Given that you may well encounter resistance from middle management in launching a project like this, especially in small to medium companies, it could be a good tactic and help make the report more acceptable if as many as possible of the middle and lower grades of management are mentioned. It will reassure them that they have been noticed, as well as giving them enhanced status.

Finally, to conclude the analysis of the first section, the CBI suggests a statement of general company objectives and policies. In principle it is an excellent idea, but some of them read as if they were written by an evangelist. So let us illustrate one of the better efforts — one done by Serck [Fig. 6] — a company whose performance in the 1970s suggests that they certainly knew where they were going.

Finance

Financial information is already disclosed in the annual report, if you know where to look. But there are three items in this section about which the CBI sounds a warning that there may be problems of confidentiality. These are total labour costs as a percentage of operating costs, adminis-tration costs as a percentage of total costs, and the costs of materials. Things would seem to have

moved fast since the CBI drafted that section. Several companies now include a value-added statement in their employee reports and this gives that information — though admittedly not in local detail and not always specifically including administration. It is worth mentioning, however, that companies like Tate and Lyle have started to give detailed financial information about their subsidiaries and now publish value-added state-ments for them. So, the above costs are being disclosed for parts of the group in some cases.

There is a belief that companies don't like telling employees when they are making a loss — that employee reports are fine when things are going well, but will prove to be a rod for the backs of management when things are going badly. One can sympathise, but it is an over-cautious view. Em-ployees have known for years that business activity fluctuates and one of the great benefits to come if employee reporting becomes a regular thing is that they will learn to take this in their stride. (And such caution would also rob management of the oppor-tunity to show considerable ingenuity in their reports — witness the extract from Avon Rubber's report (p. 82, Fig. 36) which must rank as one of the best explanations ever of a loss.)

One last point: hardly any companies put in their employee report how much the directors and chairman earn. Even those which give a detailed breakdown of labour figures — something we shall come to shortly — don't give the relevant pay figures for the men at the top. This seems to me to be a mistake, for as the late Tom Driberg MP, in his day a top gossip columnist with the *Daily Express*, is reputed to have said, "There are only three things which interest people — who is sleeping with whom, who has got what job, and how much does he earn." So put the pay figures in, they are sure to be read; but don't forget to show how much of it goes in tax, too.

Competitive position and productivity

The CBI thinks that information under the first four headings here can be given without difficulty; but the remainder of the section may cause problems. This section is obviously written with collective bargaining and briefing groups in mind, not employee reports. Nevertheless, intensive digging did uncover one or two companies which were prepared to have a go — admittedly not at the whole thing, but at substantial parts of this section.

But first the export performance. There are various ways to tackle this. You can list the countries to which you export as a percentage of the total, you can give the percentage exported of each product line, you can give direct and indirect exports, as GKN does, and you can show the increasing importance of exports to the company, with a run-down of where the new opportunities are. It does not lend itself to illustration. You can have a pie or bar chart showing the distribution of sales, which is indeed useful for at-a-glance reference. But better to take the opportunity to explain a bit about the problems of exporting — the difficulties of selling in new markets — and the relevance of these sales to the factories back home. Again, Staffordshire Potteries' report devoted a page to export sales developments.

Now, back to the difficult information, the work levels, labour costs per unit of output, production schedules and savings arising from increased productivity, which we expected to prove too hot to handle. The nearest approximation to this information was in the report of Nissen, which is a subsidiary in the United Kingdom of an American company which manufactures gym sports equipment — indeed it claims to be the largest in the world. It gave a breakdown of sales per employee, profits per employee, value added per employee, the value added per £1 of wages, the order backlog against average weekly sales and the sales per square foot; not really the same information but quite searching stuff all the same. The figures were given without a comparison for the previous year. But if they are repeated in future years it should be possible even if no comparative figures are sup-

plied for the employee to make the comparison for himself. Also on a similar theme is the information distributed internally and to shareholders by Peter Prior at Bulmers [Table 1]. Again, it does not go as far as the CBI wants, but it certainly allows the employee to relate his own efforts to the performance of the company as a whole.

Plans and prospects

This next CBI section is bound to cause more problems. No chairman could commit to print his takeover plans for the coming year — and if he did it would be a sure fire guarantee that not one of them would succeed. But a considerable amount can be done in outlining basic policy as the extract [Fig. 7] from the Crane Fruehauf report shows. Crane makes trailers for lorries, and at the time of this report had just turned in a £27,000 loss against profits of £862,000 the previous year. The Crane Fruehauf statement is easy reading but it says a great deal. It really is packed with plans, forecasts and prospects. The more conventional place for this information is in a chairman's statement. The trouble is that chairmen are naturally reluctant to lay their reputations on the line. The Fruehauf treatment, where the forecasts are presented in an unsigned statement, is somewhat easier to produce because it does not carry the chairman's name, and therefore has a degree of informality about it. It is also a more effective way of communicating, as chairmen's statements are little-enough read by

Table 1. *Information given to employees and shareholders of H. P. Bulmer*

KEY FIGURES PER EMPLOYEE

	½-year to October 1974		½-year to October 1975	
	Total amount (£000)	Average per employee (£)	Total amount (£000)	Average per employee (£)
TURNOVER				
United Kingdom	8,402	4,287	12,504	6,581
Export	426	217	338	178
TOTAL	8,828	4,504	12,842	6,759
PROFIT				
Before tax	646	330	1,833	965
Tax	319	163	993	523
After tax	327	167	840	442
Reinvested	236	120	743	391
Capital employed	8,123	4,144	9,063	4,770
Return on capital		7.9%		20.2%
Average No. of employees		1,960		1,900

shareholders, and look uninteresting and out of place in the highly simplified employee reports. So chairmen could perhaps get off the hook more often by adopting the Fruehauf approach. Certainly they cannot duck the issue altogether. Employees want to know about the future. Even if you can produce the most thoughtful and imaginative historic information at great expense it will be no substitute for a few terse words on the problems the company is facing and how management proposes to tackle them. If employee reports are ever to take off, it will be a good "plans and prospects" section that will provide the thrust.

The section on plans and prospects concludes the CBI review of information relevant to the company as a whole. It then moves on to cover information relevant to employment, by which it means manpower, industrial relations, pay and conditions and information relevant to the immediate work environment. This is, in general, much less the stuff of employee reports, but the first section on manpower is an exception.

Manpower

In the manpower section the CBI recommends the provision of information on the average number of people employed, numbers employed by sex, grade, occupation and department, labour turnover, redundancies and dismissals, absenteeism, redeployment training and retraining, and days lost through disputes.

Dunlop does all this and more, but it differs a little in that what it produces is not a report to employees in the sense that we have been talking about it. Its booklet *Dunlop at Work in Britain* is devoted entirely to employment matters. So it covers the structure of employment in the firm including the numbers employed, turnover, stability rate, with five year comparisons. Then it devotes a considerable amount of space to absenteeism, measured in terms of shifts lost, and broken down for each of the company's main operating areas. A further section covers industrial disputes and tries to estimate the profits lost in each of the company's four divisions — tyre, engineering, industry and consumer — through such disputes. It also splits these further between in-house disputes, and those in component suppliers. It rounds this section off with an estimate of the wages and salaries lost through disputes in each of the divisions. The wages theme continues and the growth in earnings over four years is plotted. Manual and staff payments are plotted against the index of retail prices (both enjoyed virtually identical pay increases and both were lagging substantially behind the retail price index). Then the final sections of this booklet cover safety and health at work, training, industrial relations and pensions. Information on such a scale would however swamp the report to employees. So it is probably better that if the Dunlop approach is followed, it is made the subject of a separate booklet.

But there is a place for some employee information in an employee report. It frequently appears high up on the list of things employees want to know. The problem is how to compress the wealth of information into a small enough space. The Hoover report [Fig. 9], discussed in detail in Chapter 6, is very interesting in this respect because it devotes relatively more space to its labour relations side than it does to finance. At the time, of course, it was having a rough ride, with trading conditions harsh and factory closures looming. But even with that proviso the degree of information given was a surprise.

More typical of what companies could achieve and which generates very good employee response is the treatment adopted by Record Ridgway and reproduced here [Fig. 8]. This particular illustration from Record Ridgway does not show days lost through disputes, whereas it did the previous year. Perhaps the report so improved industrial relations that they did not have any strikes! But perhaps not. If this had been the case, I am sure it would have said so.

Industrial relations

Of the headings in this section, safety and health crop up occasionally in reports but usually only to record the number of accidents. Actual procedures are not written about, nor is training. The number of people sent on training courses is often listed, and the company's commitment to training stressed, but there is rarely real detail. Nor would you expect it. Such information, though obviously of great importance to the employee, is not the meat of a financial report. Nor is the rest of the information in this section. Again it falls more into the province of day-to-day dealings between management and employee.

Pay and conditions

The same is true for the next section, on pay and conditions. Most of this information has to appear by law in contracts of employment, whilst the rest of the information is rooted in the cut and thrust of industrial relations. But there are two areas in this section where employee reports have a bearing. The first is in the total wage costs — bringing home to the employee that the cost of employing him is considerably more than his salary once National Insurance and pension contributions and other facilities are taken into account. Crane Fruehauf made this point with a straightforward table tucked in near the end of its report and reproduced below. It is worth doing. Few employees would believe that additional direct costs add a further 10% on his wages bill.

Table 2. *Employee costs, Crane Fruehauf*

	£		
	1973	1974	1975
Earnings	5,511,516	6,949,846	6,994,092
Other costs (NHI, Company Pensions, Life Assurance)	463,556	598,401	682,284
TOTAL	5,975,072	7,548,247	7,676,376

One other item in this section has been included in an employee report, though only rarely. That was the company share option scheme. Vaux, the brewers, produced a month-by-month chart of their option scheme under which employees could buy shares, from the date of the scheme's introduction up to the time of the report. Anyone in the scheme would be showing a thumping profit on paper — which is probably why the graph was there. But at the time the report was printed they still had 3½ years to go before they could exercise their options, unless they died or chose to retire.

Information relevant to the immediate work location

Employee reports as constituted at the moment cannot really handle this kind of information, as for most companies it would be much too localised, and so it is the kind of information best communicated through briefing channels. But it does have a bearing on the follow-up seminars which many managements use now to hammer home the message of the employee report. It is just the kind of information which could be given at such a seminar as detailed local information to back up the general financial picture.

Conclusions

The general conclusion, therefore, is that the CBI guide gives a lot of food for thought in framing a policy for the employee report, but it leans too far into grey areas of industrial relations, where policy is of necessity fuzzy at the edges. It is possible to put together a package on these lines, but as we shall see, there are much better ways to go about it. But an understanding of what the CBI is about and what the TUC wants (which is the theme of the next chapter) is a vital backcloth which someone doing this work ignores at their peril.

CHAPTER SIX

THE TUC RECOMMENDATIONS ON DISCLOSURE

The TUC laid down its policy on information disclosure in a document *Industrial Democracy*, published in 1974. It was concerned with wider issues; in the years since then much of it has found its way into collective bargaining agreements and employee reports and has been enshrined in law. The preamble to their statement conveys the flavour of the TUC's proposals. As a statement of principle the TUC says that all employees should, as of right, be given:

(*a*) all information which is circulated to shareholders at the same time as it is circulated to shareholders;

(*b*) their terms and conditions of employment, including wages, hours, holidays, pensions, sick pay arrangements and entitlement to notice;

(*c*) a job specification, including responsibilities, management structure and health and other possible job hazards;

(*d*) employment prospects, including promotion opportunities and plans to expand or contract the workforce;

(*e*) access to the employee's personal file and an entitlement to an explanation by the employer of its contents.

A second section then goes into detail. It covers disclosure to employees' representatives — a more restricted group — then to employees at large, and deals in turn with manpower, earnings, sources of revenue, costs, directors' remuneration, profits, performance indicators and the worth of the company. It concludes with a section on prospects and plans. Under each of these broad headings it lists the following specific requirements:

Manpower
Number of employees by job description
Rates of turnover
Statistics on short-time working
Absenteeism
Sickness and accident

Recruitment
Training
Redeployment
Promotion
Redundancy and dismissal
Breakdown of non-wage labour costs
Earnings
Averages and distributions by appropriate occupations and work groups of earnings and hours including, where necessary, information on make-up of pay, showing piecework earnings, etc. This information should be provided on a six-monthly basis and in the case of large companies should apply to work units or divisions as well as the whole company.

Employee representatives, declares the TUC, should also have access to whatever financial information is necessary to a full understanding of the affairs of the enterprise, e.g.:

Sources of revenue
Sales turnover by main activities
Home and export sales
Non-trading income including income from investments and overseas earnings
Pricing policy
Costs
Distribution and sales costs
Production costs
Administrative and overhead costs
Costs of materials and machinery
Costs of management and supervision
Directors' remuneration
Including country of payment
Profits
Before and after tax and taking into account Government allowance, grants and subsidies
Distributions and retentions
Performance indicators
Unit costs
Output per man
Return on capital employed
Value added

Sales per square foot of selling space (in retail sectors)
Worth of company
Details of growth and up to date value of fixed assets and stocks
Growth and realisable value of trade investments.

The TUC says that the information to be disclosed to employees or their representatives should be the subject of an information agreement which would also set out arrangements for ensuring necessary confidentiality.

Industrial Democracy goes on to declare that if worker participation in management decision-making is to become a reality, information must be provided on prospects and plans. In this context the necessary information should include:

(*a*) Details of new enterprises and locations, prospective close-downs, mergers and takeovers;

(*b*) Trading and sales plans, production plans, investment plans, including research and development;

(*c*) Manpower plans, plans for recruitment, selection and training, promotion, regrading and redeployment; short-time and redundancy provisions.

Going through these areas point by point, what does emerge strongly is the overlap of views between what the TUC wants and what the CBI seemed willing for companies to concede. As a result many of the diagrams mentioned earlier in the context of the industrialists' approach serve equally well to satisfy the TUC. Indeed, this commonality of approach found another expression in the Code of Practice drawn up by ACAS, the Advisory Conciliation and Arbitration Service, set up under the Employment Protection Act. This code of practice, which was drafted to set a norm for acceptable disclosure in industry, drew heavily on the CBI and TUC views, which were basically the same as expressed in this and the previous chapter. The ACAS guidelines went through Parliament in the early summer of 1977, and should anyone feel they would like to use these as a basis for a report, they will be able to trace them all back to either the CBI or the TUC approaches outlined in this and the previous chapter.

On the TUC guidelines, it is worth noting that though the body of information in this and subsequent sections is labelled as information to be supplied to employee representatives the TUC is adamant that information so supplied should not, and will not, be considered confidential, meaning that in all probability it will be passed on to the employees at some stage. As this is going to happen anyway, management might as well communicate such information direct to the employees through the employee report and get the credit for it.

Manpower

The information required by the first section, on manpower, as listed above, seems quite a mouthful, but this list tallies with that of the CBI. It is noticeable too how the employee report produced by Record Ridgway following lengthy discussions with the union representatives (which was described in Chapter 4) includes a manpower section which follows these recommended sub-headings virtually to the letter, and it is worth checking back to remind yourself how much information can be included in a four-page report. One would be hard pressed to think of a better way to convey the information. Indeed, the only way it could be faulted is in not breaking down the categories of employee more. But companies willing to experiment in this area have found it a major difficulty, once you start talking about labour statistics, safety, training and so on, to know where to stop. The amount of information which could be of interest is vast — enough to take over the whole of the report.

Hoover, the electrical firm, accepted this risk. In a report with seventeen pages of copy, the first six were devoted to a run-down of the financial results, a statement from the chairman and some forecasts for the coming year. But the rest, some eleven pages, was given over to manpower figures; and very well done they were too, as the sample reproduced [Fig. 9] shows.

The strengths of the Hoover report are in many ways self-evident from the pages reproduced. First, the company has taken enough space to make sure that each page looks good and contains only that small amount of information which can be readily absorbed. Second, it has taken considerable pains over design, using diagrams where they are of value, but not being afraid to present information in tabular form when this is the simplest way of putting it across. Third, the information flows logically. The company makes one or two points on each page and moves on to another topic when you turn over. Fourth, the information is comprehensive. All the areas of employee concern are covered. Finally, it does not pull its punches. When things are bad it says so.

Employees respect such honesty, even if they do not agree with it. So there can be no better guide for the treatment of employee statistics than the one reproduced here. Any company wanting to follow the same path should happily use this as a model.

Earnings

The TUC's next proposals, the section on earnings, are less easily satisfied. What it suggests is that the employees' representatives be given the average earnings and hours worked for employees, broken down by appropriate work group and occupation. This should also, where appropriate, show how much pay depended on piecework or similar output related systems. It further suggests that this information should be provided at six-monthly intervals and, where the company is large, it should be broken down into smaller, more relevant work units or divisions within the global figures. There is a general feeling among companies that this is not the stuff of employee reports. Companies do provide this information, but it has not been included in an employee report yet. Companies are always reticent on wages when asked to be specific. It is quite common for management to illustrate how the total wage bill has risen over the past five years — usually plotted against an almost equally dramatic decline in dividends — but this information is no more than they are obliged to give in the annual report. And who can blame them? In part, this reticence is commonsense. If you are dealing with a large group, there may be large pay differentials between plants, large enough to cause resentment, and demands for parity from the employees if they were brought to light. But in still greater part, the omission stems from management's wish, in an employee report at least, to step above the fray. Wages and wage claims are a continual day-to-day problem in a lot of companies and many feel that just once they would like to be able to talk about other things. The employee report they see as a marvellous vehicle for such general discussion.

Sources of revenue

Again, with the possible exception of pricing policy — which firms try not to tell even the taxman — companies have been very forthcoming on these subjects. Redman Heenan — a page of whose report is reproduced [Fig. 10] — is a classic example, perhaps because like Record Ridgway it conducted extensive research beforehand with the employees. It found a considerable pent-up demand for more information on how each company within the group was performing. Unfortunately, it stopped short of providing local profit figures because these had not been given to shareholders. But what it did produce covered very comprehensively where the products were sold geographically and which were the most important. So in two small tables it met all the TUC requirements apart from income from investments, which would be in the annual report, and the rather unlikely feature of a pricing policy statement. In another chart it also showed how exports fared as a proportion of total sales over the past five years, and what progress the group, as a whole, had made in profits over the same period. All in all, therefore, its employees were given a comprehensive picture of the firm's export record, and the importance of their own particular products in the overall performance and ultimate success of the group. In short, it gave the employees something with which they could identify, and something about which they could feel a sense of achievement — both of which are vital to the morale of anyone, inside or outside a company.

Other companies, apart from Redman Heenan, have also made their mark. But the accolade should go to Tate and Lyle and GKN, which in 1977 became two of the first really large companies to give detailed breakdowns of the sales, value-added, profit, and product performance of their subsidiaries. So important is the Tate and Lyle and GKN initiative that it will be discussed at greater length later in this book, in Chapter 15.

Costs

Even if management wanted to give all the figures in this area demanded by the TUC, it would not be that easy, if only because of the difficulties of allocating overhead costs not attributable to only one product in a way which would be seen and accepted as fair. This is also why, when big companies give a value-added statement, they have to make the definitions fairly wide, for example by putting salaries, wages, and administration into one big package. But in smaller companies it is easier, and has been done, with the best example to date coming from Nissen. It did not, it is true, give a detailed breakdown of all costs, but what it did was to produce a "hypothetical average product" and then itemised straight through from selling price to profit where the money went and what the costs were.

Costs are a sensitive area for management, as the TUC is well aware, for it returns to the subject in a later section. But there is a problem which goes beyond mere sensitivity. If cost figures were disclosed across the board it seems inevitable that customers would put pressure on companies to cut prices whenever they saw healthy profit margins. Even in a small company, with a good share of a market, you might be vulnerable to this sort of pressure, if only because it is harder for a small company to say no, and big companies, with big customers, would face it all the time. So while one can see the value of the information from the trade union side (they can use it as a guide to the company's health and efficiency), it is unlikely to be supplied very often. If it is it will probably be on the lines of the Nissen statement, where no actual costs are disclosed, there is no relation to a specific product, and an average for costs is struck across the whole company.

Directors' remuneration

Directors' payments are the next item on the TUC list with an added qualification which they must have relished in Congress House, "including country of payment". Perhaps 99% of the directors in this country would have no objection at all to stating where they were paid. They might even state where they would like to be paid if they were allowed the choice. And, frivolity apart, there is a strong case for supplying information of directors' gross and net remuneration. It might give a bit of momentum towards getting top rates of tax down if more people knew how much marginal rates meant in hard cash.

Profits

The second item in this section, distributions and retentions, causes no problems — even private family companies seem happy to tell employees how small dividend distributions are, how they are dwarfed by retained profit, and how that retained profit is a key element in financing the future investment and growth of the company. But dealing with the Government is another matter. *The Corporate Report* suggested that company annual reports should produce a statement of money exchanges with government. Some companies, admittedly very few, have tried this. One example, from Blackwood Hodge, which modelled its annual accounts on *The Corporate Report,* was reproduced as Fig. 1. But it has not caught on in employee reports, and I think there are several reasons for this. The first is that when people are talking and writing about taxation they tend to get hot under the collar, and some of the earlier employee reports, particularly, got rather carried away on the subject. One (which had better remain anonymous) even explained to its employees how

the amount it paid in tax quite dwarfed its total profits, and indeed it did. But what it failed to explain was that included in this tax figure was the vast sum of PAYE, which it had paid, but which was really the employees' tax payment. Such treatment threatened to give employee reporting a bad name for a time, and there has been a tendency since for companies to keep well away from mentioning governments and anything else which might be termed political. The notable exception to this is GKN, which seems positively to relish telling the Government what it is doing wrong. But then GKN is bigger than most.

This nervousness about politics means that companies tackle tax on profits, and some even struggle with deferred tax, but there is rarely, if ever, a mention of investment grants or other Government allowances, many of which are worth considerable sums of money. But there are some exceptions. Dowty, which does a lot of Government work, was one of the few exceptions. It mentioned Government grants, but it did not quantify them. United Builders Merchants on the other hand did, and provided an interesting table on its role as a tax payer and tax collector. It listed £2.2 million VAT, £4.2 million PAYE, £2.8 million National Insurance, £1.1 million Corporation Tax and £1.2 million local rates. It then knocked off the £0.1 million it received from the State. UBM's profits that year were £2.9 million before tax, but the total tax bill just itemised was £11.4 million. This is an area where companies could do more: spelling out just how important they are to the community — their customers and suppliers — as well as to government. It doesn't take much space and it is a message worth putting across. Greenall Whitley, however, must take the cake. Its skill in relating tax paid to miles of motorway or the pay of nurses really hits home — as can be seen in Fig. 11

Performance indicators

The TUC next goes on to ask for performance indicators. It expected these to be given verbally, if at all. But some companies, particularly the small and successful ones, are prepared to supply it. Perhaps if you are small and successful you have very little of which to feel ashamed and relish providing such figures. Unhappily, most companies are not in such a position, and even if they were would very much doubt the competitive wisdom of doing so; but it is interesting to see what can be achieved, both in terms of conveying information and educating people in the process into the methods of financial control, if these figures are supplied. A page from Nissen's report [Fig. 12] takes questions which a financially aware employee might ask, and some in which the totally unsophisticated would also be interested. It then translates these into financial ratios which are in fairly common use, and gives the answers. The effect is, to say the least, startling. The weakness of this approach is, of course, knowing how many employees could understand it, given that research has proved that well over 50% of the population have difficulty in understanding their electricity bills. But when one of the major fears in these reports is the fear of patronising the employee, a chart like this has a lot to be said for it. It is well laid out, logical, and it conveys the impression to the reader that he is really getting to grips with financial controls. Admittedly there is more to it than that, but the impression that you are being let into a few secrets makes for compulsive reading — even if having read the secrets you find they were not all that startling. (One must have one reservation about this table, however, concerning the mixture of figures from different years. It is hard to see why all the ratios could not have been calculated from the same date — indeed for the sake of credibility it could be thought to be vital. But this was not done, and it creates the unfortunate impression that the figures have been "selected" to show the company in the best possible light. There is no suggestion that this was the purpose but companies must always remember that if they do choose figures in an apparently illogical way then they are defenceless against the charge that they are cooking the books.)

Worth of company

Here the TUC wants details of the growth in fixed assets and stocks, and their current up-to-date values. It couples this with a request for information on the growth in, and realisable value of, trade investments. To some extent this information is covered in the company's annual report, though valuations of fixed assets — particularly property — are often out of date, or suspect. So too with trade investments — though in recent years these valuations have been improved. The route taken in employee reports to meet this request for information is to produce the company balance sheet, or something approximating to it. Of course, this does not necessarily give complete up-to-date valuations on fixed assets. However, there are many ways of trying to put over the balance sheet, some much more successful than others, as is apparent in Chapter 12.

Prospects and plans

The TUC's final requirement does not lend itself always to employee reporting but I would commend again the statement produced by Crane Fruehauf [Fig. 7] referred to in the previous chapter as being very positive and forward-looking in terms of sales, investment and production plans — three areas of particular TUC concern. Such information, even if it does find its way into an employee report, will, however, of necessity be vague and generalised in its approach, in contrast to the specific details which would be needed for participation in decision making.

Conclusions

As a guide to management, the TUC statement has considerable value in isolating areas of concern and interest to employees. Even if the information is not going to be supplied it is worth bearing these points in mind when drawing up a programme. It would be tempting to think, having run through the CBI and the TUC approaches, that between them they must have covered every point that the employee would want to know about and management might be prepared to give, and that might be what you would expect before you actually reduce their proposals to basics. But having done the hard work and gone through all that they have said, neither set of proposals, nor even a synthesis of the two, forms the basis of a good employee report. There may be much to be said for a company, in taking its first steps into this field, to use these proposals as a guide, and the illustrations reproduced show how much can be done. But it would not, at the end of the day, be the best possible report.

The reason for this is simple. The hardest problem in drafting an employee report is deciding what to leave out and what to put in. To be effective it needs to be short, or you bore the employee in the same way that annual reports bore the shareholder. Long reports, unless they are of exceptional quality, are not read. Neither the TUC, nor the CBI, give any system of priorities for information. This is not meant to be a criticism because, in fairness to both bodies, their proposals were framed in the wider context of overall disclosure, not simply the drafting of employee reports, and it is unfair to try them against a standard which they were not trying to achieve. But it still makes them unsatisfactory as the basis for an employee report. The second weakness of both sets of proposals is that they have veered a long way from the transmission of straightforward financial information, and have instead become involved in industrial relations and the collective bargaining process. This is a vital area for the health of companies and the success of disclosure policies, but it is tangential to the success of an employee report. And the third and most telling reason why both approaches are found lacking is that, together or apart, they do not add up to a policy. If they both have a weakness it is that at their heart they are muddled. They are, at their roots, not sure if they are simply trying to conjure up a mass of information which can be used to wallpaper the room next time both sides sit down to bargain, or if they are embarking on a policy of educating the employee so that he can become an active participant in a new age of industrial democracy. Or, being still more vague, do they just think disclosure is a good thing, and if enough secrets are made public then everybody will be happier?

Basically, the weakness comes down to the lack of positive theme behind the disclosure policies. And while you may be able to get away with having no theme in a discussion document, in an employee report, if you do not know what you want to say and why you want to say it, you will produce a bad document.

But the positive point of the CBI and TUC proposals, and the reason why they are of value to anyone beginning to do work in this field, is that they do help put what you are trying to do into context. They do draw the boundaries very clearly within which you operate. So they may not tell you what you should do, but they do tell you when you have gone far enough.

CHAPTER SEVEN

THE ACCOUNTANTS' APPROACH TO DISCLOSURE

In a great many companies the job of producing a financial report for employees is going to fall to the accountant. Even in those companies where he is not left to do the whole job on his own, he is still sure to be called in at some stage to supply the figures. Accountants, by their training, bring a specific attitude of mind to information disclosure — indeed they argue with the term itself, tending instead to favour "information provision". What follows therefore is an attempt to marry the best of the traditional accountant's skills with the demands of reporting to employees.

Accountants are among the few people in the country who actually understand financial statements, but when it comes to communicating this financial information to others, this knowledge turns out to be a dangerous thing. They know too much to be able to explain simply and they have a reputation as a result for being poor communicators. Yet they face the communications problem every day of their working lives, so they should be used to it, and adept at getting the message across. To understand why they are not it is important to recognise the limit of that communications skill and the narrow lines in which it has been developed. Such skills as the profession has are confined to communicating with shareholders (for the accountant in practice) and management (for the man in industry). They have no experience of communicating with the employees. So the individual accountant has a problem, and the question is can he adjust his approach to the quite different demands of employee reporting? What does he look for in assessing the worth of financial statements in general — and how should these beliefs be adapted to employee reporting?

Some desirable qualities of accounts

The Corporate Report listed seven characteristics which accounts had to have to please accountants. These were relevance, understandability, reliability, completeness, objectivity, timeliness and comparability. The first of these was the relevance to the user of the information in the accounts. Shareholder accounts deal with groups and large organisations. But employee accounts relate to much smaller units. The employee wants information relevant to him, which means information at site level. The accounts must be broken down to relate to the employee's immediate work area.

The second characteristic is understandability. The accounts must be understood by the people who are supposed to read them. The accountant's training has led him to believe that every extra footnote helps because it adds to the available data, but in employee reporting, you can degrade the report by trying to say too much. Information blizzards can be created very easily because the existing threshold of knowledge is so low, and the simplest bit of everyday jargon will stop the reader in his tracks. A concept as basic as the balance sheet will cause the most tremendous problems, and even if you are aware of these pitfalls and skilfully avoid them, you can still blind the reader with the sheer size of the figures. People in their personal finances deal with money on a very small scale — the thousands and millions which fly around most sets of accounts are quite incomprehensible. So the last part of this chapter is devoted to ways of avoiding jargon.

The third characteristic of accounts is that they must be reliable — which means the employee must trust them. The accountant and the outside auditor pride themselves, usually quite rightly, on both honesty and impartiality. Yet, however unpalatable the fact, the accountant has to accept that the employee does not think he has these virtues any more than anybody else. The average person on the shopfloor thinks that the auditor is hand-in-glove with the management — because the audit partners and the company director have similar incomes, similar aspirations, similar life styles and similar social attitudes, and they are paid by the management. Auditors have nothing in common with the shopfloor and everything in common with the boardroom, so it is asking a lot to expect the auditor to be thought of as impartial. The in-house accountant is tarred with the same brush. The question, then, is "Who is believable?" There is no easy answer, but the CBI in some recent research claimed that employees will believe senior executives. Middle management does not have that credibility — the argument being that top management would never tell lies to employees, but might be prepared to order its middle management to do the dirty work for it. The rest come nowhere.

The fourth of the accountant's virtues is completeness, meaning that the information must give a "true and fair" picture of the company's operations. It must be a rounded picture, not over-selective and with nothing important missed out; but what is important to the accountant may be quite irrelevant to the employee, and therefore in giving the rounded picture you can go back into the information blizzard. Far more likely is that a successful employee report will be incomplete in the conventional accounting sense. It will select its information ruthlessly, and hammer home a few points very hard — even at the expense of the rounded picture.

The next point overlaps with the previous one. It says that accounts must be objective, which means that if there is selection to be done it must be done evenly — good news and bad news dispersed in equal proportions. On paper it again seems to circumscribe the employee report, where management simply wants to put over a few key facts. But in reality, it may not be quite so bad. Traditionally, employees claimed that the only time management told them the financial facts was when the news was bad. This explains the scepticism and reservation which has greeted employee reports now — half the employees are looking for a catch. So, against the tradition of only telling the bad news, even a biased employee report is an improvement, and an advance towards the standards of objectivity that accountants expect.

Timeliness is the sixth feature. Imagine what would happen if you switched on the television on a warm June evening and the newsreader calmly announced ". . . and here is the news up until last December 31st". You would switch off — or watch for the wrong reasons. But that is what you are saying to employees when you produce a financial report six months after the year end, and while such tardiness may be acceptable to shareholders (though even that is debatable) it is certainly not acceptable to employees.

Finally comes comparability — a concept of considerable relevance in accounting. It means that you can compare one year's figures with the previous year, safe in the knowledge that the basis of the calculations has not been altered to produce spurious results. It is a concept somewhat threatened by inflation accounting. Comparability is a vital ingredient in employee reports. A bold profit figure means little to an employee. He does not know whether it is good, bad or indifferent. Therefore, he wants and should be given information on the trends in the business—trends for sales, profits, employment and so on. He wants the comparability made obvious.

The above provides the intellectual framework for the accountant's approach to his task.

A consensus on content

The next problem is what does he put in? Some of the information which should go in is not the stuff traditionally found in shareholder reports. But it is not a problem which should delay us long, for out of all the debate on the information to be disclosed, some form of consensus seems to be emerging. The matrix below [Table 3] plots, albeit

Table 3.   *Summary chart of recommendations on disclosure*

Information heading	TUC	CBI	ACAS	100 Gp	DoT
Objectives	—	×	—	—	×
Employment	×	×	×	×	×
Pay, conditions	×	×	×	×	—
Productivity	×	×	×	×	—
Plans	×	×	—	×	×
Competition	—	×	—	—	—
Financial information	×	×	×	×	×
Unit-based reports	×	×	—	—	×

arbitrarily, the blocks of information recommended by the main organisations which have been in the vanguard of the disclosure debate. The organisations are the CBI, the TUC, the Advisory Conciliation and Arbitration Service (ACAS), the 100 Group (which is an influential pressure group of top accountants in industry) and the Department of Trade (adopting parts of *The Corporate Report*).

It is obvious from the matrix that there is considerable agreement on the main areas of content, all of which have been fully developed in other parts of the book. But dangers can result from following the letter rather than the spirit of the proposals. Two examples will suffice.

A statement of corporate objectives can be clear and far-sighted, but too often is woolly, not specific, and very short-term in outlook. The Serck and Crane Fruehauf statements [Figs. 6, 7] show how this can be avoided. Second, the company's competitive position. It is all too easy to duck this challenge and say that no information can be given because it will be of interest to competitors. But the point is it will also be of interest to the employees. Supposing, for example, that the company was losing market share and had been doing so gradually over several years; this could be spelt out very easily with figures and trends on the size, growth and company share of the market. If the company is doing badly the employees should know, so they at least have the opportunity of doing something about it — co-operating in new ventures to bring about recovery. If the employees are not told at first, and the slide continues, then they will have to be told later, probably the day before the firm goes bankrupt. It harks back, in fact, to the complaint voiced earlier, that management only ever tells them the bad news at the eleventh hour.

Presentation and explanation

Rules on presentation are basically common sense. First, round all numbers to two figures — £5.2 million is much better than £5,197,283. Second, if you are using columns of figures make them read downwards not across. Psychological tests have proved that they are easier to read that way. Third, wherever possible, quote averages. It helps cut down the number of figures and their size, and puts them into some kind of context. Fourth, put the biggest figures at the top of a page or column. Interest tails off very quickly, so hit the reader with the most important facts as quickly as possible. Fifth, use illustrations — particularly pounds divided into pennies — to put across ideas of how the cash is distributed. But don't use too many. Finally, make the information as personalised as possible, and relate it to the employee's experience. Management organisation charts should name the people — by Christian name. Grand Metropolitan illustrated the effect of inflation and replacement cost accounting by showing how much the cost of a bed had risen over the previous five years. To say the cost of a new hotel had risen from £5,832,170 to £8,277,132 would have meant very little, but to say that a bed had gone from £58 to £83 makes the same point more effectively. And that is what these accounts are all about — being effective.

CHAPTER EIGHT

THE SUCCESSFUL REPORT
— A CASE STUDY

It must, by now, be obvious that there are so many conflicting ideas as to content of employee reports, and such a variety of objectives, that one of the main difficulties is welding the whole into an acceptable and successful package. In order, therefore, to see what can be achieved in practice, this chapter is devoted to a case study of a particularly successful report — the one produced by Staffordshire Potteries in 1976. Not only did this receive outside recognition as the winner of *Accountancy Age* magazine's annual award, but much more to the point, it was acclaimed by the employees and succeeded, as subsequent research showed, in putting across its basic points. In other words, it did much of what it set out to do; that, in itself, is enough to set it apart from a great many reports.

The pattern of the report

Perhaps the best way of illustrating its success is simply to list the contents of the report to provide an at-a-glance guide to the scope and content of a winner:

1. A striking cover
2. An explanation of the purpose of the report
3. Value added statements
4. Cash flow statements
5. Balance sheet trends for the past five years
6. Sales and profits for the past five years
7. Information about customers
8. Information about the employees — their distribution, sex, age and years of service
9. Information about shareholders
10. An organisation chart of senior management
11. A chart of production management
12. The role of the non-production departments
13. Design problems and policies in detail
14. Export sales and developments in detail
15. Research, technical development and investment in detail.
16. Forecast from the chairman

The report was a joint effort between personnel director Richard McNamara and accountant Geoff Cashmore. It was the first time one had been produced by either them or the firm.

The cover was striking (some might say gimmicky), a railway layout of the Staffordshire Potteries Train of the title which represented the flows in the business — investment, raw materials, labour going in, profits, costs, wages going out — in fact, a working model of the accounts. Not only did this quite dramatically represent the interrelationships and flows of cash which make up any business, but, above all, it served to catch the eye and make the reader want to look inside to see what the report was all about. And in the words of Peter Parker, one of the award judges, "it had a sense of humour — which in the context of reports and accounts meant that it had a sense of proportion" [Fig. 13].

Throughout its twenty-two pages — which was on the long side — it maintained this sense of proportion. It was particularly strong on employee statistics and charts of the organisation, showing who was accountable to whom. Then it took each part of the company and explained what each was trying to do and what the problems were. So at the end of the day it left you with a feeling that here was a company where they did not expect miracles — just a fair crack of the whip.

Detailed contents

In detail, the report illustrates a great many points which seem obvious when they are made, but which many people overlook when pitched in the deep-end to do the job for themselves. The first page, inside the cover, is headed "A report to employees upon the affairs of the company", and it immediately explains to the employees what the report is, and why they should read it. To quote the opening paragraph, "We are pleased to present this, our first comprehensive report to employees.

It has been prepared to put employees of the company in the picture about the financial affairs of the company. If you have ever wondered how much of every pound we made goes to shareholders, how much to the employees and what happens to the rest of it, this report will tell you." So that is the first lesson – explain to the reader what the report is and what it is trying to do. Give them the information and leave them to decide for themselves whether or not they want to read on.

The second paragraph of the brief introduction deals with the economic climate, and explains that the figures relate to a financial year (a mystery to many people), not a calendar year. It is simple and effective, as the quote below shows. "The figures relate to our financial year which runs from 1 July 1975 to 30 June 1976. During this time the country as a whole was in a serious economic crisis. Inflation reached record levels, the value of the pound hit rock bottom, investment by industry reached an all time low, there was a worldwide trade recession and a lot of the earthenware industry was on short time working." Thus in a few short lines, national problems which almost all employees must be aware of — inflation and the sinking pound — are related to the problems of the industry and how it affects their job. It also sets the scene for management to take credit for its actions. A black picture has been painted. The problems have been posed, so what did management do? Paragraph 3 gives the answer. "How did we get on? Well, we have had a difficult time. During the autumn we were very worried. Our customers were simply not ordering. So we launched a particularly energetic intercontinental sales drive. The production units tightened their already tight belts. We streamlined and professionalised our administration. We increased the rate of new products and we kept producing."

This paragraph serves as an introduction to another general lesson. One of the major problems in industry is that the employees on the shopfloor do not know what management does and they do not know the problems management faces and resolves every day. The paragraph just quoted is a succinct example of how to explain to employees what management is about: namely, solving problems for the good of all. This company had an advantage, the policy worked. But it may well be as effective to explain in a similar way to the employees what you had tried to do even if it had not worked. It might go some way to raising the status of management in the eyes of the shopfloor. The reason that kind of paragraph works is that it is honest and down-to-earth. The management is not

claiming to have done anything brilliant — instead it is claiming to have kept plugging away just that bit harder. This is how it sums up: "To put it simply, it worked. We made a record profit — not as much as we would have done without the national problems, but pretty good in the circumstances. Don't be afraid to take some good old-fashioned pride in our achievement. It is good to be successful. And it is successful manufacturing companies who create the wealth that pays for the national health service, our schools and social services, defence and other government expenditure." If communication is to have any long term success, and if employees are to identify with a company in a meaningful way, this link between the wealth created by industry and the benefits available to society at large must be appreciated and accepted by them all. If they think the real wealth produced is being siphoned off they know not where, then they will never truly identify and will always feel distrust and resentment. So every report ought to spare a few words to bring this out and to put the industrial activities of one company into the national economic context.

Pages 4 and 5 of the report continue the theme of wealth creation, using a value added statement. It takes as a starting point the money received from customers, and deducts the cost of raw materials and services and says that the residual, some £4 million, is the wealth the company created. It then shows where the wealth went with a novel form of pie chart [Fig. 14], a plate with a Staffordshire Potteries design on it (a small way in which the company's identity comes through). This gradually gets sliced up by wages, tax, depreciation and dividends, leaving a figure for net profits. Conscious of the bad effect of figures expressed in millions, the distribution of wealth is also put another way, breaking down the pound of wealth created. It says 79p goes to employees, 9p to the Government, 9p was retained in the business (of which 6p is profit and 3p depreciation) and 3p went to shareholders. "The money that is retained in the business is investment. It is used to finance expansion and buy new plant and machinery" says the report. It then explains how this retained money is used up, under "Where the money went to and where it came from."

"During the year we had to increase our working capital in order to combat inflation and finance expansion. At the same time we invested heavily in new plant and machinery. Some of this investment came from profits retained — that has already been explained. We did not have enough money already in the company to finance all the items however. The following sections explain where the additional money came from. We needed £967,000 in extra cash to keep the business going and to invest in order to secure the future."

After this introduction, there are two charts — the first, which shows how the money went into three main items: "purchase of new plant and machinery and buildings; to finance stocks; and to finance the difference between what we are owed by customers, and what we owe to the suppliers of raw materials." A footnote explains further what is meant by finance for stocks as follows: "This is the cash needed to pay for the increased cost of raw materials, stores and part finished products in our premises on 30 June. We have paid for the raw materials, the wages and the overheads but have not sold the products. Therefore, this actual cash is necessary to bridge the gap." On the facing page is a chart showing where the money came from, divided into wealth retained in the business (as previously explained); deferred tax; new capital provided by shareholders; and bank finance. The report tackles the problem of deferred tax head-on: "The government operates a scheme which encourages manufacturers to invest. The effect of this is to allow payment of tax to be deferred. Thus the tax that is allowed for in the wealth created figures is actually ploughed back into the business." Whether that note goes far enough is difficult to say. It is unnerving to learn that what you were told on the previous page about taxation is not quite true. But at the same time, it is hard to see how else it could have been tackled, without being equally misleading in other directions. Better too, to have enlarged on the fact that at some stage in the future it will have to be paid, though as long as the company keeps investing it can put off the day of reckoning indefinitely. Otherwise employees might think it had got out of paying tax altogether. It might also be worth saying that the logic of the Government's policy is that more investment means more jobs and higher salaries in expanding companies. So the Government gets its cut by being able to take more tax off the company and employees — and avoiding having to pay out money on the dole.

The next section provides basic balance sheet information. It gives a five-year record of the growth of fixed assets and working capital; the sources of funds (loans, debentures, deferred tax and retained capital); sales performance, and profits before tax. Each of these four diagrams

tries to bring home how the company has expanded in the 1970s but the figures are not adjusted for inflation. So to some extent they give an artificial picture of the growth and stability of the company. The authors have recognised here that for a full understanding of one year's figures the employees should be told about the performance over a span of years. Employees like to see how the company has progressed and like to feel that, in the years they have been with a company, it has grown from small beginnings to thriving bustling business.

That concludes the purely financial information. "Let us now have a look in more detail" says the report "at the three groups of people who are important to the company. First of all, the most important of all, our customers. In 1975/76 we sold our products to well over 1000 different customers. The customers range from major international retail and wholesale organisations to market stall holders. More than 60 of these customers did more than £20,000 worth of business with us in the year. The companies who bought goods directly from us during the year in the home market include Boots, British Home Stores, Lewis's, Debenhams, Tesco, Woolworths and the Co-operative Wholesale Society" [Fig. 15].

This is a very important departure. Few reports give information about their customers for fear of competitors. Yet it stands to reason that it is an obvious area of employee interest. They are spending their lives making products, it is only natural for them to want to know what happens to them once they leave the factory.

But of even greater interest is the next section. "The second group of people without whom the company could not exist . . . the employees. But how many have we got? How old are they? What do they do? How long do they stay with us? And who are they?" The company provides employee statistics on a massive scale, over its next four pages. The impact of these different tables is rather overwhelming. Information is given for the head office and for each of the group's four operating divisions separately. It is possible to see, at a glance, how many people are under 21 in any part of the company; how many clerical and supervisory staff are in each division and at head office; how many men and how many women there are; how many with up to five years' or more than ten years' service; how many are full time and so on. You could not ask for much more. The weakness of these pages is one of design, not one of content. One suspects that though these pages gave a wealth of information, they probably did not make quite the impact they should have done on the employees. The TUC chapter illustrates the approach adopted by Hoover to employee statistics — how much absenteeism there was, how many days were lost through strikes, how the safety record of the factory compared with previous years and so on — and it is a better treatment. None of those areas are covered in this report. It could be that absenteeism is not a problem (strikes certainly were not). Or it could be that the authors felt that to bring in such statistics would be to strike a discordant note, for the tenor of the report is very much one of "all pulling together". Absentee figures, no matter how objectively presented, inevitably bring in a note of criticism. But in spite of these difficulties there is value in a statement which gives the average hours worked per employee and the amount of time lost through sickness, absenteeism and disputes. It is no good pretending that such things do not happen, and in companies where it is a problem, there is evidence that employees are themselves rather shocked at its scale, when it is spelt out. That shock will not bring about an improvement in itself, but at least it is a step along the way.

The report next moves on to complete its trinity:

"There is a third group of people without whom the company could not operate. They are the shareholders. You have seen on page 7 how the shareholders put extra money into the company to help finance our expansion. The money was raised by a 'placing' of shares.

"The way a placing works is that the company sold a further 250,000 shares largely to financial institutions such as insurance companies. This increased the total number of shares issued from 988,364 to 1,238,364. The current value of these shares is £1.53 which gives the company's shares a total value of £1,894,700. The average shareholder owns 1,548 shares which have an approximate value of £2,370. The dividend payable for 1975/76 was 9.5p per share. So the average shareholder received about £147 on an investment currently worth £2,370 — so the return (or interest) is just over 6%.

"One final point to remember about shareholders is that our biggest single group of shareholders is the directors. The company is therefore in the favourable position where the top management have a big personal financial stake in the company."

What are the strengths of this statement? First of all, the shareholders had put up more capital, so it was a particularly relevant time to talk about their role. Second, the treatment furthers the partnership ideal — the link between customer, employee and shareholder for the common benefit of all. Third, it is information which employees frequently say they want and there can be few areas of finance where so little is known by the man in the street as the relationship between the shareholder and the company. But there are ways in which it could have been improved. The figure for an average shareholding is too vague. It would have been better to have split the shares into those held by institutions, pension funds and trade unions; those held by the directors; and those held by the small shareholder. To the employee an average holding of £2,300 would seem a considerable amount of money. Most small shareholders have rather less than this, and it would be good to make this clear in the report, to show that holding shares is something to which the employee could himself aspire. Apparently, some employees asked later how they could become shareholders too; there could have been a paragraph explaining how anyone could be a shareholder, how little money it takes, and suggesting where any employee who wanted to could get further information.

The lack of information on the institutions was also disappointing. They are mentioned in the context of the placing, but who they are and why they should be involved is not clear. The report would have been better for an illustration of how insurance premiums and pension contributions flow into the insurance companies — how the money then flows back to buy shares in industry and promote growth and investment and get dividends which return to the employee either as a pension, or a matured insurance policy. It is important to stress that most people in the country are shareholders in industry, albeit at one remove — and that the system is interlinked and mutually supporting. At the moment employees do not understand the role of the institutions. So it makes sense to try to tell them. The institutions have names people recognise — the Prudential, Sun Alliance, Legal and General — and it brings home to the employee that the financial world is not the shadowy mysterious place he thought it was.

The throwaway line about the directors' shareholdings is also risky. If it is going to be mentioned, and it is certainly of interest, then perhaps it should be done in more detail. Directors' holdings are listed in the annual report so they should have been reproduced here — together with information about the income directors receive, not just in dividends, but in salary, and show the impact of tax on these salaries. If the directors have relatively large shareholdings and there is a strong family connection with the company, it is worth a few lines explaining how the business was founded by an ancestor (if indeed it was). Failing that, how did present directors come by their shareholdings? Did they inherit them from previous generations? Or did they buy them out of savings? It is surprising how few companies give this information to employees although it is freely available — or indeed give any other useful and sensible information about the management.

Staffordshire Potteries redeems itself on the latter score. It says "To help complete the picture it is necessary for us to consider the senior management and have a look at the way the company is organised." It then gives details of who is in charge of what, with an organisational chart showing Christian names as well as job titles. You can see at a glance how each manager fits into the hierarchy. The only addition one could suggest is details of the ages of the management team, and some facts about their length of service with the company. They are all full time, so there are no complications with non-executive directors — but if there were then the role and purpose of the non-executive director could have been explained at this point. Backing up the management structure is a well organised chart of the production management in each division [reproduced as Fig. 4]. The great value of a chart like that is that it helps all employees to see at a glance where they fit into the organisation. Many will never have realised before how the group was organised and what the chains of command were. It can only do good to tell them.

The next step also shows great awareness of the gaps in employee knowledge. Three departments were a total mystery to the shopfloor — exports, design and technical development, and the report set out to put that right. The manager of each department contributed a short statement on what problems his department had faced, what he felt it had achieved during the year and where it was going from here. Every effort was taken to relate the activities of the specialised departments, like design, to the production units — with which the bulk of the employees are familiar. Hence stress was laid on the purpose of the group's activities — design for example showed how its new designs helped to meet new tastes and fashions and was also a response to management's decision a few years earlier to break into new areas of the tableware market. They also said where they were going, and where they hoped to be in five years. Nor did they shrink from pointing out how difficult

the job was as these new products are only part of the continued cycle of development "... which will make 'Kilncraft' dinnerware a worldwide market leader within the next five years. To achieve this goal all our dinnerware products must have high acceptability in the major markets of the world. This means redesigning shapes for the USA and Europe. It means understanding colour preferences from California to Copenhagen, and also keeping a wary eye on our competitors both local, national and overseas."

Only the final page remains, and that contained a statement from the chairman in which he gave a forecast of what the current year and future years would bring. It served neatly to round off the package.

Failures and successes

Perhaps the most telling point about the report was that it was packed with information, as the summary and exposition of its contents shows, but did not appear to be. It managed to put across a mass of detail without ever appearing ponderous. With the benefit of hindsight, however, it emerged that there were a couple of areas which the authors felt could have been improved.

The first was the statement of where the cash came from and where it went. On paper it was a simple straightforward diagram — two matching bar charts — but, said Richard McNamara, almost nobody among the employees could understand it. Its point was to explain the importance of cash and the increased demand for working capital, but this failed completely to come across. Cash is, of course, important and it would be a disappointment if the section had to be omitted altogether. So attempts to explain it in future will probably be done through the text rather than by trying to simplify the balance sheet.

A few weeks after the report was published 200 of the employees were surveyed to find out what they thought of the exercise and how they felt things could be improved. The results showed an encouragingly high readership. But they also uncovered a demand for much greater detail on employee pay — they all wanted to know how the wages in one department compared to another and how the wages in one unit compared to those in another part of the factory. Supplying such information would be a major test of management's commitment to the job because it is obvious the repercussions it could have — particularly where anomalies are highlighted. But in a broader sense management ought to be able to justify objectively its pay structure across a group. If it can justify it

Fig. 1.   Blackwood Hodge: extracts from annual report (*see page 15*), cont'd overleaf

Blackwood Hodge Limited and Subsidiaries

Source and Application of Funds

	1975	1974	1973	1972	1971 *
	£m	£m	£m	£m	£m
Source of Funds					
Profit before taxation and extraordinary items	11.7	8.5	5.7	4.1	5.0
Extraordinary items	2.2	(0.6)	1.0	0.9	(0.3)
Depreciation	5.6	3.8	3.0	2.0	1.6
Exchange on fixed assets other than properties	(1.4)	(0.3)	(0.3)	(0.3)	0.1
Total generated from operations	18.1	11.4	9.4	6.7	6.4
Proceeds of share issues to minority shareholders	—	—	2.3	—	—
	18.1	11.4	11.7	6.7	6.4
Application of Funds					
Dividends paid by the Holding Company	0.7	0.7	1.0	0.7	1.1
Dividends paid to minority shareholders	0.3	0.2	0.1	—	—
Taxation paid	2.9	3.1	2.6	1.0	1.9
Net additions to fixed assets	9.1	6.4	6.9	4.1	4.8
Acquisition of new interests	—	0.1	—	0.1	0.1
	13.0	10.5	10.6	5.9	7.9
Increase (decrease) in working capital :					
Increase in stocks	30.9	19.2	10.6	2.3	5.5
Increase in debtors	8.7	3.0	10.2	5.6	1.6
Increase in creditors	(23.9)	(11.2)	(10.9)	(4.3)	(7.4)
Increase in secured loans	—	(0.2)	(0.3)	(0.2)	(0.1)
	15.7	10.8	9.6	3.4	(0.4)
	28.7	21.3	20.2	9.3	7.5
Movement in Net Liquid Funds					
Increase in net bank indebtedness	10.6	9.9	8.5	2.6	1.1

*14 months to 31st December, 1971

33

Fig. 1.　(cont'd)

Statement of Money Exchanges
Between the Blackwood Hodge Group and the United Kingdom Government

The Group's monetary exchanges with the United Kingdom Government in the year to 31st December, 1975 are contained in the table below.

In considering the information disclosed it should be borne in mind that only 21% of Group turnover (£38.5 million) is attributable to the United Kingdom and that of the persons employed by the Group at 31st December, 1975 only 1,338 (25%) are employed in this country with an aggregate remuneration for the year to 31st December, 1975 of £3,672,000.

	£000
Payments in respect of:	
Advance Corporation Tax	**424**
A.C.T. surcharge repaid	**(161)**
Corporation Tax	**61**
Tax withheld from loan stock interest	**120**
P.A.Y.E.	**758**
National Insurance contributions	**419**
Rates	**172**
Value Added Tax	**(196)**
Receipts in respect of:	
Development Area Grants	**(25)**
NET CASH FLOW TO UK GOVERNMENT	**1,572**
EXPRESSED AS AN AMOUNT PER EMPLOYEE	**£1,175**

Fig. 1.   (cont'd)

Statement of Foreign Currency Transactions

The following table details the transactions in foreign currency undertaken by the Blackwood Hodge Group during the year ended 31st December, 1975. Exports from the United Kingdom include those purchases made in this country by Group subsidiaries overseas as well as exports made directly by UK subsidiaries.

In considering the level of investment it is important to bear in mind that the inventories and accounts receivable of Group overseas companies are financed to a substantial extent by local borrowings.

	£000
Receipts:	
Exports from the United Kingdom	**37,977**
Dividends, interest and fees remitted by overseas subsidiaries	**841**
Repayment of loans by overseas subsidiaries	**7**
	38,825
Payments:	
Imports into the United Kingdom	**2,376**
Investment in overseas subsidiaries	**317**
	2,693
NET INFLOW TO THE UNITED KINGDOM	**36,132**

Fig. 1.   (cont'd)

Ten year sales record

SALES BY PRODUCT CLASSIFICATION

	1966	1967	1968	1969	1970	1971	1972	1973	1974	1975
	£m	£m	£m	£m	£m	£m	£m	£m	£m	£m
New & used equipment	21·5	22·9	25·9	32·7	42·6	46·3	44·8	67·8	81·2	**99·1**
Parts	8·3	8·3	10·6	13·3	16·4	17·7	18·3	23·4	34·5	**46·9**
Servicing	3·2	2·4	3·1	5·1	6·9	7·6	7·2	9·6	12·8	**17·4**
Hiring	1·5	1·3	1·6	2·2	2·7	3·5	5·0	6·7	8·8	**10·0**
Engine Division and	—	1·9	2·6	2·9	3·4	3·8	4·2	5·2	7·4	**10·2**
Other Divisions	—	0·2	0·7	1·0	1·3	1·1	1·1	1·2	1·7	**2·5**
Total Sales	34·5	37·0	44·5	57·2	73·3	80·0	80·6	113·9	146·4	**186·1**

Fig. 1.   (cont'd)

Employment Report

As an employer of approximately 5,400 persons throughout the world and as a concern directly involved with the sale and servicing of highly technical products the Blackwood Hodge investment is predominantly in its employees. The contribution made by each employee to Group performance is high and is shown by the diagrams overleaf.

It is important that each employee is aware of the contribution which Blackwood Hodge personnel make to the performance of the Group and an attempt has also been made overleaf to illustrate how, by incurring employment costs, paying interest to those from whom we borrow money, providing for the depreciation of our assets, paying our taxes, rewarding those who have invested money in the business, and meeting the other costs of running the business, Blackwood Hodge fulfils its role as a supplier of earthmoving and construction equipment and the vital after-sales service for that equipment.

Blackwood Hodge has subsidiary companies in 29 countries throughout the world and these companies vary in size from those which consist of a small team of managerial and technically expert employees to those larger subsidiaries such as those based in Canada and the United Kingdom where over 1,000 persons are employed. The map on the last page of this report details the location of Group employees in the countries of employment. With such a variation in size of employing company and the contrasts brought about by the differences in employment location it is considered that many employment ratios which would otherwise be appropriate would be misleading and are, therefore, not worthy of inclusion in this Report.

Fig. 1.　(cont'd)

Employment Report continued

How the Group spends the money it receives

Sales proceeds	**£186.1m**
Purchases and overhead expenses	**£136.9m**
	————
leaving an amount of	**£49.2m**
	————

which was expended as follows:

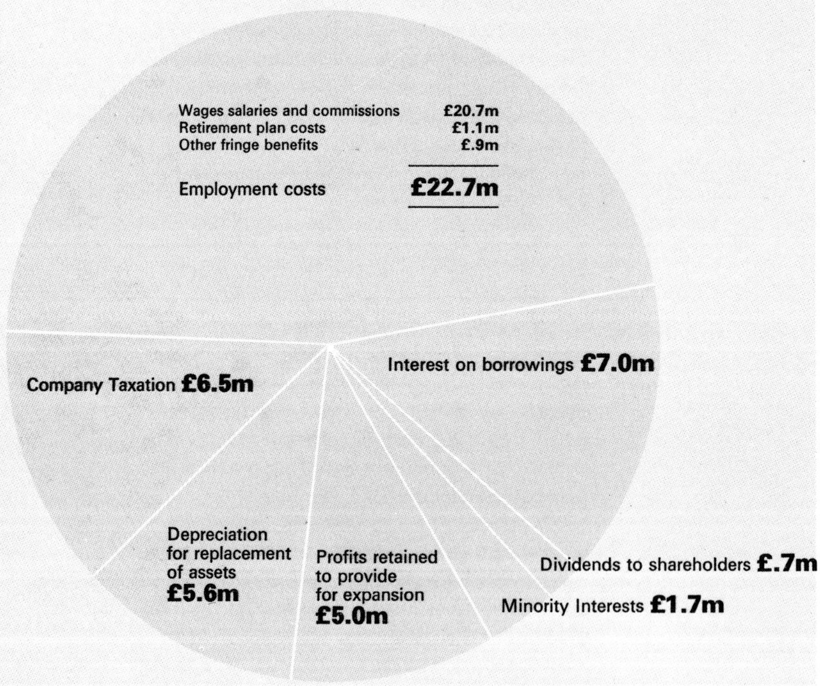

Wages salaries and commissions　£20.7m
Retirement plan costs　£1.1m
Other fringe benefits　£.9m
————
Employment costs　**£22.7m**

Company Taxation **£6.5m**

Interest on borrowings **£7.0m**

Depreciation
for replacement
of assets
£5.6m

Profits retained
to provide
for expansion
£5.0m

Dividends to shareholders **£.7m**

Minority Interests **£1.7m**

Fig. 1.   (cont'd)

Group activities expressed in amounts per employee

Sells products and services	**£34,460**
Buys products, materials and services from other organisations	**£25,334**
Pays wages, salaries and meets other costs of employment	**£4,204**
Pays interest on sums borrowed	**£1,304**
Provides for replacement of assets	**£1,045**
Pays tax on the profits	**£1,206**
Retains to provide for expansion of business	**£924**
Acknowledges that our partners in certain Group companies are entitled to profits of	**£307**
Pays dividends to shareholders of	**£136**

Fig. 2.   Cavenham: balance sheet presentation (*see page 25*)

Our Group Balance Sheet

At 3rd April 1976
And what it means

This is what we own

...and how it is financed

FIXED ASSETS

£167.5 MILLION

Land buildings, plant and machinery.

STOCK

£170.6 MILLION

Goods awaiting sale and in various stages of manufacture.

BANK DEPOSITS AND CASH

£76.2 MILLION

DEBTORS   £46.7 MILLION
Money owed to us by our customers.

INVESTMENTS   £17.6 MILLION
Money invested in other companies.

BUILDINGS AND PLANT AWAITING SALE

£6.2 MILLION

AMOUNTS RECEIVABLE   £9.9 MILLION
Cash to be received for assets already sold.

GOODWILL   £5.5 MILLION
The amount we paid for businesses over the value of their assets (such as plant, buildings and stock.) for the on going use and benefits of brand and trading names such as Bovril, Liptons, etc.

Total £500.2 Million

SHARE CAPITAL AND RESERVES

£129.5 MILLION

Money invested by Shareholders in the Company together with profits ploughed back into the Company in earlier years by the Shareholders.

MINORITY INTERESTS   £34.9 MILLION
Money put up by local Shareholders in some of our operations (like Grand Union) where Cavenham has a controlling share but outside investors still have a stake.

LOAN CAPITAL

£159.7 MILLION

Money lent to the Company on a long or medium term basis by banks and other institutions.

CREDITORS

£152.2 MILLION

Money we owe for goods and services already received but not yet paid for.

BANK OVERDRAFTS   £13.2 MILLION
Money borrowed from the banks on a day-to-day basis.

TAXATION   £8.4 MILLION
Tax payable at a future date.

DIVIDENDS   £2.3 MILLION
The part of the annual dividend to shareholders not yet paid.

Total £500.2 Million

The information in this Report is taken from The Annual Report and Accounts. If you would like a copy of the full Report, please ask your local manager.

Designed and produced by Financial Presentations Limited and Printed by Kelly & Kelly Limited.

Fig. 3. Record Ridgway: extracts from employee report (*see page 26*), cont'd overleaf

 **Record Ridgway Limited**

SALES & PROFITS

		1975 £	1974 £	1973 £	1972 £
Sales					
UK Companies	Home	5,968,802	4,775,443	4,218,668	4,474,320
	Export	3,903,548	2,543,244	2,200,615	1,851,885
		9,872,350	7,318,687	6,419,283	6,326,205
Overseas Companies		2,120,606	1,888,101	1,191,150	926,422
		£11,992,956	£9,206,788	£7,610,433	£7,252,627
Profits					
UK Companies		1,016,808	591,316	543,723	642,650
Overseas Companies		347,916	412,227	193,398	141,485
		£1,364,724	£1,003,543	£737,121	£784,135

Markets to which we sold

1975	1974
£11,992,956	£9,206,788

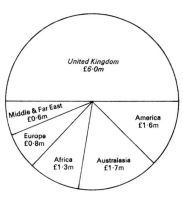

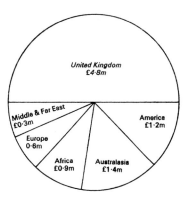

OUR BALANCE SHEET

Our assets	£	Our liabilities	£
Land, buildings and machinery	4,125,837	Money we owe to suppliers	1,701,439
Money owed to us by customers	2,764,678	Taxation we owe to Government	1,559,810
Stocks and work-in-progress	3,782,094	Money borrowed from the bank	1,072,812
Investments	650	Shareholders interests	6,339,198
	£10,673,259		£10,673,259

Fig. 3. (cont'd)

Record Ridgway Limited

VALUE ADDED STATEMENT

The best way of showing profit in its proper perspective is to show the wealth which the Company and its employees have created by their efforts and how each has been rewarded for that effort. This is shown by a value added statement.

	1975 £	£ per employee	1974 £	£ per employee
Sales	11,992,956	6,707	9,206,788	4,879
Less				
Bought-in materials and services	6,159,203	3,445	4,535,874	2,404
Value added	5,833,753	3,262	4,670,914	2,475
Less				
Wages, salaries, pension contributions	4,094,482	2,290	3,304,181	1,751
Directors salaries, pension contributions	86,552	48	69,686	37
Bank interest	148,756	83	146,852	78
Depreciation of assets	139,239	78	146,652	77
Profit before taxation	1,364,724	763	1,003,543	532
Less				
Taxation	627,773	351	551,208	292
Profit after taxation	736,951	412	452,335	240
Surplus on stock revaluation	—	—	417,887	221
Less				
Profits for minority shareholders	22,972	13	25,469	13
Dividends to shareholders	233,733	130	207,738	110
Amount reinvested in the Company	£480,246	£269	£637,015	£338

A comparison of the two year's figures highlights the distortion created by the three day week in 1974, and the resultant low level of output per employee. 1975 reflects a more normal pattern of productivity, but the effects of inflation and price restraints can also be seen. Of particular concern is the effect of inflation on the cost of materials and services (such as rates, power, freight, maintenance, etc.) which increased by 35% compared with a 30% increase in sales.

There is clearly a need for capital investment to reduce both labour content per unit of output and the high level of bought-out materials.

WHAT WE SPENT ON NEW PLANT AND EQUIPMENT
(i.e. outright purchase, lease or rental)

	Land and buildings £	Plant, fixtures and equipment £	Total expenditure £	Total adjusted for inflation £
1975	13,780	226,192	239,972	239,972
1974	1,208	165,047	166,255	198,840
1973	43,471	266,679	310,150	517,640
1972	27,016	218,281	245,297	450,120

Total expenditure is adjusted for inflation by using indices which show the increase in the replacement cost of plant and this demonstrates the extra cash which is required to maintain a level of capital expenditure. Whereas total capital expenditure in 1972 was £245,297, the cost in 1975 of the same items is almost double at £450,120.

Fig. 3.   (cont'd)

Record Ridgway Limited

EMPLOYMENT STATISTICS

Number employed

	at the year end	Average for the year
Australia	48	51
Canada	17	16
South Africa	53	57
United Kingdom	1,593	1,664
	1,711	1,788

Average hours worked per employee

Company	hours per week	hours o/time per week
Record Ridgway Tools	38·3	2·9
Bestmore Tool	34·8	1·9
United Kingdom	38·1	2·8
Record Tools (Canada)	45·8	1·6
Record Tools (South Africa)	44·0	0·3
Ridgway-Tesco (Australia)	45·8	4·1
Overseas	45·0	2·0
Total Company	38·7	2·7

Number of days lost

	No. of days	per employee
Absence	16,600	12·7
Accidents and sickness	20,992	16·0
Industrial dispute —local	3,647	2·8
—national	—	—
	41,239	31·5

Age distribution of employees

Age		
Under 20		7%
Over 20		19%
Over 30		16%
Over 40		22%
Over 50		28%
Over 60		8%

Length of service

Yrs		
Under 5		50%
Over 5		20%
Over 10		14%
Over 20		10%
Over 30		3%
Over 40		3%

Total employee costs

	Overseas £	United Kingdom £	Total £
Total wages and salaries	413,139	3,650,172	4,063,311
Pension contributions	15,481	102,242	117,723
	£428,620	£3,752,414	£4,181,034
Cost per employee	£3,457	£2,255	£2,338

Costs per employee were 53% higher in overseas companies than in the United Kingdom but this was partly due to 18% more hours being worked in the overseas companies.

Labour turnover

Labour turnover as a % of average numbers employed	23·2%
Employees made redundant	113

Training

Number of days spent on training internally	8,620 days
Number of days spent on training externally	1,200 days

Printed by Balding + Mansell, Wisbech

Fig. 4.   Staffordshire Potteries: management diagram (*see page 32*)

Production Management

You have already seen in this report that we had a difficult year. You will also have seen that we came out of the year very well. The success would not have been possible without the success of the production function and the people who work in it. Whilst we do not miss the point that the production management did not achieve this success by themselves, we thought you would be interested to know who the people are who manage the various production departments across the group.

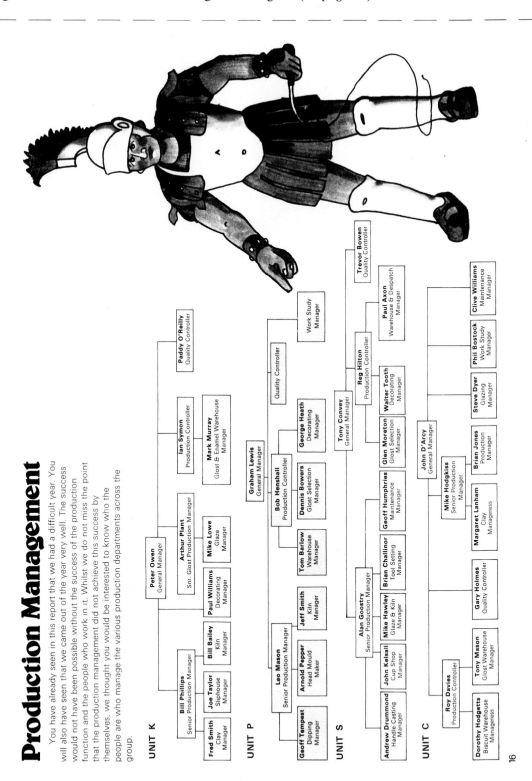

Fig. 5.   Norcros: role of shareholders explained (*see page 32*)

Where do Shareholders fit in?

12,233 people work for Norcros in the United Kingdom.

10,210 people own Norcros Ordinary Shares.

Both groups are vital to the creation of a successful Norcros. The directly employed by using their energy and skills and the shareholders through the money they invest in Norcros.

How many Ordinary Shares have been issued and who has them?
On the 31st March 1976 we had issued 54,512,806 Ordinary Shares of 25p each.
This does not mean our shareholders paid this price. The market price paid for them varies from day to day and you can see the changes in the City pages of many daily newspapers. At the close of business on 31st March 1976 the Norcros Ordinary Share price was 77p. This meant our business was valued at £41,974,860.

Who owns Norcros Ordinary Shares?

9,416	Private holders	Own	15,849,297 shares amounting to	29·1%
184	Limited companies	Own	1,213,170 shares amounting to	2·2%
31	Insurance & Assurance Companies	Own	7,430,059 shares amounting to	13·6%
288	Trustees & Public Authorities	Own	2,909,864 shares amounting to	5·3%
233	Nominees	Own	18,239,955 shares amounting to	33·5%
25	Pension Funds	Own	3,916,529 shares amounting to	7·2%
33	Investment & Unit Trusts	Own	4,953,932 shares amounting to	9·1%
10,210			54,512,806	100·0%

9,416 private holders mean that 92% of Norcros Ordinary shareholders are members of the general public who put their faith in Norcros by investing in us.

On the other hand the remaining 8% of shareholders hold more than 70% of our shares. The majority of these shareholders are banks, insurance companies and pension funds who believe that an investment in Norcros represents an opportunity to take a part in the Group's long term growth and profitability.

Some of our Principal Ordinary Shareholders:

Airways Pension Fund Trustees Limited
Bank of Scotland (Stanlife) London Nominees Limited
Barclays Nominees (Aldermanbury) Limited
Barclays Nominees (Save & Prosper Group) Limited
Charifund Nominees Limited
Church Commissioners for England
COIF Nominees Limited
Commercial Union Assurance Company Limited
Eagle Star Insurance Company Limited
Friends Provident Life Office
General Accident Fire & Life Assurance Corporation Limited
London Office Royal Bank of Scotland Nominees Limited
M & G Group (Lombard Street) Nominees Limited
Midland Bank Trust Company Limited
Norwich Union Life Insurance Society
Pearl Assurance Company Limited
R. F. Nominees Limited
Royal Exchange Trustee Nominees Limited
Scotcom Nominees Limited
Strand Nominees Limited
Sun Life Assurance Society Limited
The Imperial Tobacco Company Pension Trust Limited
The Port Employers & Registered Dock Workers Pension Fund Trustees Limited
The Prudential Assurance Company Limited
The Scottish American Investment Company Limited
West Unit Nominees Limited
West Yorkshire Metropolitan County Council

Fig. 6.   Serck: statement of company objectives (*see page 33*)

Our Purpose in Business

Serck, a major public company, has responsibilities and obligations, for example:

★ We employ more than five thousand people directly and many others indirectly in suppliers' factories. Together with their families, we are providing a livelihood for several times this number.

★ We are a key producer in Britain's vital engineering industry, providing many essential goods and services.

★ More than half our output arose from sales to our overseas customers; we are contributing significantly to our national economy and the balance of payments.

Thus we need a clear "purpose in business". We continue to see that purpose in the following way:

"Our purpose in business is to create wealth, to make money, to build a better company.
For this to be possible we must please our customers and enjoy the confidence of our shareholders and employees.
We must make good profits, so that after providing for taxes and dividends (and in present conditions financing inflation) there is available enough money to keep our factories and equipment modern and to enable us to grow in strength and maintain or improve our market position. We endeavour to provide good, satisfying employment for our people.
Creating wealth and building a better company is our contribution to better standards of living."

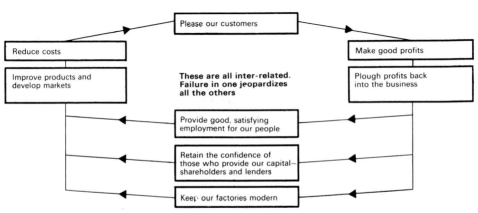

The above "Purpose" was first published in 1971.

Fig. 7.   Crane Fruehauf: statement of future plans (*see page 34*)

Our plan of action in 1976

CF's objective is to restore profitability and to return to healthy growth.

★   Throughout the Group to increase competitiveness by reducing costs, increasing investment, improving productivity.

★   CF Trailers plan to re-equip significantly on new plant and equipment at Oldham to maintain and improve the effectiveness of the manufacturing process.

★   Further extensions will be made in the CF Trailer product range with the object of reducing cyclical fluctuations in the demand for the company's products.

★   CF Containers plans to increase its penetration of overseas markets.

★   CF Containers, having successfully engineered and manufactured the GRP Van, will extend its range and options still further.

★   The range of services and facilities offered through CF Service & Equipment's network of Service Centres will be further extended.

★   A significant programme will be launched to achieve greater penetration of the parts market both at home and abroad.

★   At Imperial Coachbuilders further extensions of the product range are planned including re-frigerated and insulated models.

★   RenTco Nationwide plans to increase its contract hire fleet significantly and develop new areas of business.

★   CF Overseas aims to build up its network of distributors in export markets.

★   The Dennison companies in Ireland, having been fully acquired by CF, will continue to be run from Ireland but with a much improved co-ordination of effort in the marketing area.

★   Forfreight International formed to develop business opportunities from shipment of CF Group products overseas.

★   CF Finance plans to increase its volume of business with the introduction of new services and to increase effectiveness by bringing into operation a new computer based financial and administration system.

Fig. 8.   Record Ridgway: employment information (*see page 35*)

EMPLOYMENT STATISTICS

Number employed

End of September 1975	1976	Average for 1976	Company	hours 1975	O/time hours 1975	hours 1976	O/time hours 1976
1,525	1,537	1,515	Record Ridgway Tools	38.3	2.9	36.3	2.0
68	51	54	Bestmore Tools	34.8	1.9	38.2	1.5
N/A	94	94	Platts Forgings	—	—	39.6	2.4
1,593	**1,682**	**1,663**	**U.K. Total**	**38.1**	**2.8**	**36.8**	**2.5**
17	22	22	Record Canada	45.8	1.6	37.4	0.3
53	44	57	Record South Africa	44.0	0.3	44.9	0.3
48	44	48	Ry Tesco Australia	45.8	4.1	37.6	2.4
1,711	**1,792**	**1,790**	**Group Total**	**38.7**	**2.7**	**37.0**	**2.2**

Average hours worked weekly per employee

Age Distribution of employees

%	Age
8%	Under 20
19%	21 - 30
15%	31 - 40
20%	41 - 50
29%	51 - 60
9%	Over 60

Length of Service   years

%	years
47%	0 - 5
20%	6 - 10
17%	11 - 20
9%	21 - 30
4%	31 - 40
3%	Over 40

Number of days lost

	No of Days	Per Employee
Absence	8927	8.6
Accidents and Sickness	16319	15.7
	25246	**24.3**

LABOUR TURNOVER

Labour Turnover
as a % of Average Numbers Employed   **17%**

Employees made redundant   **13**

TRAINING

Nos of days spent on Training internally   **7145 DAYS**

Nos of days spent on Training externally   **2373 DAYS**

Fig. 9.   Hoover: employment information (*see page 38*), cont'd overleaf

Recruitment & labour turn-over both show decreases

Although the total number of employees went down we still had to recruit some new people. A total of 912 new employees was taken on and this was only one fifth of the number taken on in 1973. This again reflects the economic climate of 1975. The chart below shows how the totals of new employees engaged have moved over the last three years.

1973	4670
1974	3122
1975	912

LABOUR TURNOVER

As expected in this sort of climate there was a drop in labour turnover, except in those areas where redundancy took place. The following figures show the numbers of people who left during the year out of every 100 people employed.

	MEN			WOMEN		
	1973	1974	1975	1973	1974	1975
PERIVALE	33	33	16	21	25	17
CAMBUSLANG	22	25	14	22	22	33
MERTHYR	8	16	6	5	4	5
ADMINISTRATION AND DISTRIBUTION	28	24	18	29	30	23
ENGINEERING	14	9	8	76	12	6
MARKETING	23	19	17	43	38	30
OVERSEAS OPERATIONS	8	20	15	47	34	42

Fig. 9.   (cont'd)

Fewer people changed Jobs

The Stability Index (i.e. the index which shows how many people who were employed at the beginning of the year were still employed at the end of the year) reflected the same general trend of events.

The overall increase in the index indicates that fewer people chose to change their jobs. The level of stability among women would have been higher had it not been for redundancy.

STABILITY INDEX			
	1973	1974	1975
Men	86.4%	83.9%	93.80%
Women	79.8%	84.7%	82.96%
Men & Women	84.4%	84.2%	90.24%

Changes in absenteeism

Absenteeism during the year showed some slight overall improvement when compared with 1973 (the 1974 figures do not provide a good comparison due to the strike and lay-off of that year).

Absenteeism among men at Perivale and Merthyr was greatly improved, but at Cambuslang absence among men and women was even worse than before.

Women's absence in most of the company was significantly higher than that of men and the absence pattern of women continues to show consistent peaks in the early spring, mid summer, autumn and year end.

	MEN			WOMEN		
	1973	1974	1975	1973	1974	1975
PERIVALE	6.9	5.5	5.5	9.7	7.4	9.2
CAMBUSLANG	9.0	10.3	10.7	15.8	15.2	17.3
MERTHYR	8.3	7.2	7.3	8.8	7.4	8.8
ADMINISTRATION & DISTRIBUTION	3.0	3.0	2.7	7.4	7.2	6.0
ENGINEERING	2.4	2.3	2.0	7.1	2.7	4.1
MARKETING	2.1	2.0	1.4	4.3	5.2	3.3
EXPORT	0.4	0.5	2.4	4.9	3.7	4.0

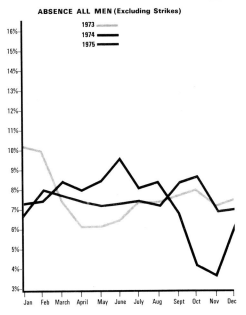

ABSENCE ALL MEN (Excluding Strikes)

1973
1974
1975

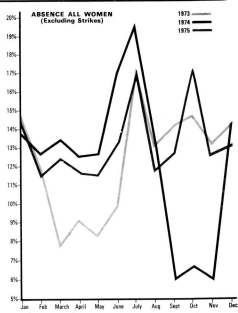

ABSENCE ALL WOMEN (Excluding Strikes)

1973
1974
1975

9

Fig. 10. Redman Heenan: sources of revenue statement (*see page 39*)

In 1974 we sold the output of our work to give the group an income of £22,085,000 which has been, or will be, paid to us by our customers. This income can be split showing where we sold the goods (by territory) and what we sold (by product):

Our income

BY TERRITORY	£	%
United Kingdom	13,614,000	61·6
E.E.C. countries excluding U.K.	2,574,000	11·7
Comecon countries	2,785,000	12·6
Remainder of Europe	1,129,000	5·1
North and South America	522,000	2·4
Australasia	123,000	0·6
Asia	910,000	4·1
Africa	428,000	1·9
	22,085,000	100·0

BY PRODUCT	%	£
Hydraulic and mechanical press plant	20·6	4,561,000
Contract engineering and procurement	25·2	5,556,000
Open steel flooring and fabrication	18·7	4,132,000
Dynamometers and test plant	10·1	2,233,000
Variable speed drives and couplings	10·4	2,297,000
Other precision and general engineering	15·0	3,306,000
	100·0	22,085,000

Fig. 11. Greenall Whitley: illustration of tax paid (*see page 40*)

GREENALL WHITLEY AS TAX COLLECTOR

TOTAL TAX BILL £52½ m

To illustrate just how much this is, we've calculated that it would buy the following:

45 MILES OF MOTORWAY

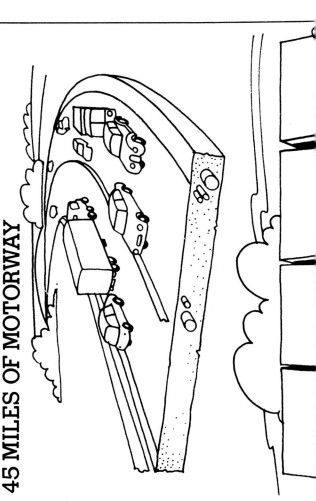

TAX PER EMPLOYEE £12,096

We pointed out, in our report last year, what an enormous amount of tax we pay and collect. Over 50% of our sales, or over 50p in every £ we receive across the counter, finds its way back to the Government in some form of tax (i.e. Excise Duty, Corporation Tax, Rates, P.A.Y.E. and V.A.T.).

The total amount of tax paid and collected last year was £52½ million. To give you an idea of what this means, we have calculated that it would buy the following:

Fig. 12.   Nissen: performance indicators *(see page 41)*

Some Questions & Answers on . . .
Objectives, Controls and Performance.

WHAT TO LOOK FOR	CONTROL RATIO/ MULTIPLE OR %	OUR 1975 RESULTS
Is the Business Profitable? 1. What are the Net earnings of the Owners?	✱ $\dfrac{\text{Current Retained Earnings} \times 100}{\text{Net Worth}} = \%$ (Total Assets less Total Liabilities)	£ $\dfrac{99,009}{373,314}$ × 100 = 26.5%
2. What is the Gross Return on Total Capital Employed?	✱ $\dfrac{\text{Before Tax Profit} \times 100}{\text{Total Capital Employed}} = \%$ R.O.I.	£ $\dfrac{216,509}{409,852}$ × 100 = 52.8%
Is the Business Solvent? 3. Can the Business pay its way immediately? (Acid Test)	$\dfrac{\text{Liquid Assets}}{\text{Current Liabilities}} :$ Ratio	£ $\dfrac{392,454}{202,955}$ = 1.9 : 1
4. Can the Business pay its way in near future? (Current Ratio)	$\dfrac{\text{Current Assets}}{\text{Current Liabilities}} :$ Ratio	£ $\dfrac{660,646}{202,955}$ = 3.3 : 1
How is the Business Financed? 5. Is there excessive reliance on borrowed money? (Gearing)	$\dfrac{\text{Long Term Loans}}{\text{Paid up Capital \& Reserves \& Long Term Loans}} :$ Ratio	We have no Long Term Loans. We are financed entirely out of paid up Capital, retained earnings and deferred taxation.
6. What Credit is being taken by the business?	$\dfrac{\text{Trade Creditors}}{\text{Average Weekly Purchases}} =$ Weeks	£ $\dfrac{66,279}{12,792}$ = 5.2 Weeks
How are the Funds being used? 7. What proportion of *total* finance available is invested in Fixed Assets?	† $\dfrac{\text{Fixed Assets}}{\text{Total Capital Employed}} :$ Ratio	£ $\dfrac{100,104}{557,795}$ = 1 : 5.6
8. What proportion of *working* capital is tied up in inventory? (Stock)	† $\dfrac{\text{Inventory (Stock)}}{\text{Working Capital}} :$ Ratio (Current Assets less Current Liabilities)	£ $\dfrac{268,192}{457,691}$ = 1 : 1.7
Are the Funds wisely deployed? 9. Are debts being collected promptly enough?	$\dfrac{\text{Trade Debtors}}{\text{Average Weekly Sales}} =$ Weeks	£ $\dfrac{189,566}{28,179}$ = 6.7 Weeks
10. What is the velocity of Inventory (Stock) Turnover?	$\dfrac{\text{Inventory (Stock)}}{\text{Average Weekly Sales}} =$ Weeks	£ $\dfrac{268,192}{26,734}$ = 10 Weeks
Is the Trading Position OK? 11. Under or Over trading or just right for working capital?	✱ $\dfrac{\text{Sales}}{\text{Working Capital}} :$ Ratio	£ $\dfrac{1,390,145}{331,396}$ = 4.2 : 1
12. Are they generating enough business?	✱ $\dfrac{\text{Sales}}{\text{Total Capital Employed}} :$ Ratio	£ $\dfrac{1,390,145}{409,852}$ = 3.4 : 1
13. Are the Sales they are making, worth making?	$\dfrac{\text{Pre-Tax Profit} \times 100}{\text{Sales}} = \%$	£ $\dfrac{216,509}{1,390,145}$ × 100 = 15.6%
14. Is the Gross Profit on Sales adequate?	$\dfrac{\text{Gross Profit} \times 100}{\text{Sales}} = \%$	£ $\dfrac{532,190}{1,390,145}$ × 100 = 38.3%
15. What Sales are produced by investment in Fixed Capital?	✱ $\dfrac{\text{Sales}}{\text{Fixed Assets}}$	£ $\dfrac{1,390,145}{78,456}$ = 17.7 : 1
What's their Productivity like? 16. What are their sales per employee?	$\dfrac{\text{Sales}}{\text{No. of Employees}} = £$	£ $\dfrac{1,390,145}{116}$ = £11,984
17. What are their profits per employee?	$\dfrac{\text{Pre-Tax Profits}}{\text{No. of Employees}} = £$	£ $\dfrac{216,509}{116}$ = £ 1,866
18. What is the Value Added per employee?	$\dfrac{\text{Sales less Materials}}{\text{No. of Employees}} = £$	£ $\dfrac{887,634}{116}$ = £ 7,652
19. What is the Value Added per £1 Wages & Salaries Paid?	$\dfrac{\text{Sales less Materials}}{\text{Total Wages \& Salaries}} = £$	£ $\dfrac{887,634}{421,350}$ = £ 2.11
How's the Order Situation? 20. Is the order back-log OK for plant capacity?	$\dfrac{\text{Outstanding Orders}}{\text{Average Weekly Sales}} =$ No. of Weeks	£ $\dfrac{250,767}{26,734}$ = 9.4 Weeks
Are they Over/Under Housed? 21. What are the Sales per sq. ft.?	$\dfrac{\text{Sales}}{\text{Total Sq. Footage of ALL space}} = £$	£ $\dfrac{1,390,145}{27,711}$ = £50.17

✱ At start of the Year † At Year-End

Fig. 13. Staffordshire Potteries: cover design (*see page 46*)

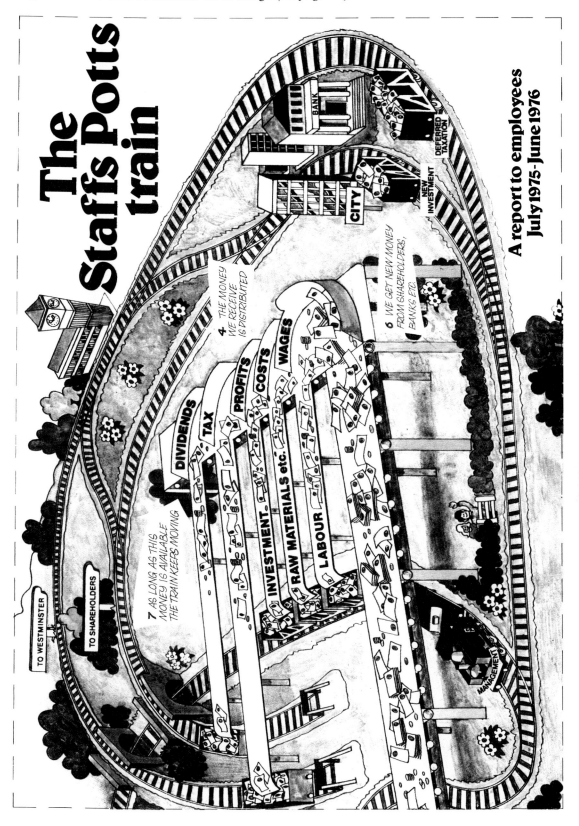

Fig. 14. Staffordshire Potteries: part of value added statement (*see page 47*)

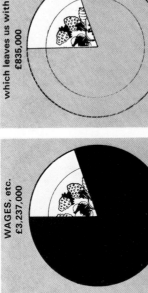

What happens to this wealth?

We pay ourselves a large proportion of it! £3,237,000 went in wages, salaries, N.I. contributions, sick pay, etc.

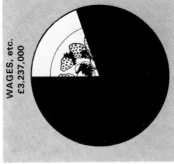

WAGES, etc.
£3,237,000

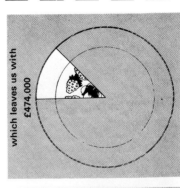

which leaves us with
£835,000

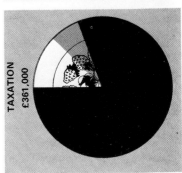

TAXATION
£361,000

which leaves us with
£474,000

TAXATION takes £361,000

The first section of the report presents the figures from the annual report in a way which we hope is clear to the layman. The figures are exactly the same as those in the annual report, which is required by law and independently audited.

So, let us have a look at what money we made in the year and where it went to.

In 1975/76, our customers paid us £7,441,000 for what we sold to them. It cost us £3,369,000 to buy the materials and services (clay, glaze, electricity, rates etc.) needed to make our products.

That leaves us with £4,072,000, which is how much we received for what we sold after paying for raw materials. It is the wealth that Staffordshire Potteries created.

Wealth Created
£4,072,000

4

Fig. 15. Staffordshire Potteries: importance of customers explained (*see page 48*)

Let us now have a look in more detail at the three groups of people who are important to the company. First of all the most important of all, our customers.

In 1975/76 we sold our products to well over 1,000 different customers. The customers range from major international retail and wholesale organisations to market stall holders. More than 60 of these customers did more than £20,000 worth of business with us in the year.

The companies who bought goods directly from us during the year in the home market include Boots, British Home Stores, Lewis's, Debenhams, Tesco, Woolworths and the Co-operative Wholesale Society.

Fig. 16. Dowty: cover design (*see page 78*)

DOWTY
GROUP

Summary of
Report and Accounts
YEAR ENDED 31st MARCH 1976

Fig. 17. Automotive Products: cover design (*see page 78*)

What happens to the money we earn as a company.

A report for employees on Automotive Products Limited in 1975

Fig. 18. Coubro & Scrutton: cover design (*see page 79*)

Fig. 19. Thorn: cover design (*see page 79*)

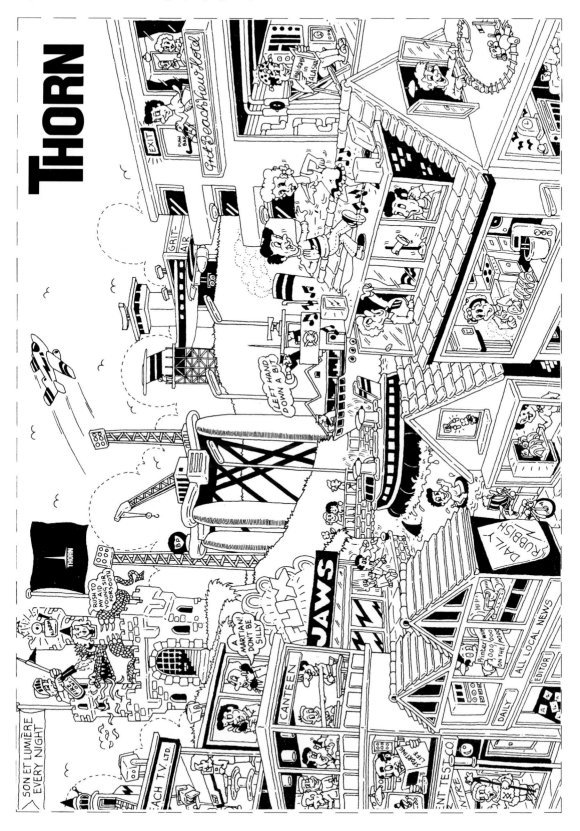

Fig. 20. Metal Box: cover design (*see page 79*)

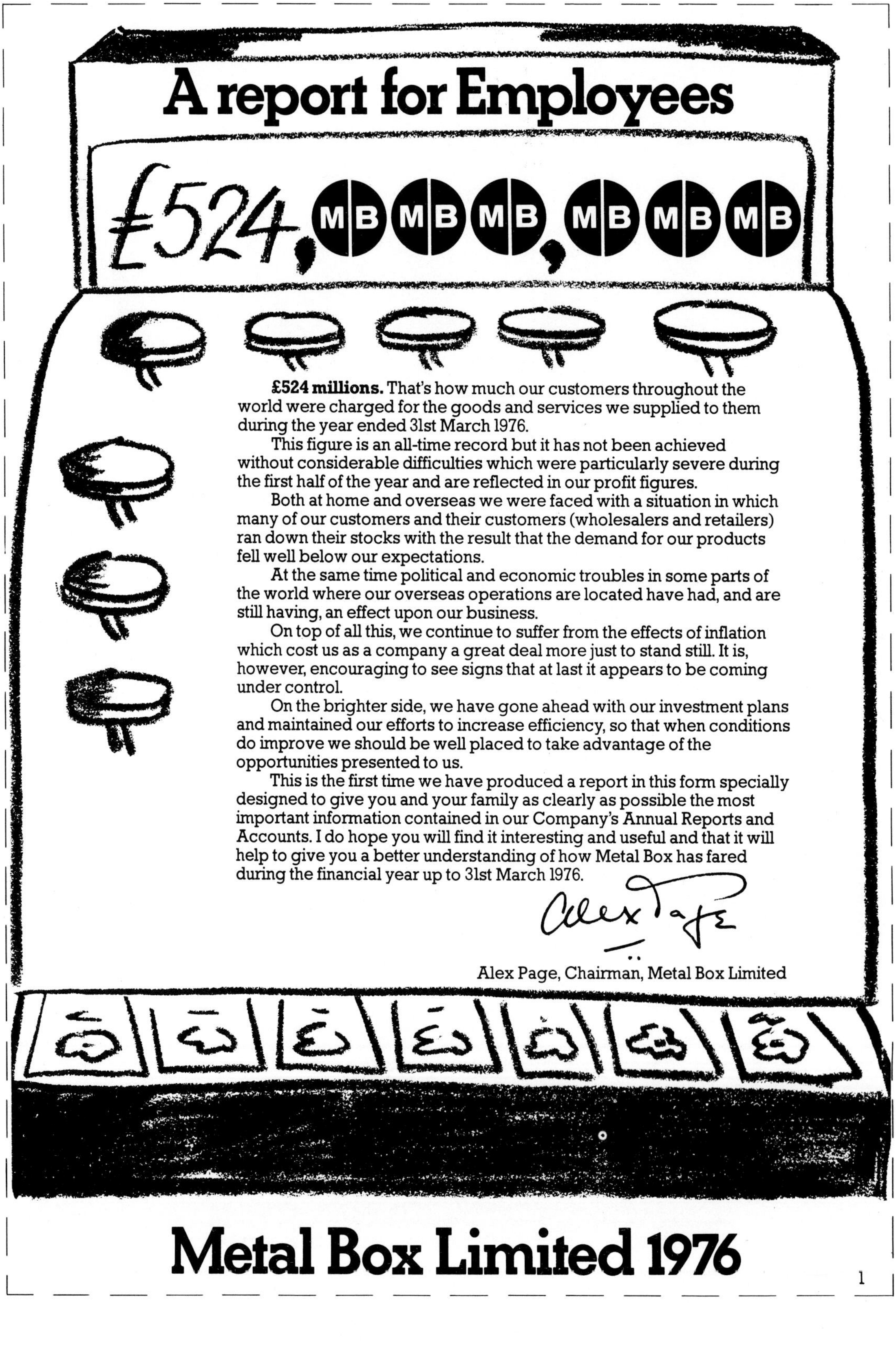

A report for Employees

£524, MB MB MB, MB MB MB

£524 millions. That's how much our customers throughout the world were charged for the goods and services we supplied to them during the year ended 31st March 1976.

This figure is an all-time record but it has not been achieved without considerable difficulties which were particularly severe during the first half of the year and are reflected in our profit figures.

Both at home and overseas we were faced with a situation in which many of our customers and their customers (wholesalers and retailers) ran down their stocks with the result that the demand for our products fell well below our expectations.

At the same time political and economic troubles in some parts of the world where our overseas operations are located have had, and are still having, an effect upon our business.

On top of all this, we continue to suffer from the effects of inflation which cost us as a company a great deal more just to stand still. It is, however, encouraging to see signs that at last it appears to be coming under control.

On the brighter side, we have gone ahead with our investment plans and maintained our efforts to increase efficiency, so that when conditions do improve we should be well placed to take advantage of the opportunities presented to us.

This is the first time we have produced a report in this form specially designed to give you and your family as clearly as possible the most important information contained in our Company's Annual Reports and Accounts. I do hope you will find it interesting and useful and that it will help to give you a better understanding of how Metal Box has fared during the financial year up to 31st March 1976.

Alex Page, Chairman, Metal Box Limited

Metal Box Limited 1976

Fig. 21. Tarmac: cover design (*see page 79*)

A REPORT FOR EMPLOYEES

How we fared in a tough year-when one in twenty of the U.K. workforce had no job.

1975

The information in this booklet is also contained in the Annual Report and Accounts of Tarmac Limited (see back cover) which is published simultaneously with this document

Fig. 22. EMI: cover design (*see page 79*)

EMI 1976

Money and People

These are some of the things the people of EMI
did in the financial year ended 30 June 1976

Jobs

EMI provided jobs for 49,900 people
inside the Group. We also provided
work for many people outside the
Group by buying £463 million of materials and services from suppliers

Sales

We sold £671 million of goods and
services throughout the world

Wages

We earned £143 million in wages for
ourselves and our families

Taxes

We paid £31.2 million in taxes — the
equivalent of full old age pensions for
28,000 couples for a year

Exports

We exported £87 million of goods and
services from the United Kingdom —
enough to import petrol to run all private cars in the UK for six weeks.

Future

To help secure our jobs in the future
We invested £30 million in new assets
We spent £25 million on technical effort
related to research and development

Fig. 23. Electronic Rentals: cover design (*see page 79*)

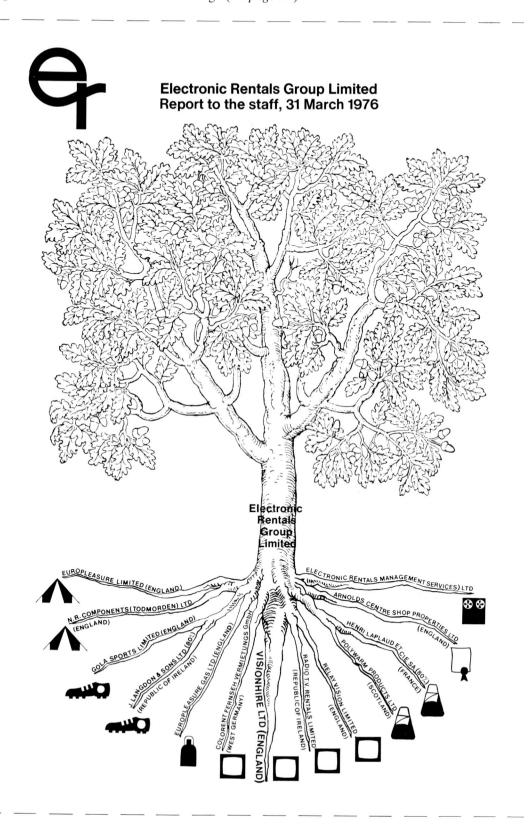

Fig. 24. Macarthy Pharmaceuticals: sales illustration (*see page 80*)

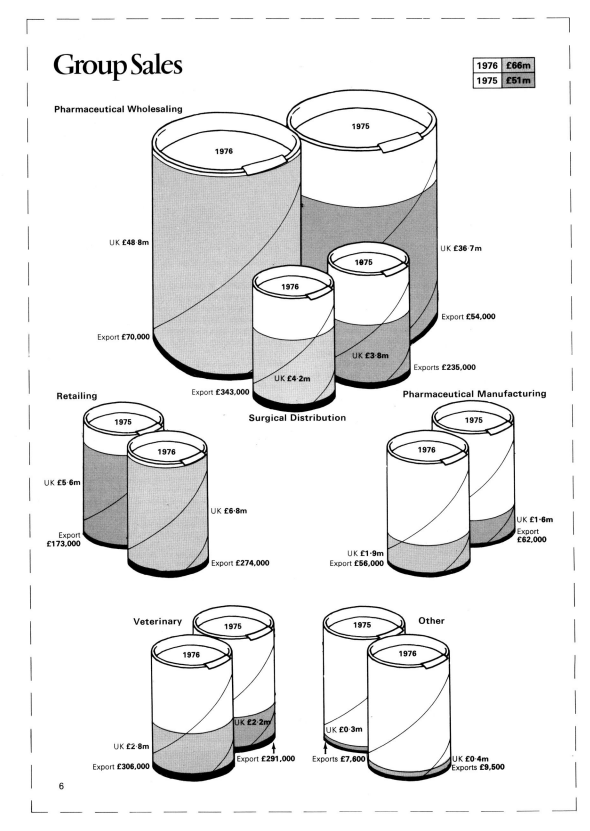

Group Sales

| 1976 | £66m |
| 1975 | £51m |

Pharmaceutical Wholesaling

1976

1975

UK £48·8m

UK £36·7m

Export £70,000

Export £54,000

1975

1976

UK £3·8m

UK £4·2m

Exports £235,000

Export £343,000

Surgical Distribution

Retailing

1975

1976

UK £5·6m

UK £6·8m

Export £173,000

Export £274,000

Pharmaceutical Manufacturing

1975

1976

UK £1·6m

Export £62,000

UK £1·9m
Export £56,000

Veterinary

1975

1976

UK £2·2m

UK £2·8m

Export £291,000

Export £306,000

Other

1975

1976

UK £0·3m

Exports £7,600

UK £0·4m
Exports £9,500

Fig. 25. Gestetner: sales income illustration (*see page 80*)

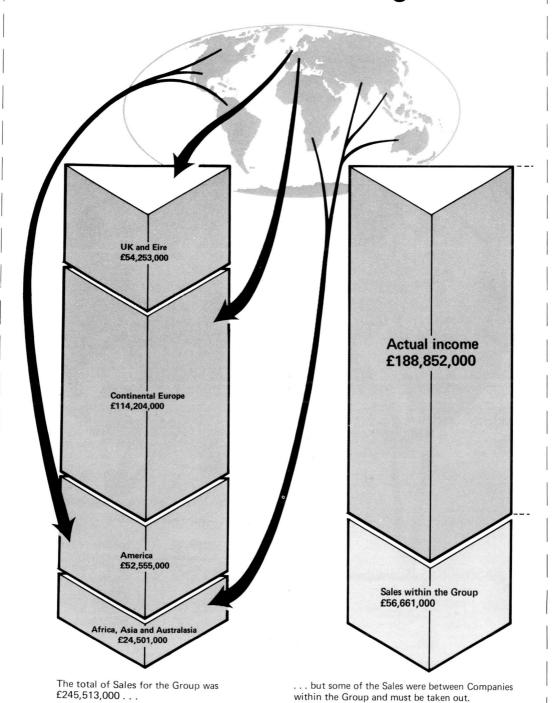

The income from sales of our goods

UK and Eire
£54,253,000

Continental Europe
£114,204,000

America
£52,555,000

Africa, Asia and Australasia
£24,501,000

Actual income
£188,852,000

Sales within the Group
£56,661,000

The total of Sales for the Group was
£245,513,000 . . .

. . . but some of the Sales were between Companies
within the Group and must be taken out.

Fig. 26. EMI: sales income diagram (*see page 80*)

How the EMI cake is made
There are four main ingredients to EMI's £503 million sales cake

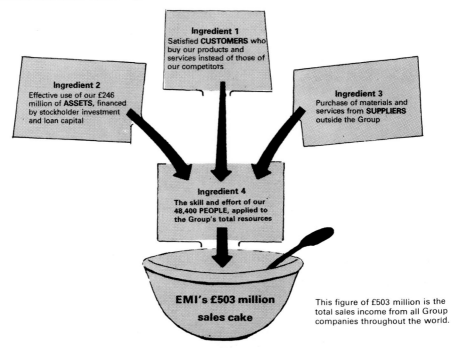

Ingredient 1
Satisfied **CUSTOMERS** who buy our products and services instead of those of our competitors

Ingredient 2
Effective use of our £246 million of **ASSETS**, financed by stockholder investment and loan capital

Ingredient 3
Purchase of materials and services from **SUPPLIERS** outside the Group

Ingredient 4
The skill and effort of our 48,400 **PEOPLE**, applied to the Group's total resources

EMI's £503 million sales cake

This figure of £503 million is the total sales income from all Group companies throughout the world.

How it turned out this year
After being baked in the furnace of competition, the £503 million sales cake turned out like this

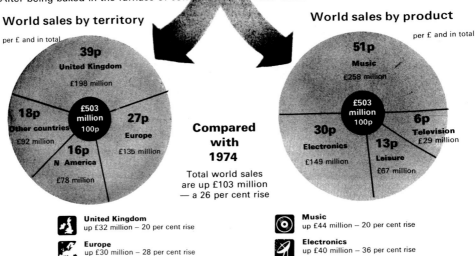

World sales by territory
per £ and in total

39p United Kingdom £198 million

18p Other countries £92 million

£503 million 100p

27p Europe £135 million

16p N America £78 million

Compared with 1974
Total world sales are up £103 million — a 26 per cent rise

World sales by product
per £ and in total

51p Music £258 million

£503 million 100p

6p Television £29 million

30p Electronics £149 million

13p Leisure £67 million

United Kingdom
up £32 million — 20 per cent rise

Europe
up £30 million — 28 per cent rise

North America
up £11 million — 16 per cent rise

Other countries
up £30 million — 50 per cent rise

Music
up £44 million — 20 per cent rise

Electronics
up £40 million — 36 per cent rise

Leisure
up £13 million — 24 per cent rise

Television
up £6 million — 26 per cent rise

Fig. 27. J. Lyons: profit and loss presentation (*see page 80*)

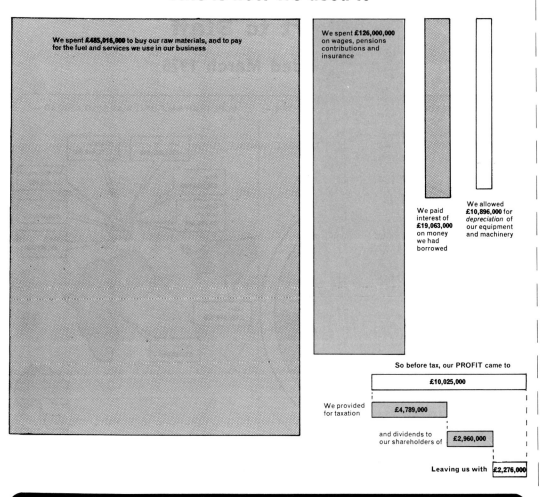

What we received and what we spent

During 1976, the total sales by the J. Lyons Group came to £651,000,000.

This is how we used it

We spent **£485,016,000** to buy our raw materials, and to pay for the fuel and services we use in our business

We spent **£126,000,000** on wages, pensions contributions and insurance

We paid interest of **£19,063,000** on money we had borrowed

We allowed **£10,896,000** for *depreciation* of our equipment and machinery

So before tax, our PROFIT came to £10,025,000

We provided for taxation £4,789,000

and dividends to our shareholders of £2,960,000

Leaving us with £2,276,000

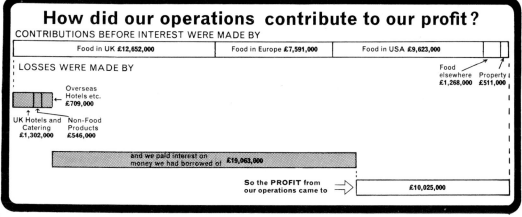

How did our operations contribute to our profit?

CONTRIBUTIONS BEFORE INTEREST WERE MADE BY

| Food in UK £12,652,000 | Food in Europe £7,591,000 | Food in USA £9,623,000 | | |

Food elsewhere £1,268,000   Property £511,000

LOSSES WERE MADE BY

Overseas Hotels etc. £709,000

UK Hotels and Catering £1,302,000

Non-Food Products £546,000

and we paid interest on money we had borrowed of £19,063,000

So the PROFIT from our operations came to £10,025,000

Fig. 28. EMI: profit and loss diagram (*see page 81*)

Our operating profit of £65 million

Where it comes from

By territory

3.2p	United Kingdom	£21.8m	
2.2p	Europe	£14.5m	
2.0p	North America	£13.1m	
2.3p	Other countries	£15.6m	
9.7p	Total	£65m	

9.7p £65million

Compared with 1975

— up £5.3 million — 32 per cent rise
— up £4.9 million — 51 per cent rise
— up £6.0 million — 85 per cent rise
— up £5.6 million — 56 per cent rise

By product

4.1p	Music	£27.3m	
3.9p	Electronics	£26.4m	
0.8p	Leisure	£5.6m	
0.9p	Television	£5.7m	
9.7p	Total	£65m	

9.7p £65million

— up £7.5 million — 38 per cent rise
— up £11.8 million — 81 per cent rise
— down £259,000 — 4 per cent fall
— up £2.7 million — 90 per cent rise

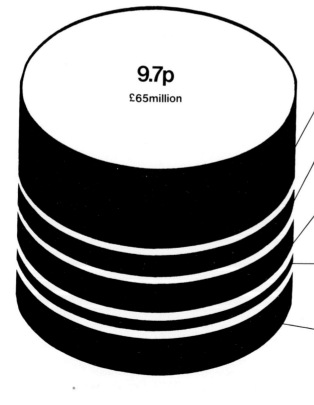

9.7p £65million

Where it goes

4.7p Taxation £31.2m
goes to governments to help pay for public and social services
Compared with 1975 up £11.7m

0.8p Interest £5.6m
paid on money borrowed from banks and loan stockholders
Compared with 1975 down £2.6m

1.0p Dividends £6.6m
paid to our ordinary and preference stockholders
Compared with 1975 up £600,000

0.5p Minorities £3.6m
belongs to minority shareholders of companies in which EMI has a majority shareholding
Compared with 1975 up £1.4m

2.7p Retained £18.0m
put into reserve to re-invest in the business

Fig. 29. Molins: profit and loss presentation (*see page 81*)

From the sale of tobacco machinery and paper and packaging machinery . . .

	PERCENTAGE OF TOTAL SALES
• *£11 million in the United Kingdom*	12·9
• *£42 million in the Americas*	51·5
• *£16 million in Continental Europe*	19·0
• *£7 million in Asia*	8·5
• *£4 million in Africa*	5·5
• *£2 million in Australasia*	2·6

We received £82·1 m

MOLINS

We spent £76·8 m

FOR EVERY £100 SPENT
£47·4 SUPPLIERS
£44·9 WAGES
£5·1 TAX
£2·2 INTEREST
£0·4 DIVIDENDS

• *Our suppliers charged us £36.4 million*
• *We paid out £34.5 million in wages and employment costs*
• *The tax man wants £3.9 million*
• *Our bankers got £1.7 million in interest on loans*
• *The shareholders received £0.3 million in dividends*

✱ *Leaving a balance of £5.3 million.*

Of that balance, £1.4 million was earmarked for the replacement or maintenance of buildings and machinery, leaving a £3.9 million "surplus" available to offset the effects of inflation and to expand the business.
It was not enough, as page 6 of this Report illustrates.

4

Fig. 30. M.K. Electric: profit and loss diagram (*see page 81*)

1. What we earned, spent and saved
in the year ended 27 March 1976

Every £1 of sales income was made up as follows . . .

	YEARLY TOTALS £000	
	THIS YEAR	LAST YEAR
FROM U.K. CUSTOMERS FOR:		
Electric Wiring Accessories	18,494	16,733
Plastic Mouldings	1,656	1,544
FROM OVERSEAS CUSTOMERS FOR:		
Electric Wiring Accessories	3,111	3,300
Plastic Mouldings	53	9
	23,314	**21,586**

. . . And this is how much was spent and saved:

	THIS YEAR	LAST YEAR
Materials & Services	10,599	10,705
Wages & Salaries	9,422	8,737
Interest on Borrowings	303	409
Depreciation of Fixed Assets	819	952
	21,143	20,803
Taxation to Government	1,122	356
Dividends to Shareholders	567	241
Retained for Expansion	482	186
	2,171	783
	23,314	**21,586**

The figures above represent a summarised version of our profit and loss account and show that margins improved during the year due to economies in costs and the effect of price increases.

Amounts spent and saved are shown in two groups. The first four items totalling £21,143,000 are the costs relating to the sales income of the year and include a charge 'Depreciation of Fixed Assets.' This is a proportion of the original cost of Buildings, Machinery and Vehicles spread over their estimated useful lives.

The second group of figures totalling £2,171,000 represents the profit for the year and shows how this will be divided into corporation tax, dividends and amount retained for expansion. The prior year profit of £783,000 includes an extraordinary receipt of £108,000.

Fig. 31. Norcros: profit and loss diagram (*see page 82*)

Income and Expenditure

To our total group sales figure of £155.9 million we add investment income of
£0.7 million making our total income for the year £156.6 million.

Out of each one pound of our total income we spent:

25p	**42.7p**	**13.1p**	DEPRECIATION 1.5p	INTEREST 2.2p	ASSOCIATED COMPANIES COSTS 7.8p	**7.7p**
WAGES AND SALARIES	**MATERIALS**	OTHER COSTS				**SURPLUS**

Wages and Salaries
£39.2 million was paid
to 13,403 employees
who work for Norcros
Companies in the United
Kingdom and Overseas.

This is 25%
of our income.

Materials
£66.9 million was paid
for raw materials
necessary to produce the
products we make in the
Construction, Consumer,
Engineering, Printing
and Packaging Divisions
and in our Overseas
Companies.

This is 42.7%
of our income.

Other Costs
£20.5 million was paid
for other costs which
includes statutory
payments such as
National Insurance
contributions, local rates
etc., administration costs,
advertising, distribution,
insurances, maintenance,
research and
development etc.

This is 13.1%
of our income.

Depreciation
£2.3 million has been set
aside to replace old and
outdated machinery and
equipment.

This is 1.5%
of our income.

Interest
£3.4 million was paid in
interest charges on
mortgages and to banks
and other people who
have loaned us money.

This is 2.2%
of our income.

**Associated
Companies Costs**
£12.2 million was our
share of the total costs
incurred by our
Associated Companies.

This is 7.8%
of our income.

Surplus
Out of our total income
figure of £156.6 million
before allowing for tax
we were left with a
surplus of £12.1 million,
which amounts to 7.7%
of our total income.

4

Fig. 32. Smiths Industries: profit and loss illustration (*see page 82*)

What we earned, spent and saved last year – and

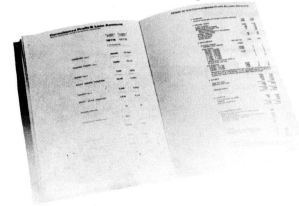

Our sales TURNOVER amounted to £180.8m

£72.1m

We spent £72.1m
on Raw Materials
Components, etc.

£25.0m

£64.2m

CONSOLIDATED PROFIT AND LOSS ACCOUNT
(REPORT & ACCOUNTS PAGE 12)
This statement combines the results of the operations of all the businesses of SI (Smiths Industries Limited and Subsidiary Companies) in the UK and Overseas during the financial year ended on 31st July, 1976. The figures are shown to the nearest £1,000.

	£000	
TURNOVER		
The amount we have charged to customers for goods and services supplied to them.		180,850
Operating Costs: –		
Raw Materials, components and products bought for resale.	72,123	
Services and other expenses such as fuel and power, rates, rent, insurance premiums etc.	25,019	
Payroll, including social security and pension contributions, welfare and training.	64,145	
Depreciation – the amount set aside each year to recover the original cost of machines and equipment over their working lives.	2,067	
Total Operating Costs	163,354	
TRADING PROFIT		17,496
Interest – the net amount payable on borrowings.	1,328	
PROFIT BEFORE TAXATION		16,168
Taxation – payable to UK and overseas governments.	8,330	
PROFIT AFTER TAXATION		7,838
Minority Interests – some shares of certain Australian subsidiaries are owned by others. This is their share of the profit.	32	
Dividends – payments to Shareholders as a return on their investment.	3,030	
RETAINED PROFIT		4,776
Extraordinary Items – special items unrelated to the trading results.	+424	
PROFIT including extraordinary items.	5,200	

£25.0m
on Services

£64.2m
on Payroll

£1.3m
on Interest

We provided £8.3m
for Taxation

£3.0m
for Dividends

We saved £2.1m
Depreciation

£4.8m
Retained Profit

Earnings per share
Profit after tax divided by the number of issued shares **17.3p**
This is one way in which the financial performance of companies is measured.

2

Fig. 33. Dowty: profit and loss diagram (*see page 82*)

Our income, expenditure and savings

(Group Profit and Loss Account
—Report and Accounts, page 14)

This summary shows the consolidated results of all Group companies
at home and abroad during the year ended 31st March, 1976.

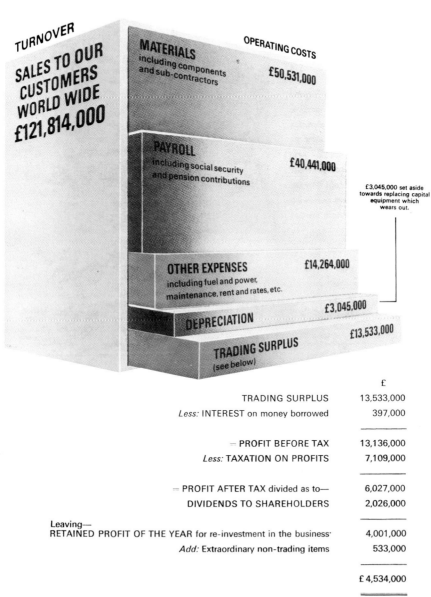

TURNOVER
SALES TO OUR CUSTOMERS WORLD WIDE £121,814,000

OPERATING COSTS

MATERIALS
including components and sub-contractors £50,531,000

PAYROLL
including social security and pension contributions £40,441,000

£3,045,000 set aside
towards replacing capital
equipment which
wears out.

OTHER EXPENSES £14,264,000
including fuel and power,
maintenance, rent and rates, etc.

DEPRECIATION £3,045,000

TRADING SURPLUS £13,533,000
(see below)

		£
	TRADING SURPLUS	13,533,000
Less: INTEREST on money borrowed		397,000
= PROFIT BEFORE TAX		13,136,000
Less: TAXATION ON PROFITS		7,109,000
= PROFIT AFTER TAX divided as to—		6,027,000
DIVIDENDS TO SHAREHOLDERS		2,026,000
Leaving— RETAINED PROFIT OF THE YEAR for re-investment in the business·		4,001,000
Add: Extraordinary non-trading items		533,000
		£ 4,534,000

PROFIT AFTER TAX PER SHARE—
i.e. Profit after tax divided by number of issued shares — 16·1p per share
(An increase of 22% over the previous year)

8

Fig. 34. Ransome Hoffmann Pollard: profit and loss illustration (*see page 82*)

WHERE EACH RHP £1 WAS EARNED

Group turnover by markets

UK

69p

The Americas

10p

Europe EEC

5·7p

Australasia

4·8p

Africa

4·3p

Rest of Europe

3·3p

Asia

2·9p

WHERE EACH RHP £1 IS SPENT

Wages and salaries

46¹⁄₂p

Materials, services and expenses

41¹⁄₂p

Capital investment

6p

Retained profits

1³⁄₄p

Interest

1¹⁄₂p

Tax payable

1¹⁄₂p

Dividends

1¹⁄₄p

Edited and designed for Ransome Hoffmann Pollard Limited by IH Publications, Rapier House, Lamb's Conduit Street, London and printed by Greenaways, London.

Fig. 35. J. Lyons: explanation of subsidiaries' losses (*see page 82*)

Why MUST we be so big today?

To survive, we must be strong enough to compete with big European and International Companies.

This is why we had to expand, both inside and outside the UK.

And there are other advantages.

It is because we are such a diverse organisation that our more profitable operations can help to tide over any which suffer temporary setbacks and lose money.

This graph shows how some of our operations have increased their profit contributions while those of others have decreased.

In 1971/72 our hotels and catering were making money and could support our bakeries, which were losing it. Today the picture is different. Tomorrow it may well be different again.

It is only because we operate in so many fields that we can support temporary losses in some of our operations.

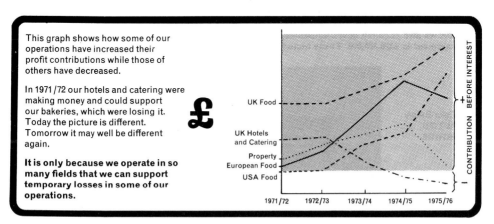

Our operations are subject to fluctuation — for example, in a warm summer, we sell more ice-cream and soft drinks.

In the present economic climate, our hotel and restaurant businesses are losing money. We believe the situation will change, and they will again become profitable.

OUR OVERSEAS VENTURES ARE MAKING A GOOD OVERALL CONTRIBUTION

1975/76 Food Products	SALES	CONTRIBUTION BEFORE CHARGING INTEREST
Europe	£185,000,000	£ 6,894,000
U.S.A.	£139,000,000	£ 9,193,000
Others	£ 15,000,000	£ 1,268,000
Hotels & Catering Overseas	£ 7,000,000	— £ 695,000
TOTAL	£346,000,000	* £16,660,000

plus share of associated companies' profits of £1,113,000

The money made by our overseas ventures helps us all.

We believe that they will continue to expand, and so increase the strength of the whole Group.

THE PROSPERITY AND STRENGTH OF THE GROUP AS A WHOLE IS IN THE INTERESTS OF STAFF IN ALL PARTS OF THE GROUP.

Fig. 36. Avon: explanation of loss (*see page 82*)

THE AVON £

How a fraction of 1p
multiplied 72 million times
becomes a £1/2 million Loss

**Income
100p**

29p
Tyres

26p
Motorway

18p
Industrial
Polymers

13p
Overseas

9p
Bridgend

3p
Inflatables

2p
Medicals

The column on the left shows how the Avon £ was earned.

A comparison with the column on the right shows that for every £1 we earned in the last financial year we spent one pound and seven tenths of a penny on keeping the company going and thus ended up with a deficit of £502,850 on our turnover of almost £72 million.

To cover this loss the company had to borrow money from our bankers, who were prepared to lend it to Avon having faith in the future of the Group and in its ability to make a profit in the years ahead.

The position could have been far worse but for some good financial house keeping. We achieved a £¾ million reduction in stocks and the amount of money owed to the company. The cash saved was then invested in fixed assets (buildings, plant and machinery) thus strengthening Avon's overall position.

*'Annual income £20,
annual expenditure
£19·19s·6d,
result happiness.
Annual income £20,
annual expenditure
£20 ought and 6d,
result misery'*

— Mr Micawber

**Expenditure
100·7p**

66p
Materials
& Services

30·6p
Salaries,
Wages &
Associated
Costs

4p
Interest &
Depreciation

0·1p
Dividends

Fig. 37. Nuffield Nursing Home Trust: profit and loss linked to balance sheet *(see page 83)*, cont'd overleaf

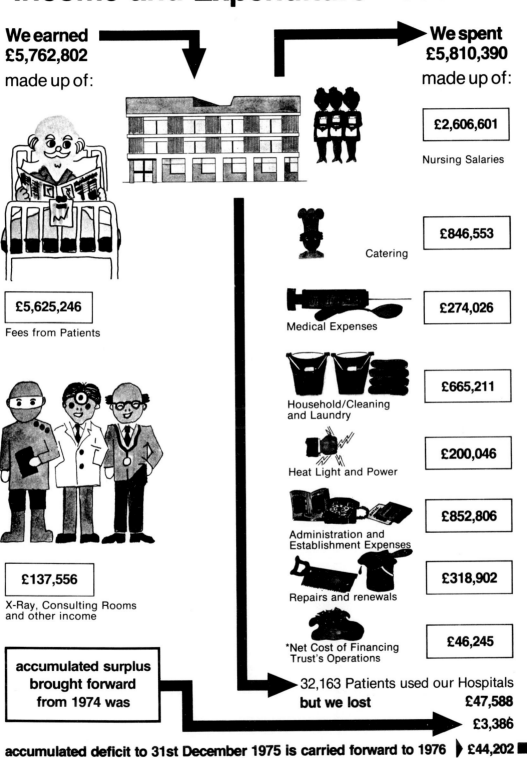

Income and Expenditure Account

We earned
£5,762,802

made up of:

We spent
£5,810,390

made up of:

£2,606,601

Nursing Salaries

£846,553

Catering

£274,026

Medical Expenses

£665,211

Household/Cleaning
and Laundry

£200,046

Heat Light and Power

£852,806

Administration and
Establishment Expenses

£318,902

Repairs and renewals

£46,245

*Net Cost of Financing
Trust's Operations

£5,625,246

Fees from Patients

£137,556

X-Ray, Consulting Rooms
and other income

accumulated surplus
brought forward
from 1974 was

32,163 Patients used our Hospitals
but we lost £47,588

£3,386

accumulated deficit to 31st December 1975 is carried forward to 1976 ▶ £44,202

*(*See notes overleaf)*

Fig. 37. (cont'd)

Balance Sheet

Source of funds and liabilities

Employment of funds

Accumulated Fund*

£8,108,065

£12,083,192 Fixed assets and buildings in progress

LESS

From income and expenditure account **£44,202**

New Homes deficit equalisation account* **£162,222**

Investments/loans to Nursing Homes

£128,774

Secured debenture loan & unsecured loan

£4,200,000

Stocks

£348,008

Creditors and accrued charges

£809,320

Debtors and short term deposits

£642,952

Repairs and renewals provision*

£589,847

Bank accounts and cash

£297,882

£13,500,808

Fig. 38. Grand Metropolitan: balance sheet presentations (*see page 83*)

Printed in England by Brown Knight & Truscott Ltd.

Fig. 39. Dowty: balance sheet illustration (*see page 83*)

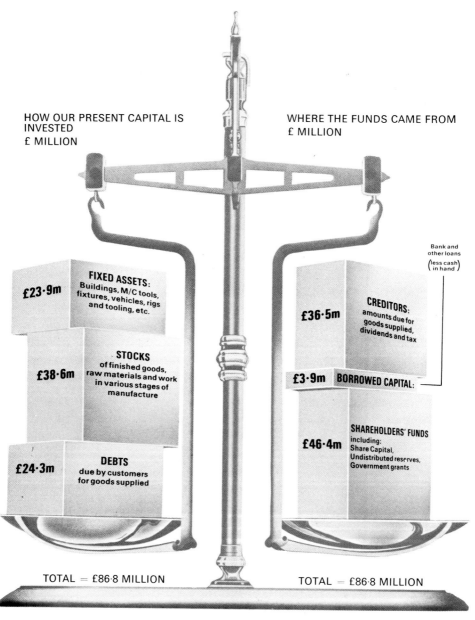

State of affairs at 31st March, 1976

Including the new investment during the year shown opposite (page 11)

(Group Balance Sheet
—Report and Accounts, page 15)

HOW OUR PRESENT CAPITAL IS
INVESTED
£ MILLION

WHERE THE FUNDS CAME FROM
£ MILLION

Bank and
other loans
(less cash
in hand)

£23·9m **FIXED ASSETS:** Buildings, M/C tools, fixtures, vehicles, rigs and tooling, etc.

£36·5m **CREDITORS:** amounts due for goods supplied, dividends and tax

£38·6m **STOCKS** of finished goods, raw materials and work in various stages of manufacture

£3·9m **BORROWED CAPITAL:**

£24·3m **DEBTS** due by customers for goods supplied

£46·4m **SHAREHOLDERS' FUNDS** including: Share Capital, Undistributed reserves, Government grants

TOTAL = £86·8 MILLION

TOTAL = £86·8 MILLION

Fig. 40. Babcock & Wilcox: balance sheet diagram (*see page 83*)

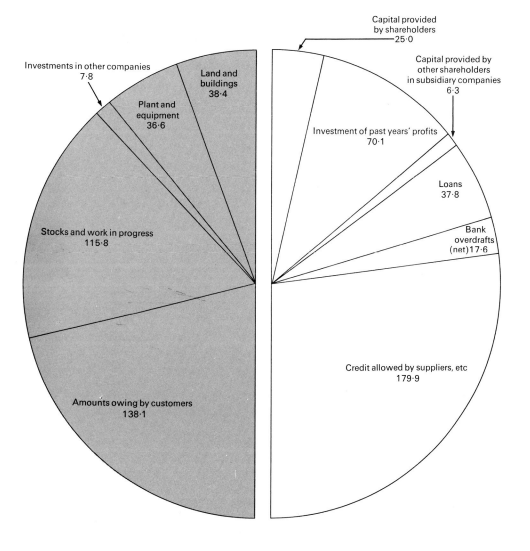

Our financial position at the end of 1975

What we own
£ million

How financed
£ million

Investments in other companies
7·8

Land and
buildings
38·4

Plant and
equipment
36·6

Stocks and work in progress
115·8

Amounts owing by customers
138·1

Capital provided
by shareholders
25·0

Capital provided by
other shareholders
in subsidiary companies
6·3

Investment of past years' profits
70·1

Loans
37·8

Bank
overdrafts
(net)17·6

Credit allowed by suppliers, etc
179·9

Total   **£336·7 million**   **Total**   **£336·7 million**

Fig. 41. Smiths Industries: balance sheet diagram (*see page 83*)

Our Financial position at the end of July 1976

FIGURES ARE TAKEN FROM THE BALANCE SHEET AND THE TEN YEAR REVIEW (REPORT AND ACCOUNTS PAGES 14 & 20)

Assets

What we owned at 31st July 1976 and what others owed us.

Fixed Assets
This includes land and buildings, which were valued in 1974 at £20m, plant and machinery, vehicles, furniture and fixtures (less accumulated depreciation) and investments.

£34·1m

Stocks
Finished goods awaiting sale, raw materials and products at various stages of completion, including the value of any work we have done on them.

£58·6m

Debtors
Money owed to us by customers who have received our goods and services but have not yet paid for them.

£35·1m

Finances

What we owe others and how we finance the balance.

Current Taxation
See note below.

£6·5m

Deferred Taxation
See note below.

£13·8m

Creditors
Money owed to suppliers for goods and services that they have supplied to us.

£32·5m

Net Borrowings

£10·5m

Shareholders Funds
Comprises
Share Capital **£23.4m**
Reserves **£41.1m**

£64·5m

Note: Taxation takes more than half the profits, but we do not have to pay it all immediately and may never have to pay some of it.
Current Tax – we know that we owe and will have to pay **£2·9m** — *this year.*
unless the law is changed we will have to pay a further **£3·6m** — *next year.*
Deferred Tax – by taking advantage of certain allowances we have been allowed to defer the payment of a further **£3·4m** till — *sometime.*
The rest **£10·4m**
relates mainly to stock relief under the 1975 Finance Act and capital gains on property revaluation and is deferred until some unspecified date, – or maybe — *never*

Fig. 42. Nissen: balance sheet explained (*see page 84*)

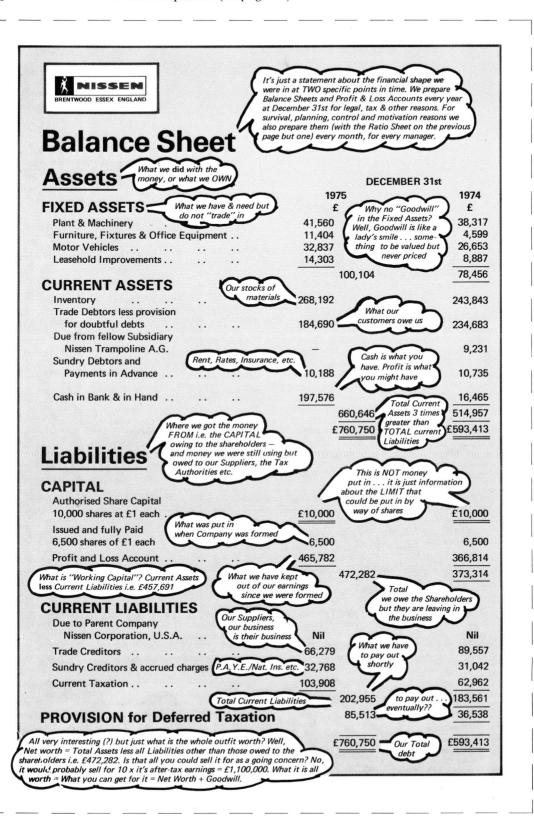

Fig. 43. H. P. Bulmer: value added diagram (*see page 84*)

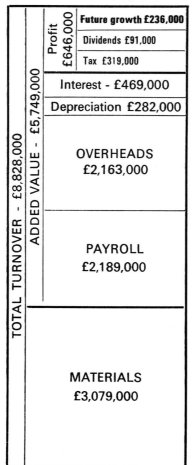

½-Year to October 1975
Total turnover £12,842,000

Future growth £743,000	
Dividends £97,000	Profit £1,833,000
TAX £993,000	

Interest - £452,000

Depreciation £321,000

OVERHEADS
£3,121,000

PAYROLL
£2,877,000

MATERIALS
£4,238,000

ADDED VALUE £8,604,000

TOTAL TURNOVER £12,842,000

H.P. BULMER GROUP

STATEMENT OF ADDED VALUE

½-Year to October 1974
Total turnover £8,828,000

Profit £646,000

| Future growth £236,000 |
| Dividends £91,000 |
| Tax £319,000 |

Interest - £469,000

Depreciation £282,000

OVERHEADS
£2,163,000

PAYROLL
£2,189,000

MATERIALS
£3,079,000

ADDED VALUE - £5,749,000

TOTAL TURNOVER - £8,828,000

Fig. 44. Smiths Industries: value added illustration (*see page 84*)

how VALUE ADDED was applied

A Statement of **VALUE ADDED**
*has been included in the Report & Accounts
this year for the first time (page 11). This statement
shows how the wealth created by the efforts of
the Company and its employees has been shared
between employees, providers of capital,
governments and retained for re-investment.*

A sales income of **£180.8m**

Less £ **97.1m** paid to suppliers of raw materials and services

gives an added
value of £ **83.7m**

For every £1 of value added

77p goes to pay **Employees** wages,
pensions and employee benefits.

1½p goes to pay **Interest** on the
money we have borrowed.

10p goes to **Governments,** UK and
overseas to pay taxes.

3½p goes to **Shareholders** in dividends.

and we save

8p to provide for **Inflation,**
for the **Maintenance** of existing
facilities and further **Investment.**

3

Fig. 45. Metal Box: value added diagram (*see page 84*)

...and what happened to it.

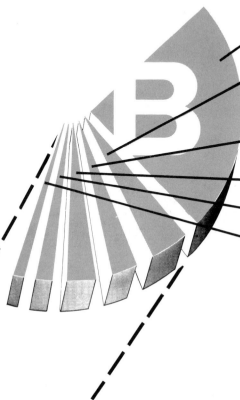

The total wealth created of £134 millions was divided as follows:

£85 millions (63%):
Wages and salaries paid to the 29,600 U.K. employees (3,200 of whom were part-time workers).

£16 millions (12%):
Other payments for the benefit of employees: the company's national insurance and pension fund contributions, canteen subsidies, sick pay, welfare and surgeries.

£10 millions (8%):
Depreciation: the amount set aside towards replacement of buildings, machinery and equipment.

75% of the wealth created, therefore, is for all of us in Metal Box

£12 millions (9%)
Set aside for **taxation** payable to the Government.

£7 millions (5%)
Retained in the business for expansion and job security.

£4 millions (3%)
Dividends to stockholders: total dividends payable to stockholders were £7 millions, of which £3 millions came from the Metal Box Overseas Limited dividend to Metal Box Limited. Therefore, the amount taken from UK created wealth for dividends was reduced to £4 millions. Dividends to stockholders were higher this year because additional cash of £24 millions was obtained from stockholders through a Rights Issue and we had to offer an increased rate of dividend to attract their money. The cost of the increased dividend was partly offset by lower interest payments on temporarily reduced borrowings made possible by the Rights Issue.

This is the Home profit before taxation shown on pages 3 and 16 of the Annual Reports and Accounts.

The Stockholders

The table below is a summarised version of the table on page 9 of the Annual Reports and Accounts.

	Number of Holders	Amount of Stock Millions of £s	%
Individuals			
Range of holdings			
1-500 units	35,812	£ 7	13
501-1,000 units	6,213	4	7
over 1,000 units	3,268	11	19
	45,293	£22	39
Institutions			
Banks, Nominees & Trustee Companies	3,589	£18	32
Insurance Companies & Pension Funds	278	15	26
Other Companies and Foreign Holders	757	2	3
	4,624	£35	61
TOTAL	49,917	£57	100

Rights Issue

In July 1975 a further £24 millions were raised from stockholders by the issue of 11½ million £1 units of stock at a price of £2.10 each.

Largest Stockholders

The two largest stockholdings in Metal Box are owned by the Prudential Assurance Company with 2·1% of the issued capital and the Co-operative Insurance Society with 1·8%.

Fig. 46. Tate & Lyle Refineries: value added diagram (*see page 84*)

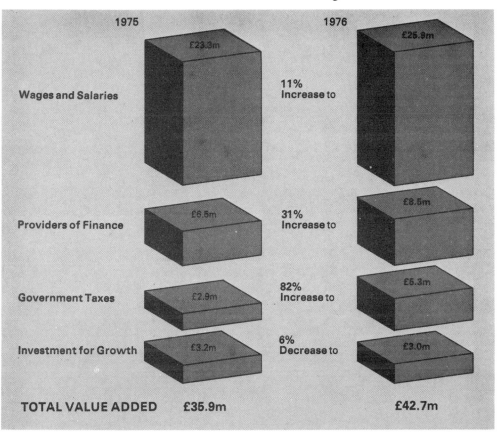

Tate & Lyle Refineries 1976

The use of value-our two year record

	1975		1976
Wages and Salaries	£23.3m	11% Increase to	£25.9m
Providers of Finance	£6.5m	31% Increase to	£8.5m
Government Taxes	£2.9m	82% Increase to	£5.3m
Investment for Growth	£3.2m	6% Decrease to	£3.0m
TOTAL VALUE ADDED	**£35.9m**		**£42.7m**

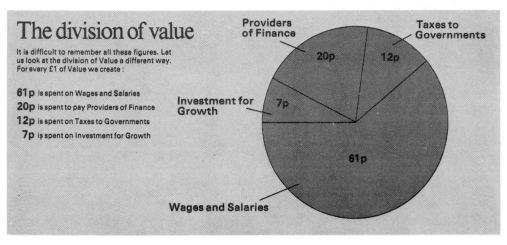

The division of value

It is difficult to remember all these figures. Let us look at the division of Value a different way. For every £1 of Value we create:

61p is spent on Wages and Salaries
20p is spent to pay Providers of Finance
12p is spent on Taxes to Governments
7p is spent on Investment for Growth

Providers of Finance   20p

Taxes to Governments   12p

Investment for Growth   7p

61p

Wages and Salaries

Fig. 47. Johnson Group: cash flow illustration (*see page 85*)

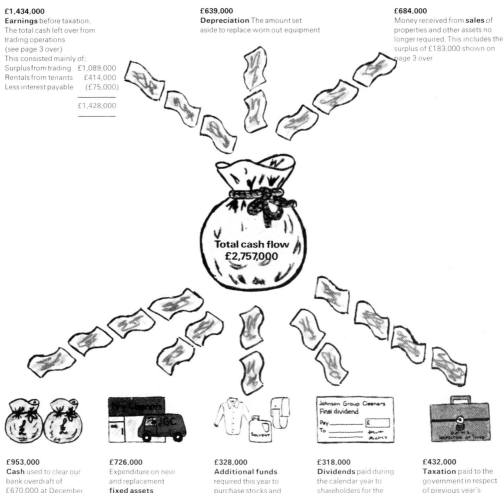

How did our cash flow in 1975?

This statement shows where our cash resources came from in 1975, and how they were used within the Group. The figures are based on the details of sources and application of funds shown on page 22 of the published Accounts

How our cash flowed in

£1,434,000
Earnings before taxation.
The total cash left over from
trading operations
(see page 3 over)
This consisted mainly of:
Surplus from trading £1,089,000
Rentals from tenants £414,000
Less interest payable (£75,000)
_____
£1,428,000

£639,000
Depreciation The amount set
aside to replace worn out equipment

£684,000
Money received from **sales** of
properties and other assets no
longer required. This includes the
surplus of £183,000 shown on
page 3 over

**Total cash flow
£2,757,000**

£953,000
Cash used to clear our
bank overdraft of
£670,000 at December
1974 and provide funds
for growth in 1976

£726,000
Expenditure on new
and replacement
fixed assets

£328,000
Additional funds
required this year to
purchase stocks and
finance the day-to-day
running of the business

£318,000
Dividends paid during
the calendar year to
shareholders for the
use of their money.
These were the final
payment for 1974 and the
interim payment for 1975

£432,000
Taxation paid to the
government in respect
of previous year's
earnings

How our cash was used

6

Fig. 48. Turner & Newall: cash flow diagram (*see page 85*)

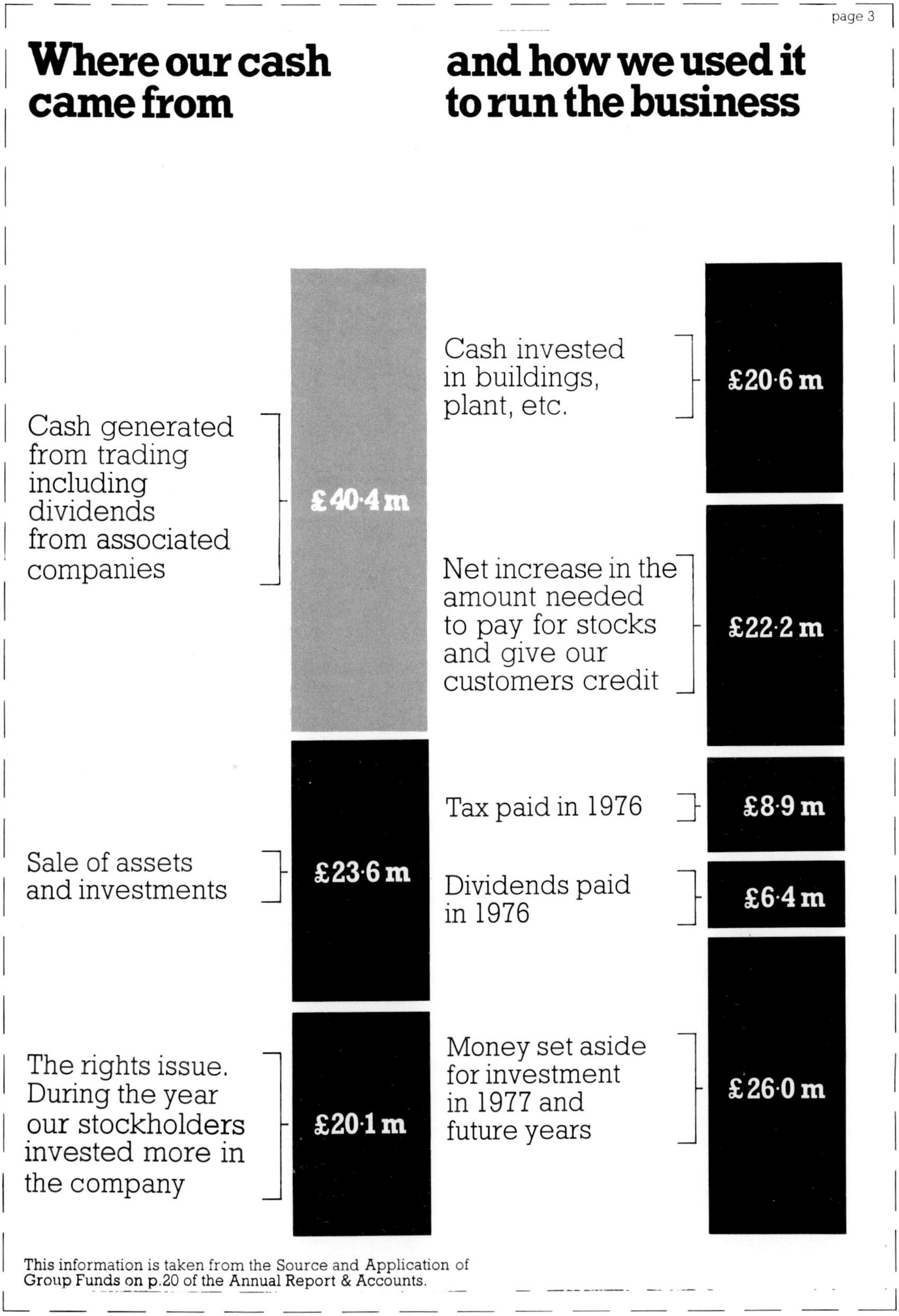

Where our cash came from

and how we used it to run the business

Cash generated from trading including dividends from associated companies

£40·4 m

Cash invested in buildings, plant, etc.

£20·6 m

Net increase in the amount needed to pay for stocks and give our customers credit

£22·2 m

Sale of assets and investments

£23·6 m

Tax paid in 1976

£8·9 m

Dividends paid in 1976

£6·4 m

The rights issue. During the year our stockholders invested more in the company

£20·1 m

Money set aside for investment in 1977 and future years

£26·0 m

This information is taken from the Source and Application of Group Funds on p.20 of the Annual Report & Accounts.

Fig. 49. Dowty: investment illustration (*see page 85*)

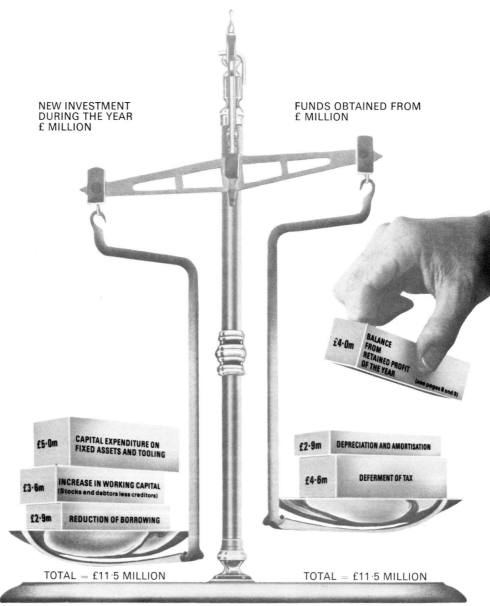

New investment during the year 1975–76 and sources of funds

(Group Source and Application of Funds
—Report and Accounts, page 24)

NEW INVESTMENT
DURING THE YEAR
£ MILLION

FUNDS OBTAINED FROM
£ MILLION

£4·0m BALANCE
FROM
RETAINED PROFIT
OF THE YEAR
(see pages 8 and 9)

£5·0m CAPITAL EXPENDITURE ON
FIXED ASSETS AND TOOLING

£2·9m DEPRECIATION AND AMORTISATION

£3·6m INCREASE IN WORKING CAPITAL
(Stocks and debtors less creditors)

£4·6m DEFERMENT OF TAX

£2·9m REDUCTION OF BORROWING

TOTAL = £11·5 MILLION

TOTAL = £11·5 MILLION

11

Fig. 50. Smiths Industries: investment diagram (*see page 85*)

Investment

Over the last 5 years: We have achieved a turnover of **£685.6m**
and earned a profit (after tax) of **£29.6m**

Over the same period: We have invested in the business a sum of **£42.1m**
We have bought companies for the sum of **£22.7m**
We have spent the sum of **£31.0m**
on research, development and product
engineering, which is another kind of
Investment for the future —

making a total of : **£95.8m**

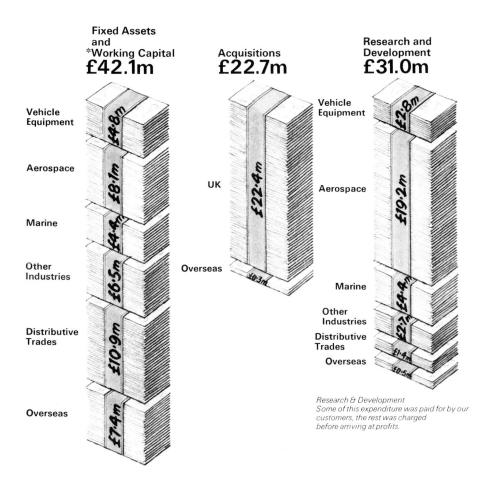

**Fixed Assets
and
*Working Capital
£42.1m**

**Acquisitions
£22.7m**

**Research and
Development
£31.0m**

Vehicle
Equipment — £4.8m

Aerospace — £8.1m

Marine — £4.4m

Other
Industries — £6.5m

Distributive
Trades — £10.9m

Overseas — £7.4m

UK — £22.4m

Overseas — £0.3m

Vehicle
Equipment — £2.8m

Aerospace — £19.2m

Marine — £4.4m

Other
Industries — £2.7m

Distributive
Trades — £1.4m

Overseas — £0.5m

*Research & Development
Some of this expenditure was paid for by our
customers, the rest was charged
before arriving at profits.*

*Working Capital — is made up of:— Stocks + Debtors less Creditors.

In his Chairman's Review Mr. E. R. Sisson states —
"... with the rate of inflation during the year a higher level of profitability or a change in the
basis of taxation is necessary if companies are to be enabled to accumulate adequate funds for
further investment."

Fig. 51. Macarthy Pharmaceuticals: investment diagram (*see page 85*)

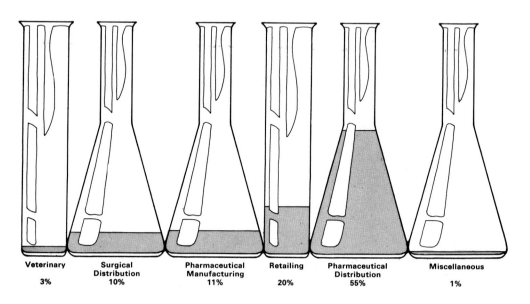

Where we invested our money in 1976

Veterinary	Surgical Distribution	Pharmaceutical Manufacturing	Retailing	Pharmaceutical Distribution	Miscellaneous
3%	10%	11%	20%	55%	1%

and what we invested it in

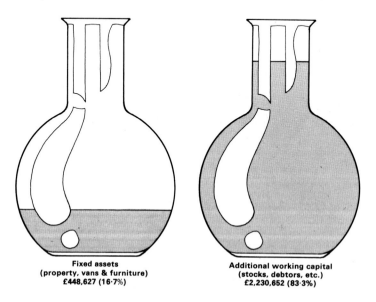

Fixed assets
(property, vans & furniture)
£448,627 (16·7%)

Additional working capital
(stocks, debtors, etc.)
£2,230,652 (83·3%)

Fig. 52. Tate & Lyle: investment diagram (*see page 85*)

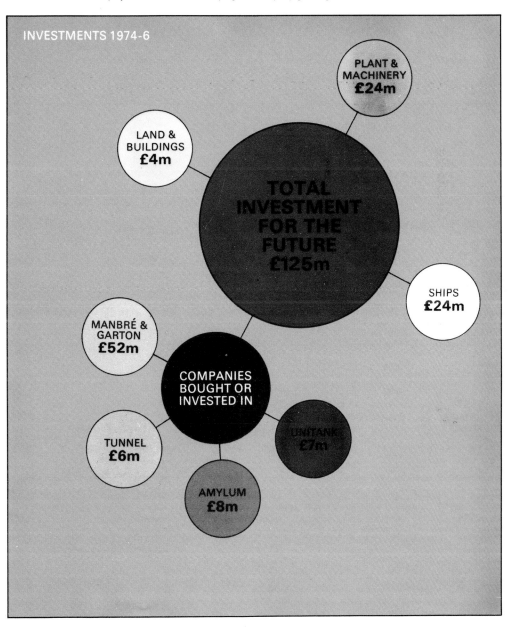

Tate & Lyle Limited 1976

The future depends on investment

If we did not invest money in new plant and machinery; if we did not renew our vehicles and ships; if we did not invest in new projects, the Company would soon start to decline. Over the last two years we have spent over £125 million investing for the future, keeping the company growing and prospering. This money has been spent in a number of different ways.

INVESTMENTS 1974-6

PLANT & MACHINERY £24m

LAND & BUILDINGS £4m

TOTAL INVESTMENT FOR THE FUTURE £125m

SHIPS £24m

MANBRÉ & GARTON £52m

COMPANIES BOUGHT OR INVESTED IN

UNITANK £7m

TUNNEL £6m

AMYLUM £8m

7

Fig. 53. Grand Metropolitan: inflation illustration (*see page 92*)

4.
How inflation affects reported profits

Profits disclosed in the report so far have been calculated according to a method that has been operative in this country for many years—the historic cost method; from the sales value of the period is deducted the cost of achieving those sales and the resultant figure represents the profit (or loss). However, such costs may have been incurred some time before the date of the sales—for example, materials may have been purchased several months before their conversion into a finished product; similarly, certain machines may have been purchased 10 or 20 (or even more) years ago but are still employed in manufacturing products. In times of inflation, if these 'old' costs are used to calculate profits, the true profitability of the Company is seriously distorted and two simple diagrams illustrate why.

Amounts put aside out of profits based on original cost are inadequate for replacement of machinery

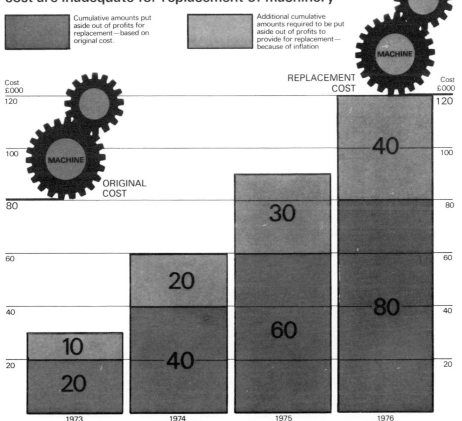

A machine costing £80,000 at the beginning of 1973 will cost to replace in 1976 (say) £120,000. Under historic accounting, £20,000 each year would be put aside out of profits (representing the depreciation charge) so that £80,000 would have been 'saved' by the time replacement is required, but £80,000 is clearly inadequate and inflation accounting requires that a further £10,000 each year be put aside in order to provide for the replacement cost of £120,000.

Fig. 54. (cont'd)

5.

How inflation
affects reported profits (continued)

Amounts put aside out of profits based on original cost are inadequate for replacement of stock

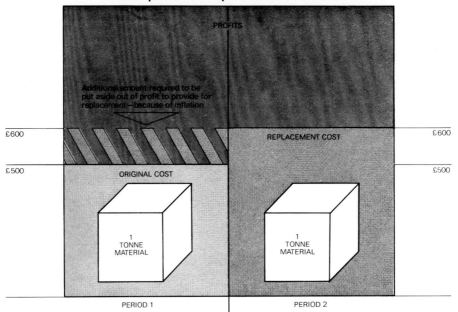

PROFITS

Additional amount required to be put aside out of profit to provide for replacement—because of inflation

£600

REPLACEMENT COST

£600

£500

ORIGINAL COST

£500

1 TONNE MATERIAL

1 TONNE MATERIAL

PERIOD 1

PERIOD 2

One tonne of material costing £500 is consumed in period 1 requiring replacement of the material in order to fulfil further customers' orders but the cost in period 2 is now £600. To ensure that 'profit' is not consumed or distributed thus denying the opportunity of replacing the one tonne of stock at new prices a further £100 (on top of the £500) must be put aside out of period 1 profit to pay for period 2 requirements.

Current cost accounting

The effect of inflation on reported profits has been the subject of much concern and discussion in recent years and the Government appointed a Committee to look into the subject under the Chairmanship of Sir Francis Sandilands. The Committee reported in June 1975 concluding that a system of 'current cost accounting' should be introduced to show a more realistic picture of profit by charging against sales the current costs of the assets consumed in earning them. This would have the effect of making a more appropriate contribution out of profits to provide for the replacement cost of both stocks and fixed assets.

Even though the details are still being developed by the accountancy profession, a new accounting method should emerge in the near future.

M.K. Group profits-current cost adjusted

Using current costs as opposed to historic costs, the profits of the M.K. Group for the year ended 27 March 1976 would require the following adjustments:

	£000	£000
Profit under the Historical Cost Convention		2,171
Additional charges based on Current Costs:		
Depreciation—Fixed Assets	490	
Cost of Sales—Stock	270	
		760
Profit under the Current Cost Accounting Convention		1,411

INFLATION ACCOUNTING
and what it means

'INFLATION accounting' has been much in the papers recently and we have all got to understand something about it if we are to know what the RHP figures mean or understand what is happening to British industry as a whole.

Last year RHP sold its products for £78m, an improvement of about 20% on the previous year's figures of £63m. From these sales we made a profit of £5.1m compared with £5.8m in the year before. Have the returns we earned in the past two years been satisfactory?

Last year, about half our reported profits were needed merely to replace raw materials at higher prices, and we *must* do this to keep our factories busy since the physical volume of our stocks has already been reduced as far as possible. Similarly, most of the rest of our profit is needed to replace our machinery, at a much higher cost now, to produce the same volume of product. The profit of £5.8m last year which you might have expected to see as extra cash in the accounts was wholly taken up in maintaining the business. At the end of the year we had not a penny more in the bank than at the beginning.

Cash confusion

The difference between profits and cash under conditions of inflation has confused almost everyone—Government, managers, employees and the media alike. It is inflation that is responsible for this, since it has destroyed the meaning of the reporting system that has traditionally been used. For instance, in the past if the sales figures went up it meant more sales had been made, whereas now the sales in real terms may very well be less, even if the figures are more. Similarly, in the past, if the figure for stocks went up there were more stocks on the shelves, but now you cannot tell what has happened unless you know how much the stocks went up in value.

The serious effect of inflation on business profits has now been recognised by the Government which set up the Sandilands Committee to decide what changes in company accounts reporting were necessary. This report was published about a year ago and within the last fortnight the Accounting Standards Committee have issued new guidelines for inflation adjusted accounts.

Inflation accounting recognises the problem by measuring the earnings of a business against the amount that is needed to maintain it by replacing its assets. The assets of a business are its stocks (of raw materials, work in progress and finished goods), its plant and its buildings.

In non-inflationary conditions traditional accounting methods easily show how to cover costs and earn enough profit to put aside for replacing worn-out assets and the proverbial rainy day.

When we have a situation of high inflation with costs rising rapidly the new accounting proposals give us a much more realistic basis for measuring success. In the last twelve months the cost of our major raw material—steel—rose by an average of 35%, with quite a few individual increases above 50%. If cost increases like this are not recovered the business is bound to decline, it will end up smaller in size, output will go down and some of the people in it will lose their jobs.

Shrinking businesses

This is happening to many companies today. Their accounts show some profits, the value of their stocks and sales rise and they appear to have some money in the bank. Nevertheless, in real terms the output of their business is shrinking and they cannot keep their factories or work force fully employed.

So how *does* a company achieve genuine profitability under inflation? It must price above current costs to make a real profit, though naturally it will have to work its hardest to bring down these current costs by increased productivity. It is not possible in the world market place just to increase prices in line with costs if our competitors costs are lower than ours—hence the vital importance of productivity.

The true facts

This new form of accounting is important because there is widespread misunderstanding about the real nature of business profit, particularly during inflation, and in consequence much ill-informed pressure on industry to invest in excess of its real financial capability. At present, industry—particularly manufacturing industry—hardly makes a real profit as opposed to an accounting profit in today's terms. We who work in industry must understand the true facts and be able to explain them to others.

The problem is important and relevant to RHP because our real profit is much lower than that shown by today's accounts and our ability to finance investment, expansion or distribution of profits can easily be overestimated.

In 1977 we need to make a larger profit in better market conditions and this profit, together with the Government loan, will all be needed to finance the planned expansion.

Fig. 56. Gestetner: inflation diagram (*see page 92*)

How inflation affects the cash we need to run our business

Our sales bring in money so we have CASH IN HAND. This is needed for the day to day running of our business and is called WORKING CAPITAL.

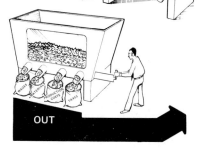

All looks well but then . . .

. . . we have to make payments to keep us going and pay our taxes, so our WORKING CAPITAL is reduced . . .

. . . until our customers pay and income from our sales tops up our WORKING CAPITAL.

All is well again but . . .

. . . next time we make payments we find:
    wages have risen,
    cost of raw materials has risen,
    taxes have risen,
as inflation starts to bite. Our WORKING CAPITAL is very low so . . .

. . . we have to get more cash in. Our increase in sales income helps but is not sufficient, so we have to increase our borrowings to top up our WORKING CAPITAL.

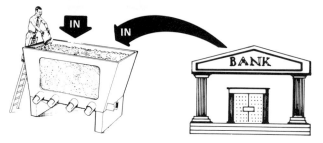

5

Fig. 57. EMI: inflation diagrams (*see page 93*)

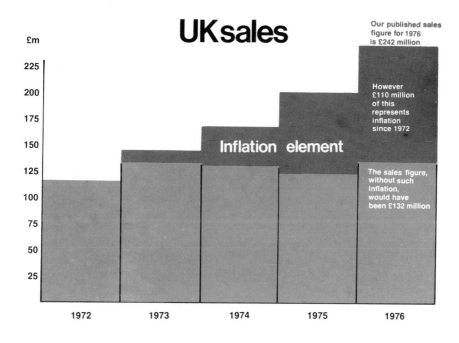

How inflation affects our UK business

UK sales

£m

Our published sales figure for 1976 is £242 million

However £110 million of this represents inflation since 1972

Inflation element

The sales figure, without such inflation, would have been £132 million

225
200
175
150
125
100
75
50
25

1972   1973   1974   1975   1976

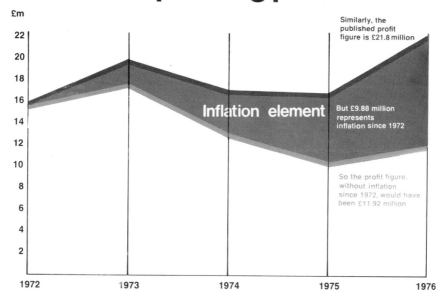

UK operating profit

£m

Similarly, the published profit figure is £21.8 million

Inflation element

But £9.88 million represents inflation since 1972

So the profit figure, without inflation since 1972, would have been £11.92 million

22
20
18
16
14
12
10
8
6
4
2

1972   1973   1974   1975   1976

Fig. 58. UBM: effects of inflation explained (*see page 93*)

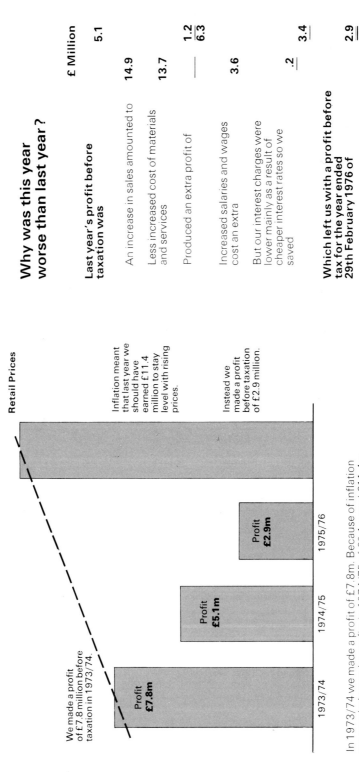

How we've failed to keep pace with inflation

Retail Prices

We made a profit of £7.8 million before taxation in 1973/74.

Inflation meant that last year we should have earned £11.4 million to stay level with rising prices.

Instead we made a profit before taxation of £2.9 million.

Profit **£7.8m**

1973/74

Profit **£5.1m**

1974/75

Profit **£2.9m**

1975/76

In 1973/74 we made a profit of £7.8m. Because of inflation we needed to make profits in 1974/75 of £9.1m and £11.4m in 1975/76 just to maintain 1973/74 levels.

Instead we made profits in 1974/75 of £5.1m and £2.9m in 1975/76. In real terms our profits for 1975/76 are therefore only about a quarter of those earned 2 years ago.

Why was this year worse than last year?

	£ Million
Last year's profit before taxation was	5.1
An increase in sales amounted to	14.9
Less increased cost of materials and services	13.7
Produced an extra profit of	1.2
	6.3
Increased salaries and wages cost an extra	3.6
But our interest charges were lower mainly as a result of cheaper interest rates so we saved	.2
	3.4
Which left us with a profit before tax for the year ended 29th February 1976 of	2.9

Fig. 59. Tate & Lyle Truck Services: employee report (*see page 97*)

Tate & Lyle Transport 1976

 T LT TRUCK SERVICES

A review of 1976

By Bob Foskett, General Manager

1976 was a difficult year for the Truck Services Division. The transport industry is very dependent upon the condition of the economy and the problems affecting the UK last year are reflected in our own financial performance. During the previous few years we had expanded rapidly, and our choice of workshop locations did not always fit the customer demand for our services. Consequently, we have had to rationalise our operations during the year, reducing both the number of premises and, regrettably, the number of employees working for us.

I believe, however, that we can face the future with optimism:

First, we have concentrated our resources, and we now possess well sited workshops which can offer a full, efficient service to prospective and existing customers.

Secondly, we have developed the "Truck Centre" concept which provides purpose built commercial vehicle facilities equipped with an efficient communications system, and the most up-to-date diagnostic and servicing equipment. The first centre was officially opened at Coatbridge in Scotland on January 21st, 1977.

Thirdly, we are amending our franchise arrangements to enable us to sell the right type of truck in the right type of market.

Finally, we have developed a new management team and I have every confidence, not only in their judgement, but in the skills and commitment of all our employees.

In short, I believe that we are well organised to meet the coming year. But organisation by itself is not enough.

We are in business to attract, serve and maintain our customers; without them we have no

money to pay wages, to maintain our workshops or equipment and to invest in the future. The customer is the most important person in our lives, and all our efforts should be put at his disposal.

If we all act on this basis then I am sure that 1977 will prove a successful year. I would like to finish by thanking you all for your hard work, and enthusiasm during 1976 and offering you my best wishes for the coming year.

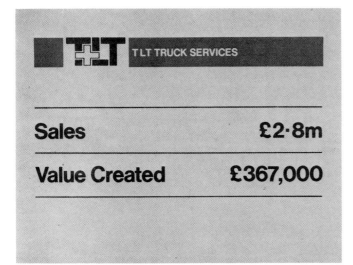

T LT TRUCK SERVICES

Sales	**£2·8m**
Value Created	**£367,000**

A diagnostic pit at the Coatbridge Truck Centre.

The new Truck Centre at Coatbridge, Scotland.

Fig. 60. Tate & Lyle Transport: value added statement (*see page 97*)

Tate & Lyle Transport 1976

Value of £8·2 million created by Tate & Lyle Transport in 1976

In the year which ended on 30 September 1976 the Value created by all of us working in Tate & Lyle Transport amounted to £8.2 million.

Value is the difference between the cost of all the fuel, spares and bought in services we need to operate our transport fleets and the total sales income we receive.

Value serves to reward all those who work for the business, makes a contribution to our society and helps to ensure our future growth and security.

While we believe that Value is the true measure of our success we must strive by increasing the size of the cake to increase that part of Value known as 'profit'. Profit indicates the amount of money we have available to plough back into the business and the degree of support we can expect from our shareholders. Only if we remain profitable will we be able to raise further funds to finance our future growth and job security.

In 1976 the value created by us and how it was used was as follows :

	£million
TOTAL INCOME FROM SALES	**17.9**
The money we receive from the sale of our transport services	
minus	
TOTAL COSTS	**9.7**
The money we paid suppliers for fuel, spares and sundries	
gives	
VALUE	**8.2**
This Value is used to pay for a number of different things.	

But we are judged by profit

Our ability to retain our capital and attract the use of further funds depends upon our ability to provide an adequate reward to those who provide capital. This reward comes from that part of Value known as pre-tax profit.

As you can see, profit is only part of Value but it does indicate the amount we can use for the future development of the company.

In 1976 we used our pre-tax profits as follows :

Providers of Finance in the form of Dividends	£300,000
Taxes to Government	£300,000
Retentions	£200,000
	£800,000

£6.4m — **TO PAY OURSELVES** Wages and National Insurance and Pension Contributions

£0.2m — **TO PAY THE PROVIDERS OF FINANCE** a) Interest on Loans b) Dividends to Shareholders

£0.3m — **TO PAY TAXES TO THE GOVERNMENT**

£0.3m — **TO PROVIDE INVESTMENT FOR GROWTH** a) RETENTIONS Money retained to invest in future growth

£0.2m — b) DEPRECIATION Money put aside to renew equipment and machinery when it wears out

£0.8m — **TOTAL VALUE ADDED £8.2 million**

Pre Tax Profit £0·8m

The use of value

Another way of looking at our performance is to show how each £1 of the Value we created was spent.

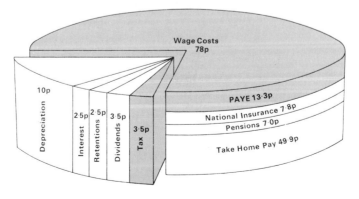

Wage Costs 78p

10p Depreciation
2·5p Interest
2·5p Retentions
3·5p Dividends
3·5p Tax

PAYE 13·3p
National Insurance 7·8p
Pensions 7·0p
Take Home Pay 49·9p

then it should be able to cope with the pressures resulting from disclosing the information. If it cannot justify its pay policies then it should be seeking anyway to make them justifiable and pressure for this information might be just the catalyst it needs.

So much for possible improvements. What can we learn from the report as it stands. From its success seven rules emerge. First, it was complete and consistent. The report started at the beginning and worked progressively through the company. It was all-embracing in its coverage, and in its attempts to provide information of interest. And it was consistent — the tone and attitudes of the first page were maintained right through the report. Second, it tried to relate everything to the readers' experience. Even when it was dealing with millions of pounds it talked about the figures in pay packet terms. Or it talked about customers who could be found on every High Street. Nowhere did it take refuge in jargon. Third, it made a few basic points well, rather than a lot of points badly. It emerged clearly that the company had done well in the past, there were a lot of people involved in trying to make sure that it continued to do well in the present, and it was in everybody's interest to make

sure it did well in the future. Fourth, each section was concerned with putting over one idea, but only one. Fifth, the illustrations had impact — though they were not to everybody's taste — but they never got in the way of the message. Six, it knew where it was going. It chose a theme for the report and stuck to it. Digression is not just boring, but also bewildering! And finally, it was the work of one person, the personnel officer, with the accountant supplying the figures and the chairman keeping an eye on both. That is quite enough. A committee would have destroyed the flavour of the report.

By following these rules the report achieved what John Garnett, head of the Industrial Society, thinks are the two prime objectives of employee reports: first, that they put across the message that in national terms, of every £1 of value added 7p goes to shareholders and 93p to employees; second, to put across what he calls the "common purpose" — the realisation that everybody concerned with the company is in the same boat, and that the purpose of the exercise is to create value, wealth, call it what you will, for the good of all concerned.

PART THREE

PRODUCING A REPORT

CHAPTER NINE

THE INITIAL DECISIONS

Planning an employee report means taking decisions in four key areas, each of which will be discussed in turn in this and the following chapters. It involves, first of all, establishing a policy stating why the company is producing an employee report and what its objectives are. Then the company can take a decision on the form of its report — whether it is going to adapt existing channels of communication, like its house journal, or whether it is going to opt for something different and who should get it. From this it is then in a position to decide who should be involved in the production of the report, whose job it should be and how it should be produced. And finally, only after having settled that can the company decide on the content, which is the subject of the next four chapters of this book.

It is obvious, therefore, that the whole process can take a lot of time. In an ideal world a company could usefully start planning six to nine months in advance, though in fact this never happens and some companies start to plan their employee report only after they have finalised the annual report, effectively tying the hands of the author. But when the two reports are planned side by side, the cross-fertilisation of ideas will not only lead to the compatability of information, but also to greater clarity in the shareholders' report.

Aims and objectives

Michael Branden, already mentioned in Chapter 4, who is a committed advocate of employee reports, has frequently to his horror found that companies have taken no formal decisions as to what they are trying to achieve and consequently measures of success never go beyond whether employees found the communications interesting or understandable. As he once wrote, "If these are the only criteria then *Playboy* would win every time. There has to be more to it than that." He has isolated three distinct managements whose style makes it difficult to think clearly about objectives.

The first type excuses the absence of objectives by stating that it wants to avoid all suggestion of propaganda, or indeed anything which might suggest manipulation. This is very much the auditors' and accountants' approach, where every figure must be directly traceable to the audited accounts, and all should be given equal treatment. No ratio or figure should be played up at the expense of another. But there should be no reason why being coldly factual rules out the setting of objectives. One company taking this line still had as its objective to increase the awareness of employees to the true level of profit. Before its report only about 20% of the employees were remotely near the figure — after the exercise nearer 40% were "warm". So that was a simple objective which the company had gone some way to achieving.

The second company is the one where management is going to produce a report for employees because pressure of legislation and general social and industrial relations difficulties have forced them to, but it is sure it is going to disclose only the very minimum it can get away with. These companies too have an objective — to keep as much as possible out of print. But it is hardly an objective in keeping with the "spirit of the Act" — even if it is easy to measure your success rating. These are the companies by and large which also have plans to deluge the trade unions with information the moment the unions ask for it — because they understand clearly that too much data can be just as confusing as too little. They plan what I have described in another chapter as an information blizzard. There is not a lot which can be done in this kind of company. Paranoia in management breeds still more paranoia in employees, so both sides probably get the industrial relations they deserve.

The third kind of company is the most common. It is the one which wants to be open with its employees. In this company there is nothing, or very little, about which management will not provide information. Where such companies do draw the line, if they do, is on matters like cost details and investment plans, along with salary details. The problem here is also self-evident — if management is going to come clean on everything indiscriminately, you will quickly end up with a vast amount of unrelated information rolled together so that no clear pattern can emerge, so it too will create an information blizzard, although this time it will do so unintentionally. It is therefore not enough simply to be "open" because it will do no good at all if the employees fail to understand what is going on — any more than if you gave a speech laying bare all the company's secrets, but in a foreign language. Indeed the critics of employee reports say you are doing just that — making a speech in a foreign language, and they maintain further that this can lead to worse, not better, industrial relations because it adds to the frustration felt by some employees.

The need for objectives therefore is fairly clear cut. The next step is to consider what sort of objectives, and what kind of employee report. The objectives are not that difficult; they depend really on what every company wants to say. But here are just a few examples.

One objective could be to enhance awareness of the key indicators that are relevant to wage bargaining; a second could be to prepare the ground for some major changes — be it the disruption of a massive capital spending programme, or the disaster of redundancy. A third might be to improve teamwork and a fourth might be a shot in a campaign to cut down waste or absenteeism by raising morale. The common factor in them all which emerges clearly is that each objective, if it is achieved, will result in a change of attitudes which will make the management of the business that much easier. And if the message is put together correctly it should make the employee aware how his day-to-day life plugs into the company's finances, how behaviour of one sort or another will affect performance and how performance will affect pay, working conditions, job satisfaction and job security.

At the end of the day the pros and cons of this debate come back to whether the management is trying to educate the employee, or whether it is trying to inform him. Informing him is hard work, basically because he will only absorb what he wants to know, and he will furthermore only absorb it in the way that suits him — which may be quite a different thing from what would suit management. Education, on the other hand, implies bringing about a change in the employee's attitude — by the use of facts and figures and the organisation of information and arguments. You

may or may not be trying to bring him round to your point of view — though most managements are — but you are certainly trying to give him the tools with which he can form his own, hopefully better balanced, judgement.

In any company there are a lot of people who will want to be involved with the employee report, particularly in the first year. Later, we will deal with who ought to be involved, but for the moment let us deal with the reality, which is that in any company producing a report will involve several or all of the following: the managing director (or chairman); the personnel director; the marketing and sales directors; the chief accountant; several production managers and the company public relations consultant. This is obviously an unwieldy group but it may be politically impossible at first to get it any smaller. If a report is ever to be produced, therefore, four stages need to be gone through. The first is to set up a working party to do the work which will report to the full committee listed above. The second step is to secure agreement among all concerned as to what are the objects of the programme (the business objectives just discussed) coupled with the legitimate interests of the employees. Third comes the selection of the information and fourth is the choice of communications methods to be used — whether the report will be accompanied by audio-visual presentations, etc. This procedure can be represented diagrammatically as in Table 4.

Table 4. *Primary stages in producing the report*

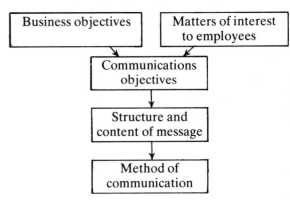

To explain the above terms further, the communications objective is quite simply the message you want to put across. The following is an example:

"The employee should understand that:
   job security depends on sales;

sales depend on prices;

prices depend on wages.

Therefore, excessive wage increases could imperil job security."

The message structure tells you how you are going to convey this objective in detail. So, to continue the above example, the message structure would be as follows:

1. A general introduction explaining what the report was.
2. What influences sales volume? — the relative impact of prices, quality, delivery, customer service.
3. How can we increase sales? — by new products?
4. Can we hold prices by squeezing profits?
5. What is management proposing to do about the problem?
6. What are the future prospects?

This message structure in short gives you the table of contents for the report.

But there is one observation which must be made about the specific example above and that is that the approach results in a quite different style of employee report from that which has conventionally been produced. This report is, in fact, the kind produced using the business objectives approach which was discussed in Chapter 4.

Form and channels of communication

The next question is what form this employee report should take. Should it be a supplement or special issue of the house journal? Should it be a supplement to the shareholders' accounts? Or should it be a separate production in its own right? The house journal has three points in its favour. The first is the cost, or lack of cost, in devoting pages to finance instead of the usual editorial. The second is time — it can be printed quickly. And third, something frequently expressed but disturbingly patronising, is that it is in the same tabloid format as the popular press — the *Sun* and the *Daily Mirror* — and the employees are at ease with that format. The British Institute of Management estimates that there are probably 2000 house journals operating in the UK, with a nominal readership running into millions. So in theory they ought to be the natural vehicle for a company communications programme. But there is a question mark hanging over their ability to do the job. Can they ever write effectively about anything other than the social life of the company? If they were to do so, there would have to be considerably

more editorial freedom than is the norm. True editorial freedom is an ideal which does not apply to the vast majority of house journals. Put at its most simple, the editor as an employee is part of the company hierarchy and must inevitably be compromised. To do his job effectively he needs equal status with the senior management so that he can deal on equal terms with them, and get real information from them. Only then would the magazine begin to gain credibility with the non-managerial readership. The editors, by and large, do not have either such freedom or such credibility. A BIM survey of the content of a sample of journals over a six-month period showed that the primary concern of the papers was to report social and general news items. But the areas which could be thought to be "sensitive", like manpower and industrial relations, were given barely a mention. And in the 29 journals in the sample only 0.8% of the available space was devoted to industrial relations. So, in general, house journals fail to reflect real-life issues. To quote an article in *The Director,* "they too often tend to be a chronicle of social trivia, a mélange of sentiment and silliness". So if there is more than a grain of truth in that allegation it makes it hard to support the house journal as a method of communicating financial information.

The house journal loses the great advantage which the employee report gives management. This is to show that it is doing something special and trying to establish a new line of direct communication with the employees. House journals are familiar and well known, and the publication in there of the annual results will raise no more than a passing eyebrow. The receipt of a new, once-a-year document will self-evidently produce a much greater impact. Even the best house journals are not particularly widely read, so you have immediately lost a large part of your employee audience by putting the information in there and there alone. The house journal can certainly report on the results, and give the basic information, but it is desirable, if not essential, for employee reports to be produced as well; Metal Box, Smiths Industries and many others take this line.

It is worth deciding at this early stage, too, just who is going to receive the employee report and who will get the shareholders' report. One point is that if you produce an employee report you must also give the employee the option to get hold of the annual report, so that he can see for himself if he so desires that the figures are the same in both. In practice this is not a problem and most companies tell employees how to get a copy of the annual report, or include a card or coupon for them to fill in if they want it. The second decision is whether to send shareholders the employee report. If you do, it has the great advantage of complying with the stipulation which says you ought to tell shareholders everything that you tell the employees. Companies which have done it normally comment that the shareholders get a lot more out of the employees' report than the employees seem to — and that is probably true, even if sad reflection on the existing state of information sent to shareholders. There are only two problems. First, it will put the cost up a lot — and therefore each company has to decide whether it thinks it is worth it. Second, and more intractable, is that one company may produce a whole range of employee reports for its different divisions. Tate and Lyle and GKN, looked at in detail in Chapter 15, already do this, while Courage produces its own reports but is virtually wholly owned by the Imperial Group. What would Imps shareholders make of getting a copy of the Courage report to employees? What would a GKN shareholder do with 125 employee reports?

The solution has to be a compromise. Where a single group document exists, then it is undoubtedly to the shareholders' liking to receive it. But as the number of documents multiplies, then their benefit to the shareholder diminishes as he starts to be confused. At this point management should let the shareholder know that the documents exist, but only make them available on request. The alternative is to produce one document which meets the needs of shareholders and employees together. In a way this flies in the face of the concept of employee reports as such, though as we have seen it ties in with the thinking of Peter Prior of Bulmers who insists that there is no evidence that the shareholders understand more or less in accounts than the employee. But it denies the fact that they have different interests and different perspectives, and that to try to combine the two creates a bulky and rather jumbled report. In this respect it is worth referring back to the annual accounts of Blackwood Hodge, who took *The Corporate Report* as the model. Their experience was that the employee-oriented information was well received by shareholders but seemed not to make an impact with employees. No matter what the content, the annual report will always appear a pretty intimidating document to the outsider. The joint report, then, is a non-starter. But in passing it is worth drawing attention to Ash and Lacy, whose annual report consisted of the traditional report and with it, stitched in, the employee report; in other words, two separate reports in one. Many others have taken a similar line, with the employee report in such form that it can be suitably inserted into the annual report.

The employee report need not, and perhaps should not, be an annual event. Indeed, it may inhibit its development if it is tied too closely to the company's financial reporting year. You may find you do a better job producing a series of reports to come out quarterly, half-yearly — perhaps even monthly. When and if this happens the employee report's connection with the annual report will be tenuous in the extreme. It is much more likely to be plugged into the management accounting system and information flow, when it will then be topical and relevant. In an age of television this is what people have come to expect. If an industrial giant like Unilever or ICI reports every three months to shareholders, then there is a pressing logic that it should report at similar intervals to its employees. It is a decision for each management to take according to its own circumstances. Frequency is important and will become more so. For the moment, however, according to the Norkett survey (*see* Chapter 3), the majority of companies providing accounting information do so once a year to employees (45% of companies surveyed, as against 31% which do so more frequently and 24% who do nothing at all).

One other point comes to mind in considering the form of these documents, and that is their size. Currently they come in all varieties, from the sensible to the absurd, but the bulk are A4, the standard size for annual accounts and a size which, to quote one personnel manager, "cannot easily be thrown away". Perhaps not, but it cannot easily go in the employee's pocket either, so in the absence of a briefcase how does he carry it home? Fluidrive, the engineering company featured later, produces a report roughly the size of a wallet which will slip into the inside pocket. It thinks it amazing that other companies persist with the larger documents. At the other extreme, some firms produce reports which unfold like a map; when they are unfolded, they are generally quite unmanageable. It should be compulsory for whoever produces them to try unfolding and reading them on the top deck of a crowded bus just to see how impossible they are to handle.

Personnel to be involved

The CBI found in a survey that the greatest obstacle to be overcome before an effective communications network could be set up was not hostility by trade unions but hostility by management. While union officials were generally quite adept at passing on information to the membership, the lower tiers of management often do so only with the greatest reluctance. This reluctance at a lower level is a reflection of what has been seen historically as a general unwillingness by management to communicate. And though this may no longer be the case, there are sufficient tensions in any hierarchy between senior and middle management, between personnel and line, between personnel and accounts and so on, still to cause severe problems. For this reason, the wholehearted commitment and backing of the chief executive is vital. Without it there is little chance of a satisfactory report emerging. And from the point of view of the end product too he has to be seen to be committed. The shopfloor is much more likely to believe something if the man at the top tells them, than they are if it comes merely from their immediate boss.

A problem at the moment is that because this is a new field it has yet to become the established prerogative of any one section of management. Indeed, quite the opposite. Most want to wash their hands of it. But there is also the contradictory fact that employee relations belong to everybody to a greater or lesser degree — be it personnel, production management, the public relations officer, or finance director. So it is difficult if not impossible at first glance to see who is going to give way to whom. In any factory there are the following people who could legitimately claim to be involved: the chief executive, the finance director, the internal accountants, the external audit personnel, sales, marketing, line management and internal and external public relations consultants. That is on the management side. Then there are the employee representatives — unions, shop stewards, members of staff associations or whatever. But we have to start somewhere. So let's look at the typical company where the chief executive, having taken the decision, will look to the accountant and the head of personnel to do the work.

To consider the accountant's role first: the coming years are going to be difficult times for accountants. Traditionally they have supplied the figures management asked for, interpreted in the way management wanted them interpreted. Traditionally too, they have prepared annual accounts with the interests of the shareholder uppermost — though there has been a tendency to ignore the small shareholder in favour of the big institutional investor. There is a tendency, too, for accountants

to carry these attitudes with them into the boardroom when they become finance directors. They know what has to be put into accounts to meet the legal requirements. They know what has to go in to ensure that profit is properly calculated, and they know what has to be done to ensure a stable capital base. What they lack is the human view — the imagination — for effective communication. There is a notable reluctance among some people in business to give the finance directors their heads on employee reporting, particularly when the finance directors are accountants. Indeed, it has been rather unkindly suggested that accountants and auditors got us into this mess in the first place by making published accounts incomprehensible, and therefore they must be kept well away from reports to employees if these are not to go the same way. Similarly, few firms of auditors are equipped yet to assist in this field. There are notable exceptions — firms like Turquands, Barton, Mayhew, Arthur Young, Touche Ross, and Spicer and Pegler, who are already thinking hard about what contribution they can make to move the science forward. But they do have grave conceptual problems. It really is hard to see the mind which produces the annual accounts being able to do a good job on the employees' version. There are exceptions to this as there must be to every generalisation. But as a rule of thumb it is better to leave the accountants to supply the figures, and to allow someone with a non-financial background to do the interpretation.

The personnel officer on the other hand is the man in the company who knows what the employees want and what they will stand for — or at least, he should do. However, the report he prepares will reflect his perspective and will be more heavily inclined towards the employment report concept — with information on the labour force rather than information derived from the balance sheet. This is not the real problem, however. The real problem is the relationship of personnel with the branches of line management. In a lot of companies there is a gulf between the personnel department and the line manager. The personnel officer may feel that an individual production manager has a very poor and inadequate communications system with the employees in his department. The production manager, on the other hand, feels that his success or failure is measured in terms of profits, and that if this is the yardstick then it is up to him and nobody else as to what sort of management style he chooses to operate and the personnel officer should have no power to impose a communications policy on an unwilling and sceptical production manager. This is where the commitment of the chief executive comes in again — to give personnel the backing he needs to get the job done. It has to be recognised, however, that he will face hostility from other managers as well as from the trade unions. This hostility needs to be overcome if the exercise is to be successful. But first, you need to understand the reason for the hostility.

In part, as suggested above, the report is seen as irrelevant to the production manager's problems. But the other part of the problem is that the report is also seen as a threat. It is a threat because, unless he is exceptional, the middle manager will have no particular skill at understanding accounts, and very little idea of what the turnover and profit figures are for the company. He does not have this information himself but he is being asked to co-operate on a project to give it to the shopfloor. It is not surprising he feels undermined — managers these days have little enough authority as it is, without gratuitously giving away what little they have. There you have the problem. Somehow you have to make sure that production and personnel are both agreed on the need for a report to employees and, having secured agreement, that they are further agreed on what the purpose of this report is.

There is a further problem. We have established that you are asking for trouble if you do not involve your production people in the planning process. With a small company this involvement might be quite easy to arrange because the numbers are small. With a larger company it is impossible to meet all those who have an interest. It is at this point that many companies wash their hands of the whole business and call in an external PR consultant to resolve the problem — in exactly the same way as management consultants are called in to say what management wants to say, but cannot for political reasons. The great advantage of the external PR man is in his objectivity. Not being emotionally involved with the company, he can see its strengths and weaknesses, its successes and problems probably in much better perspective than can the hard-pressed director who has to live with it all the time. It is also easier perhaps for the outside consultant to draw together the different threads of management thinking into a policy programme for the report to employees — much as a management consultant operates. The specialist PR firms are doing an increasing volume of this work and are learning all the time. The bad ones, of course, will have one style of report into which they will try to force all companies, regardless of their different problems and philosophies. But the good ones are responsive to the subtleties of individual companies.

However, an external PR firm can create problems too. Time and again it is said that they fail to interpret the theme laid down by management and what they do produce tends all too often to be inaccurate. The case for the defence is that the public relations expert is the specialist in communications and that part of the criticisms results from management's own shortcomings in not fully understanding communications techniques. So there are two solutions — either that you hand the project and a degree of control over to an outside specialist with a proven track record, or you employ a PR firm with a non-financial background, but keep it firmly on the production side, well away from the interpretation.

Larger firms have their own public relations executive internally. Indeed, some of the most obviously gifted work in-house. They therefore know the company politics, the company line, and the company problems. But their difficulty is that they are employees too and so have trouble in pushing their view hard enough in the face of a hostile director, or in bringing a sufficient degree of objectivity to the job. Their problems are, in fact, similar to those faced by the editors of house journals, the shortcomings of which were discussed earlier in this chapter. It is truly hard for an employee to be tough enough with his own bosses.

So much for mistrust among management. What about the union side? Any employee report which is to break down the barriers of mistrust is going to need union co-operation. This could be at the planning stage in deciding on the content, at the writing stage, by giving the union a page for their comments, or at the distribution stage by allowing the union to distribute and interpret the information provided. But the unions have to be involved somewhere along the line because if they are not brought into the project, then they will resist it and if they resist it much of the benefit will be lost. The way out of the problem, as we suggested earlier, is to form a consultative committee (with a limited life) right at the start of the project. This has to take the key decision as to the theme of the report, where to show, for example, that profits are too low, that a new product line is to be introduced or that the company cannot afford a wage increase. The way to develop such a theme is simply a matter of establishing priorities. Personnel will probably incline towards a safety message, or the problems of labour turnover and absenteeism. Production might want more information on the relationship between output wages and job security. The corporate planning side might lean towards the cash problems and the financing of investment. But whatever theme is finally chosen — and it is up to the chief executive to ensure that it is the right theme — then it is vital that this is accepted by all the departmental heads, so that they will all give the project their blessing. Once this has been established the consultative committee could and should be disbanded. The project then becomes a job between personnel, finance (or company secretary), chief executive and the writer — be he in-house or outside consultant, or one of the first three.

Working with the chief executive the consultant draws out the company policy and story to match, the finance director is needed to check that the figures have not been distorted in the process, and the personnel director is consulted to make sure the employees are not going to be offended or patronised by the results. It is as much a juggling act as any branch of management.

CHAPTER TEN

CONTENT — GENERAL PRINCIPLES

Other chapters in this book have outlined different approaches to information disclosure. The management approach, based on the CBI proposals, the employee approach, based on TUC recommendations and now backed by ACAS, the straightforward accountants' approach and the approach adopted by big firms all in their own way indicated what the content of the report should be. This chapter, therefore, is going simply to draw some general lessons from the debate so far, while the next will give specific suggestions for the content and put the report into the wider industrial context.

Levels of effective communication

The first thing you have to consider is the audience. Who are they and what are they interested in? The answer is not as simple as it seems. True, the audience is the employee, but we are almost all employees these days, and the report will be going to a range of people of quite different educational attainment. The problem is how you provide one report which will be understood by the mass of the people, but will achieve this understanding without alienating any other section.

First though, let me make the general observation that there is a great deal of nonsense talked about the level of comprehension among employees and what they will understand. The *Sun* and the *Daily Mirror,* it is argued, are simple. *The Sunday Times* and *The Daily Telegraph* on the other hand, are complicated and too difficult for the manual worker. But this opinion is, in fact, not borne out in practice. The *Sun* and *The Sunday Times* are effectively pitched at the same level of comprehension. They are written using the same journalistic techniques — a fact which explains the typical journalist's ability to switch newspapers without having totally to change his style. What is different between the *Sun* and *The Sunday Times* is nothing to do with the words used. The contrast is in the content — the stories which are selected, the length of those stories, their detail, and the way

in which the page is laid out, and the use made of pictures.

This, though it may be surprising, can be proved by the application of what is known as a "Fog Index" in the United States and a "Clarity Index" in Britain. It is a method of analysing a piece of writing to see how effective it is in putting the message over and at what level it is pitched. The *Sun* writes its leader column at around the 30 mark on the Clarity Index, and so does *The Sunday Times* Business News; 30 is the average reading level of a 16-year-old. This has a marked relevance for authors of employee reports. If you ask the professional public relations men who produce a lot of these what level they aim at, they will usually say "O" level standard. And that, of course, ties in with the 16-year-old reading age. This means in practice that you should not face any problems in pitching your report if you aim for this level, for this is the level for effective communication with the vast bulk of the people. If you get more complex you will very quickly overstep the mark and lose your audience.

But another lesson of the *Sun* and *The Sunday Times* is that design is important. So, if your managers feel patronised by the employee report, and feel it is far too simple, it is not because they understood the balance sheets before and did not need to have them simplified, and it is not because the prose was too simple, it was because you have got the design wrong — probably overdone the illustrations, the bar charts, and the diagrams. Design is explored elsewhere in this book; suffice it to say here that there is little justification for different grades of employee report for different grades of management. It can, on the contrary, be quite divisive, in that it is bad for internal morale, and it is, without question, patronising. Also, and perhaps most importantly, there is no evidence at all to suggest that the highly skilled engineer knows any more about accounts than the barely skilled labourer.

There is a case, however, for additional reports

on top of the basic employee report to go to people with special interests. *Dunlop at Work,* which is published annually and runs to about 16 pages, is an example of this. It does not mention the annual accounts and makes no attempt to explain them. What it does is to review every aspect of employee relations on a company-wide basis, so it covers the structure of employment, which includes trends in the numbers employed over the past seven years, labour turnover and the amount of natural wastage and redundancy. It goes into some detail about stability rates. A further chart shows the absenteeism at the different plants round the country. It then goes into detail on industrial disputes, and as well as calculating the days lost, tries to show how much profit was lost in each division through internal and external disputes, and how much was lost in wages and salaries. This is followed by detailed information on wages and salary movements. Employees are split into two categories, manual and staff, and their wage progress plotted against the retail price index. Further sections deal, again in commendable detail, with health and safety at work, industrial relations, training, and finally, pensions.

There seems little doubt that a lot of this information would be of considerable help and interest to employees. It is worth noting, however, that the Dunlop document is toughly worded and quite uncompromising. It does not make any concessions to employees' sensibilities. Instead it spells out forcibly what happens, and what management thinks of what happens. So how good an effect it has on employee relations, or how effective it is, is a moot point. It is quite obvious that the average employee report cannot go into such detail on basic employee statistics, but there is a place for them on a more limited scale along with the annual accounts. Hoover have shown that a lot can be squeezed into a relatively small space in the example referred to in Chapter 6 [Fig. 9].

What interests the readership?

The next thing to establish is what the employees are interested in. The CBI can provide some help here, with a survey published in 1976. This suggested, interestingly enough, that pay is not the factor uppermost in employees' minds and that junior and middle management tend to overstress the importance of pay to the employee. In this survey the employee was given 21 factors relating to job satisfaction which he had to rank in order of preference, and the four which came out on top were:

Interesting work	54%
Job security	51%
A feeling of worthwhile accomplishment	45%
Good pay	44%

The survey says that this points the danger of overestimating interest in pay alone. However, it must also be recognised that factors like a feeling of accomplishment may well be desirable but they tend to be thin on the ground. So pay re-emerges as the focus of interest in the absence of loftier pursuits. The survey also highlighted a split between large and small firms. In small firms, the emphasis was more towards interesting work, accomplishment and having a boss to respect. In larger firms, job security and satisfactory physical conditions assumed more prominence. Obviously, this underlines the remoteness from the group which the employee in a large organisation feels. The survey also highlighted a split between men and women. Women rated physical conditions and pay highest, men opted more for the feeling of accomplishment, having a say in how the work gets done, and having a chance to develop their own abilities. Other conclusions also apply to employee reports. There was a feeling among employees that being informed was part of job satisfaction, and very few had any objection to direct communication from management provided what they were told was relevant to them and also provided management were not telling them how to vote.

The difficulty of using junior management to communicate financial information was also highlighted. The survey suggested that they were ill-equipped to play a key role, partly because of their misconceptions about what the employee was interested in, partly because, like the shopfloor, they greatly overestimated the profit being made by the company and failed to understand why it needed to be increased, and partly because junior management displayed a lack of confidence in senior management.

The British Institute of Management tended to reinforce these findings. It isolated four categories of problem.

1. Structural difficulties owing to the nature of the company.
2. Disillusion by management following lack of success.
3. Problems attributable to management.
4. Problems attributable to employees and unions.

By structural difficulties it meant problems which arise from the size, spread, product diversity and timing of releases. A particular problem is the gulf between the profit centre information which the company is geared to produce and the information relevant to the local labour market which tends to be what employees and unions want. The second difficulty is again a real one. It has been said before, and it is worth repeating, that it is very easy to become discouraged when producing employee reports. But more and more companies accept that the passing on of information is one of the responsibilities and it has to be tackled. The problems attributable to management are those of internal dissension — the gulf between personnel and line for example — and the general disinclination in many tiers of management towards communication with employees. The BIM suggested that getting the commitment of top management was the greatest obstacle to any programme, and that three times as many problems arose through management's reluctance to pass on information as arose through hostility or misinterpretation by employees and unions.

Varying viewpoints on the type of information required

The BIM split the information of relevance to employees into four areas:

(*a*) personnel data;
(*b*) income data;
(*c*) general performance;
(*d*) future plans.

The detailed classification was as follows:

Personnel data
Number of employees
Turnover and absenteeism
Manpower plans
Income data
Details of pay scales
Make-up of pay
Directors' fees
Executive salaries
General performance
Details of unit costs
Sales revenue
Profits before and after tax
Government grants and subsidies
Rate of return on capital
Value of the company
Future plans
Expansion policy
Mergers and takeovers
Factory and unit closures

It was not suggested that all this information be included in an employee report. But it does provide a very clear guide to what an employee is likely to want to know.

The second code of practice, produced by the Advisory Conciliation and Arbitration Service, highlights the following five areas:

(*a*) pay;
(*b*) conditions;
(*c*) manpower;
(*d*) productivity;
(*e*) financial.

These break down as follows:

Pay
structure, job evaluation, etc
earnings/total
fringe benefits, non-wage labour costs
Conditions
recruitment
redeployment
training
promotion
equal opportunity
appraisal
safety, health, welfare
redundancy
pensions
Manpower
numbers
turnover
absenteeism
planned changes
manpower plans
Productivity
production efficiency data
savings
return on capital
sales
state orders
Financial
cost structures
profits
balances
allocations
transfer prices
inter-company loans

This is primarily for collective bargaining purposes. But the disclosure principle is the same.

The CBI survey also produced what it termed "general assertions" about the way the economic system works, and it was felt that these should form a basic core of what is desirable for employees to understand. These assertions were explained in the introduction to their report as follows:

"What every employee should know
The distribution of today's wealth must give first priority to investment to create tomorrow's wealth.
Job security depends on investment and investment will be adequate only if profits are adequate. If too much added value goes to consumption (through wages, tax used for social services and so on), jobs will be lost.
It is good to pay dividends to shareholders
Shareholders are a useful source of capital for the investment needed to maximise job security. Dividend payments to shareholders are usually less burdensome than interest payments on borrowed money.
Economic prosperity is improved by flexibility in labour deployment
Change in the demand for skills is inevitable, particularly if living standards are to improve year by year. But such changes will not always benefit everyone concerned and some conflict of interest is unavoidable, not just between the company and groups of workers but also between one group of workers and the rest of the workforce.
An economy's ability to generate new job opportunities and develop new industries depends on its ability to stimulate entrepreneurs.
The successful development of new economic activity requires entrepreneurial talent as well as land, capital and labour.
Managerial decision-making and business planning are not simple matters of computation
Management — including management science — is an art. The important decisions are rarely clear-cut and call for the skilful exercise of judgement. Managers make a valuable contribution to economic performance by identifying problems and initiating action in situations that are ill-defined, uncertain and often fraught with risk. There is rarely enough information from market research or planning exercises to make decision-making a simple matter."

However, an understanding of these general assertions is not enough. A more specific understanding of how these general assertions relate to their own particular situation is needed by employees. Unless a general assertion can be related directly to a specific case then employees will not be able to see the relevance of one to the other. Experience has shown that one of the best ways of allowing employees to relate the general to the particular is to provide them with as much up-to-date information as possible on their own immediate workplace.

It is emerging also that it is no longer easy to say no to requests for information from employees. And if you do say no, the union side will do its own research anyway — which could result ultimately in the serious embarrassment of the management. The basic decision the company has to take when looking to its disclosure policies in their widest sense, therefore, is what sort of industrial relations climate it wants to foster, and the basic fact it must recognise is that employees will only ultimately be interested in information which will help them to influence the decisions of management. Anything else, ultimately, is irrelevant. The CBI came close to accepting this in its evidence to the Bullock Committee on industrial democracy when it said employees needed information regularly:

(*a*) to be aware of the reasons for decisions by management;
(*b*) so management can find out what employees think *before* decisions are taken;
(*c*) so employees can be informed about the condition and health of the business.

This, in turn, links up to the thinking of life-long student of industrial relations Lord McCarthy, who sees four approaches to disclosure:

1. Education and involvement.
2. Brainwashing and blinding with science.
3. Enemy intelligence.
4. Part of problem-solving.

The first is a managerial approach, the second and third are union approaches and the fourth is, if anything, a move to a wider horizon.

The educational approach has been discussed already. What it says is that if the employee is better informed then he will take a greater interest and will assist management for the greater good of the enterprise as a whole. The second attitude which McCarthy isolates occurs when people receive a slab of information which they feel must be important but which they cannot understand because it is too complicated. Therefore, they feel they are being brainwashed. The third approach is the more typical union approach which says that it wants the information to use at a crucial moment in the bargaining process — so that it can chuck in facts and figures which will wrong-foot the management. But this approach is a little naïve, McCarthy thinks, because no legislation in the world, and certainly not the ACAS code, will force employers to give unions information they do not want to release. Instead, they will give what suits them and what supports their arguments. And, if pressed for more information, they will, if it suits them, claim that they can't find it. Thus, the unions, though they may find the day-to-day power on the shopfloor consolidated, will be as far as ever from having power at the strategic level where corporate decisions are taken.

McCarthy's analysis is at its strongest, however, in its fourth point, which is where he sees disclosure of information in the context of problem solving. He says that one of the reasons why employees tend not to react to information is that it is not given to them with any purpose in mind. Genuine communication, like any real conversation, has to be a two-way flow. The management have actually got to present information in such a way that the employee has to respond. The easiest way of seeing this in action is in the context of problem solving. In this case the management tells the employees that it has a problem, and that it has identified three ways in which the problem can be solved. The employees are then asked to consider the three ways, and a fourth if they think of one, and then say which approach they prefer and what modifications they would like. Thus the information is passed down, and more information, as a result, is passed back up. The weakness in this idealised view, apart from the practical problems of setting it up, are that it only works as a one-off event with a particular problem. It is not a continuous process. It does point a way, however, to killing the belief that collective bargaining is a zero-sum game — a process in which nothing is created and one side's gain must necessarily be the other side's loss. What McCarthy hopes is that the joint approach on problem solving will develop into a new approach in collective bargaining — the predictive bargain — which will be an attempt between management and unions to get some sort of agreement about the future, rather than continuing the present sterile preoccupation with the past.

Relating all this to the content of employee reports *per se,* enough has been said to show that there is no hard and fast body of information which can be applied to every company in every circumstance. There cannot be such a standard even for companies operating in the same industry, because the management style in every company is as different as the people in it and these reports should reflect the management style. But the overriding aim is the same, namely to try to provide all employees, white collar and blue collar, inside and outside a union, with financial informa-

tion which relates to their own company and their security and prospects within it. The trick is to do this without running foul of legislation and the Stock Exchange, and not giving your competitors so much information that they could wipe you out tomorrow.

Obviously, therefore, you cannot include all the information, and you are going to have to do some hard thinking about what information you should be including in these accounts. Others have done some hard thinking too — notably the four judges of the Employee Accounts Award given by *Accountancy Age* magazine for the first time in 1977. So let us examine what they think should go into a good set of employee accounts. The four judges were: Frank Chapple, general secretary of the Electrical, Electronic Telecommunication and Plumbing Union; Peter Parker, former chairman of Rockware, and now the head of British Rail; Derek Boothman, architect of *The Corporate Report;* and Sir John Donaldson, the distinguished judge whose special knowledge and interest in industrial relations led to his being judge in the Industrial Relations Court in the early 1970s. Between them, they seem to cover the whole spectrum of society and therefore bring to the subject a great breadth of vision.

Each expert was looking for something slightly different. Frank Chapple's view is that "the most relevant information to employees is how the company is doing in capital and revenue terms and in terms of orders". What is needed in not a simple restatement of the annual accounts which are frequently vague on such topics as above, but a report which goes into detail. Secondly, the report should be broken down so that it is meaningful to the individual in the place where that individual works — be it company, division, factory or whatever, and it should try to put across the global position of the company and explain how each individual unit fits into the overall structure. Apart from the need for the information to be clear and presented in a straightforward fashion, Chapple also makes the point that the employee report should be part, but only a part, of a co-ordinated employee information programme, which runs throughout the year.

The second expert, Peter Parker, broke down the report into its basic objectives, and following from this, the essential characteristics which were necessary to meet the objectives. The primary objective was to enable the employee to have sufficient understanding of the aims, problems and successes of the industry for him to take pride in the results — to identify himself more readily with the firm and to rebut (at least to himself) adverse criticism. Secondly, the report should form another link in the chain of communication between management and staff to create confidence in the industry and in its management. It is an aspect of this kind of communication to demonstrate that each employee matters. Third, the report should demonstrate (provided it is true) that the industry has good prospects for the future and therefore reasonable prospects of continued employment for the employees. To meet these objectives, good visual impact is essential (a point repeated by Frank Chapple). Unless the front page, particularly, is arresting and intriguing, then the bulk of employees will read no further. Brevity is the second characteristic. Even the best laid-out report will be unlikely to hold the attention of employees if it is too long and too wordy. The third characteristic is the avoidance of technical jargon. The fourth is that the structure of the business is explained in simple organisational terms. In Parker's view, the most relevant information to the employee includes the following financial information: results achieved compared to the objectives set for the year; the results achieved and how they compare with the previous year; the prospects for stability of employment and the distribution of added value for the year as between employees, shareholders, debenture holders and so on. The explanations should include the key factors which influenced the results — things like the impact of new products, the growth of new markets, higher productivity in the labour force, or the coming on-stream of a new capital plant. Then the report should provide key facts to which the employee can relate his own wage — the sales per employee, the investment per employee, the profit earned, and so on. A simple restatement of the financial accounts does not go far enough. Instead, what is needed is a block of additional information which is related to the employee's perspective and puts his role in the business into context. Parker produced score charts with which to judge the content of the report. The points he plotted were:

(a) good visual impact
(b) good design and layout
(c) clarity in graphic presentation and charts
(d) success in reflecting the company's image with style
(e) brevity and avoidance of technical jargon
(f) outline of business
(g) key facts about the business with which the employee can identify
(h) performance plans and objectives
(i) prospects for the future
(j) employee's perspective

This would seem to encapsulate the key points on content from the management's point of view.

Sir John Donaldson, while making many of the same points, also brought to the exercise the judge's objectivity. He said:

"As I see it the object of the exercise is twofold. First, to make employees aware of the fact that they are in partnership with the shareholders — it is the shareholders' capital which enables their labour to make profits and wages for each. Second, to give employees a sense of personal involvement in the success of the partnership. Such a feeling leads to job satisfaction, self-esteem and greatly increased efficiency to the benefit of both partners.

"I do not think that merely restating published financial information in a different form serves any very useful purpose. The information which an employee would consider relevant is that which bears on his security, prospects and conditions of work. Financial information should therefore be presented in a way which shows its relationship to these prime interests.

"But it should also, if possible, be presented in a form which gives the same information about capital's contribution to the venture. It should detail what are capital's prospects and rewards, and how secure it is. Some effort should then be made to interrelate the two.

"In this context I have it in mind that employees should understand that if an enterprise becomes more capital intensive it will be necessary to pay for the increased capital and that it is not true that the whole of the increased output is due to their efforts. At the same time, an increase in mechanisation or other forms of capital intensiveness may well make their task easier and they may also expect to share to some extent in the improved profitability of the enterprise."

As an accountant it was not surprising that Derek Boothman should put more stress on the mechanistic side of the accounts, and he specifically said that in his view every employee report should include a value added statement, a cash flow analysis, a balance sheet and an employee benefits and statistics statement. None of the other experts were quite so specific.

He might have added the point about verbal communication — that you can be much more open. Many managements would die rather than give detailed and written profit forecasts, in cold print. But in the course of conversation, or in answers to a question, it is much easier for a manager to be explicit about how the company is doing and what its prospects are. He can put the information in its proper context, and he can make it clear that it is a prediction, not a certainty. And in a local presentation of this nature he can provide the information without upsetting the Stock Exchange, because the Stock Exchange will never know. So the judges each had different standpoints reflecting their different backgrounds and perspectives. The report which eventually won the competition that year was produced by Staffordshire Potteries. Its case study forms the content of Chapter 8.

CHAPTER ELEVEN

CONTENT — SPECIFIC PRINCIPLES

A chapter purely devoted to the specifics of content is partly a contradiction in terms because the content of an employee report cannot be considered in isolation and no single table of contents will serve for all companies because of their innate differences. But there are some points which have a universal application.

Planning the contents

Every company must have its own information policy, which in the case of disclosure to employees should be linked to its industrial policy. The objectives of this policy must be carefully defined and must reflect the needs and desires of the users. Constant attention must be given to the way in which the information is presented. The fact that the information has been disclosed is no guarantee at all that it has been communicated, so constant attention should be paid to organising feedback and monitoring the results of past efforts.

Misunderstandings are inevitable. Any programme therefore should have some form of training built in, and some system for isolating areas of misunderstanding and overcoming them in future years. The demand for information can only increase, so that whatever you include this year it is likely that you will have to go even further next year. And inevitably this will cause some friction and problems. So it pays to spend some time thinking ahead to next year's content and taking steps to anticipate the problems before they become too overpowering. This point is particularly important, because whilst a successful information policy is a result rather than a cause of good industrial relations, nevertheless sharing information inevitably leads to pressure to share decisions. Therefore the company needs to keep a clear idea of where it stands on industrial democracy.

A starting point for any discussion on content is to consider what the employees think of the information they get already. Do they think of it as the whole truth, or the truth but only part of it? Or do they feel it can only be bad news, as management only ever tell them bad news. Or do they regard it as management propaganda and nothing else? These attitudes will vary depending on which employees you ask — both in accordance with their differing status in the hierarchy of the company and between different plants in different locations. Plants in some areas of the country are notoriously difficult. And, of course, their attitude will vary depending on what they are told and the way it is put across. The author of the employee report needs to ask himself these questions so he can develop some sort of feel for his audience and try to overcome their inbuilt prejudices if they have them — and most people have. In most companies there is a credibility gap between management and employee that undermines the efforts of management to communicate, and it is important to try to find out some of the reasons why this gap exists. It could be, rather unhelpfully, because of a traditional mistrust of bosses, and the fact that management has never tried to talk before, or, if it did talk, that it never wanted to listen. Or it could be because previous efforts have smacked too much of PR, and bear little relevance to day-to-day problems, being instead a gimmick to impress outsiders. It could be the vehicle for the information which is at fault — house journals are particularly vulnerable to the charge that they are pure propaganda sheets. Perhaps the fault is in the information itself — was it all history? Did it mix facts with opinions? Yet again, the fault could have been in the language used. It is not just accountancy terms which are confusing but technical terms and local shopfloor slang can be bewildering to anyone not in that immediate work location.

The reason these points have been made at length is that the author of the employee report has to know what he is up against before he begins to set pen to paper, or he is wasting his time. A few hours spent seeking the answer to these questions will pay dividends several times over before the report is completed. The next step is to quantify exactly what you are telling employees at the moment, under the usual, well-tried headings of legal requirements, manpower data, performance indicators and other general information. When you have done this you can see how much it costs to do what you are currently doing, and what you are getting for your efforts. You can see how you are collecting the information at the moment — how it breaks down between companies and countries, between divisions and departments, between profit centres and product areas. And you can see how closely or easily this can be adapted to meet the needs of the employees — if indeed it can — or whether all the figures are going to have to be reworked from first principles, if you are to provide the employee with facts about his own plant or production line. It is important that you can get the information easily. If it can only be obtained at great cost, or very slowly from the existing accounting machinery, then it is time certainly to revise your reporting systems, but also to look for other short-term alternatives.

While you are doing all this you need to remember the essentials of the employee report — its timeliness, its accuracy, its relevance and its ease of comprehension. Once you have established the ground rules for your own particular company you can then decide where the emphasis of your report should be placed from the following basic and well thumbed list: value added; wages; productivity; profits; taxes; export sales; cash flow; inflation; future plans and employment prospects.

But at the beginning of a report, the first thing the employee wants to read about is profits. That, however, is not the first thing you give him. The very first thing you do in this report, which arrives unheralded through his letterbox or is thrust into his hands with a half-mumbled apology from his foreman, is to explain what the report is all about, why it has been produced and what he can get out of it. When that has been got out of the way, then you can pitch in and explain about profits.

The profit or value added statement

Or can you? Just what do you mean by profits? Do you mean income, or net income, trading profit, gross profit, net profit, profit after tax, profit before tax, earnings, retained earnings or even stretching the point, value added? If you don't know, you had better decide quickly, because somehow you are going to have to take one of that list and translate it into a concept which the employee has to both understand and accept. So if you are going to sell the profit idea the choice is between value added, earnings, return on capital, contribution to the economy or contribution to society — and faced

with a choice like that it is not surprising that more and more companies are opting for value added.

Value added statements are growing in popularity because they show how companies create wealth and how the community as a whole benefits from that wealth. Several examples are referred to later in the book and give detailed breakdowns of how it can be put together. It is perfectly possible to produce a profit and loss statement *and* a statement of value added, but it is rather a waste of space as both are giving the same facts in a different form. And as the value added statement has fewer elements, and shows clearly how a surplus is arrived at, it is preferable to a straightforward profit and loss statement.

Too many reports apologise for making profits by not mentioning the word or by using euphemisms. But the employee will be looking for a figure he can label as profit and it is absurd to produce a financial report which does not give him this. Employees accept that business has to make a profit, so why avoid mentioning the word? What you are trying to do, in part at least, is to make him realise how low those profits are. The value added statement still causes difficulty in many circles, partly because of its newness, partly because of its alleged ambiguities. It is worth quoting at length from what *The Corporate Report* said, in its strong endorsement of the idea:

"The simplest and most immediate way of putting profit into proper perspective *vis-à-vis* the whole enterprise as a collective effort by capital, management and employees is by presentation of a statement of value added (that is, sales income less materials and services purchased). Value added is the wealth the reporting entity has been able to create by its own and its employees' efforts. This statement would show how value added has been used to pay those contributing to its creation. It usefully elaborates on the profit and loss account and in time may come to be regarded as a preferable way of describing performance.

"There is evidence that the meaning and significance of profits are widely misunderstood. It is not the purpose of this report to attempt to justify the profit concept. We accept the proposition that profits are an essential part of any market economy, and that in consequence their positive and creative function should be clearly recognised and presented. But profit is only a part of value added. From value added must come wages, dividends and interest, taxes and funds and new investment. The interdependence of each is made more apparent by a statement of value added.

"We recommend that business enterprises and where appropriate other economic entities within our tests of significance, include as a part of their corporate reports and in a prominent position, a statement of value added containing as a minimum the following information:

(a) Turnover
(b) Bought-in materials and services
(c) Employees' wages and benefits
(d) Dividends and interest payable
(e) Tax payable
(f) Amount retained for reinvestment.

"The statement of value added provides a useful measure to help in gauging performance and activity. The figure of value added can be a pointer to the net output of the firm, and by relating other key figures (for example, capital employed and employee costs) significant indicators of performance may be obtained. A simple illustration of the type of statement envisaged is given below:

"Illustration
A manufacturing company statement of value added

	Year to 31 Dec 1974 £M	Pre-ceding year £M
Turnover	103.9	102.3
Bought-in materials and services	67.6	72.1
Value added	£36.3	£30.2
(Applied the following way)		
To pay employees:		
wages, pensions and fringe benefits	25.9	17.3
To pay providers of capital:		
interest on loans	0.8	0.6
dividends to shareholders	0.9	0.9
	1.7	1.5
To pay Government:		
corporation tax payable	3.9	3.1
To provide for maintenance and expansion of assets:		
depreciation	2.0	1.8
retained profits	2.8	6.5
	4.8	8.3
Value added	£36.3	£30.2"

The above statement is to be regarded as illustrative only. The basic information required is already available in every enterprise and the concept is neither new nor original. It must be appreciated that the presentation of value added statements involves overcoming many of the problems also associated with the presentation of profit and loss accounts, for example, the treatment of extraordinary profits and losses. What it comes down to, at the end of the day, is that the value added statement probably means more than the traditional profit and loss account to the employees, because it represents to them the overall wealth created by their company and how it was shared out. But even value added statements can cause problems. The share given to employees, for example, can often and should be broken down into different classes of payment — and possibly different grades of employee. It depends on the company; excise duties, inter-company sales and sales taxes can all inflate these turnover figures and one must decide if, in the interests of fair presentation, these should be left in or netted out.

As we said, the value added statement does not suit everyone, although we would heartily recommend its adoption. Those companies who feel they must take an alternative course then obviously have to consider the profit and loss account. We mentioned earlier the range of possible definitions of profit, each of which has its advocates. We would opt, in the end, for trading profit, because it is the most easily grasped and the most immediately relevant to the employee, in that it reflects the operations of the company. But others are equally valid, so the main point is to be consistent — to pick one figure and stick to it.

The next problem is that in the published accounts, information is split between the statement and the notes. This format is difficult enough for the professional to follow and is obviously unacceptable in an employee report. Statements and relevant notes have to be merged into one package. Just what form this package should take is discussed in detail in the design chapter. But briefly the choice is one of a pie or a bar chart, or if it can be used, a design based on the company logo. The important thing in choosing the design is to find one which allows you to explain how the different costs and revenues build up, and how the difference between these is the profit. The success of this page depends on your skill at breaking down the profit so that the layman can see where it came from — and do the sum for himself. So all the figures must add up. Nothing must be omitted or assumed. A typical breakdown would be as follows:

OUR PERFORMANCE IN 1977
What we spent running the business
Wages, salaries and pension contributions
Depreciation — money put to one side to replace
   machinery which is wearing out
Fuel, transport, rates, water, administration and
   other overhead costs
Raw materials purchased for the manufacture of
   the product
What we received from the sale of products
From sales of product X to the USA
From sales of product Y to the USA
From home sales of product X
From home sales of product Y
From sales in other countries.

Obviously the detail in the income statement depends on the nature of the company. But the more information about the sales of products and markets the better. The two figures for sales and expenses can then be subtracted to give the trading profit for the year. It is worth also expressing this as a percentage of sales or of capital employed, or as a percentage of the wage bill or some similar measure, to put it in perspective, for few people are at ease in grappling with figures expressed in millions. That, indeed, is the point of using an illustration. All the items must have the relevant figures attached and all must be clearly explained. If there is an exceptional item then do not call it that. Spell out what it is. Equally, depreciation is understood by most people who own cars and it is worth demonstrating that the principle is the same in business by showing a particular machine and explaining how sums are set aside to replace it.

A few other pitfalls to be avoided result from the jargon. Turnover is a meaningless word simply because it has far too many meanings. If you mean sales income, say so. If you want to include income from investments, then spell it out — and explain what the investments are. There are other terms too which it is worth digressing to mention, for they all add an extra pit for the unwary. A quick listing will suffice, for all can easily be explained by the user of them, once he realises the need to do so — it is just that familiarity tends to obscure this need.

Typical accounting terms never to be used without elaboration are: minority interests, outside interests, extraordinary items, prior year adjustments, depreciation, deferred liabilities, deferred tax, accounts receivable, capital, loan capital, trade investments, inflation accounting, cash flow, dividends and balance sheet.

There are various parts of the balance sheet which would benefit from further explanations. For one thing, why should the company have cash on one side and long-term loans on the other? Why not use the cash to pay off the loans? Explaining this gives you the chance to say how the share capital, long-term loans and ploughed-back profits are what was used to put up the factory and buy the machines in the first place. And as the loans are not going to be called in, you can safely use the cash for other things. Capital is another term which causes confusion, because it is so often used as a synonym for money. It is best to use the term as sparingly as possible and, when you do use it, to make absolutely clear that it has nothing at all to do with cash.

The second part of the explanation of profits is a breakdown of how the trading profit was spent. This gives you the opportunity to deal with tax, dividends, exceptional items and retained profits.

Again, there are several diagrammatic possibilities but the most common is a pie chart — largely because it shows how small the dividends are, after taxes, and so on. Again, each item must be clearly and fully explained. This is a good opportunity too for a breakdown of sales revenue in a different way; a chart showing how every £1 of sales was used could then itemise:

raw materials and overheads;
wages and pension contributions;
depreciation;
debt interest;
taxation;
money ploughed back;
dividends.

This has the advantage of bringing home to the reader the relationship in size between the different items, and spelling out who benefits, and how, from the company's prosperity.

The cash flow statement

The 100 Group, the industrial-based chartered accountants, in their suggestions for employee reporting, strongly recommend a cash flow statement "provided it was kept in simplified terms and moved from a cash in hand position at the beginning of the period, to a cash resulting at the end of the period". Their model of a cash flow statement is shown in Table 5, and while it is at times painful in its use of unexplained jargon, it has the merits of comprehensiveness and clarity of presentation.

The great benefit of a cash flow statement is that it is a concept the employee can understand. Cash flows into the business and it flows out again. The problem is that the figures in the cash flow statement will not be the same as the figures in the profit and loss account and balance sheet. It has to be spelt out that the cash flow statement is concerned purely with cash — much of which may be owed to other people. Profits, on the other hand, are the surplus generated by the business, which need not be in cash (it could, for example, be held as additional stocks or raw material).

Much of the justification for cash flow statements at the moment is that they can illustrate very effectively the way inflation undermines the fabric of the business. Yet most employees think inflation is good for companies because they put their prices up and make bigger profits. So important is this concept that a separate chapter (Chapter 14) has been devoted to examining how companies have explained the concept of inflation and inflation accounting. Suffice it to say here that it would seem

Table 5. *Cash flow statement recommended by the 100 Group*

	Year to 31 March 1976 £000	
CREATION OF FUNDS		
Created by operations		
Operating surplus *less* tax	878	
Depreciation — provision for reinvestment	738	
		1,616
Provided from other sources		
Shares issued at a premium	61	
Loans *less* repayments	404	
		465
Other items		215
		2,296
USE MADE OF THE FUNDS		
To maintain and strengthen the company		
On new buildings, plant etc	1,355	
On acquisitions	184	
		1,539
For additional working capital		
Raw materials, products in the course of manufacture, and finished products — increase	273	
Debtors — money owed to us — increase	180	
Creditors — money owed by us — decrease	20	
		473
For payments of dividends		241
TOTAL FUNDS USED		2,253
INCREASE IN CASH		43

Note: Shown as changes on the	1975	1976
Balance Sheet		
Cash *less* money borrowed	1,212	1,412
on short-term basis	455	612
	757	800
Year's increase		43

these days to be a vital ingredient in any employee report — but there is a need for caution both in explaining how the deferred tax and depreciation figures in the profit and loss account are, in fact, sources of funds, and also in preventing the spread of concern if the table shows a major increase in corporate debt.

Trends

The next point to remember is the importance of trends. One year's profit, sales or value added means little to anyone in isolation. So it has to be put in context and the simplest way to do that is to provide information relating to the previous five years. The next page therefore should have charts showing how the current year's performance relates to previous years. These can combine various elements. The chart of sales income, for example, can also record profit, wage and raw material costs so you can see how these have grown as sales have grown. A further chart could provide similar trend information on the breakdown of profits, the amount ploughed back over the years, and how much the company has paid in tax. Examples to ram home specific points should be used. Has the company paid enough tax to build a new hospital or pay a hundred teachers' salaries? Such techniques stress the social benefits of profitable business.

The balance sheet

This is the source of more confusion and bewilderment than anything else in reports for employees. A lot of companies don't bother with the balance sheet and one cannot really blame them. Those who feel it must be included should look to Chapter 12 for some good ideas on how to put it across. There are two basic approaches. The first is the pie or bar chart which gives a "static" presentation, simply listing the various items one after the other, and explaining them as it goes along. The other is a more dynamic approach which leads the reader through the various items one after another in an effort to make him see how the balance sheet is constructed. It has to be said that both approaches have only limited success, simply because the balance sheet is such an outrageously artificial concept with no relation at all to the business itself. Few laymen, and few enough of those with a degree of financial knowledge, really understand it. Hence the appeal in the design section of those treatments like Grand Metropolitan which gave point to the balance sheet by presenting it as the "backing" for the company. The static approach mentioned just now in its usual form is a pie chart with half the pie devoted to assets and half to liabilities.

The 100 Group also advocates the balance sheet as the third of its four key elements, provided, again, that it is set out in a straightforward and uncomplicated format. Their view of how this could be achieved is shown in Table 6.

Table 6. *Balance sheet recommended by the 100 Group*

Balance Sheet — Financial position at 31 March 1976

WHAT WE OWN	
Fixed assets	*£000*
Land and buildings	1,510
Plant and equipment	4,304
	5,814
Intangibles, such as goodwill of businesses we have acquired, patents and trademarks	61
Investments in other companies	1,232
	7,107
Current assets	
Raw materials and products in the course of manufacture, and finished products awaiting despatch	3,031
Amounts due to us by customers for goods and services we have delivered, but which have not yet been paid for	2,901
Cash	1,412
	7,344
	14,451
WHAT WE OWE	
Current liabilities	
Amounts due for goods and services supplied but not yet paid for and including taxation and dividends immediately payable	2,627
Money borrowed on a short term basis from banks and other sources	612
	3,239
NET CAPITAL EMPLOYED	11,212
Represented by funds invested in the company	
Shareholders' interest	7,907
Loan capital	3,305
	11,212

It can be seen from the table that there are no easy solutions to the problems of a balance sheet, so it is with some relief that one turns to what, by common consent, is the one vital ingredient — the employment report.

The employment report

The 100 Group, in supporting the idea, stresses how this information (at last) relates to the employee and his locality — and how it ought to be given, even if it is thrown back as ammunition in the next pay round. The 100 Group got the idea from *The Corporate Report*, and its introduction to employment reports is again worth quoting at length. It says:

"Nothing illustrates more vividly the nineteenth-century origin of British company law than the way in which employees are almost totally ignored in the present Companies Act and in corporate reports. The 1967 Companies Act introduced a requirement for companies with more than 100 employees to state in the directors' report the average number of employees per week and the aggregate remuneration paid. This modest requirement barely does justice to the role of companies as the life support systems for millions of people.

"Economic entities are concerned with the use of monetary material and human resources. As employers they are accorded a position of trust by their employees who *look to the entity for employment security and prospects. In our view this relationship carries with it a responsibility to report to and about employees*. Significant information about the workforce can presently be given by simple and readily available means. We recommend that the general reporting responsibility as regards employment information be met by the publication of employment reports concerned primarily with information about time worked and numbers employed rather than money values.

"We recommend employment reports containing the following information:

(a) Numbers employed, average for the financial year and actual on the first and last day.
(b) Broad reasons for changes in the numbers employed.
(c) The age distribution and sex of employees.
(d) The functions of employees.
(e) The geographical location of major employment centres.
(f) Major plant and site closures, disposals and acquisitions during the past year.
(g) The hours/schedules worked by employees giving as much detail as possible concerning differences between groups of employees.
(h) Employment costs including fringe benefits.
(i) The costs and benefits associated with pension schemes and the ability of such schemes to meet future commitments.
(j) The cost and time spent on training.
(k) The names of unions recognised by the entity for the purpose of collective bargain-

ing and membership figures where available or the fact that this information has not been made available by the unions concerned.
(l) Information concerning safety and health including the frequency and severity of accidents and occupational diseases.
(m) Selected ratios relating to employment."

There have been several examples of employment reports referred to throughout this book and they tend to have the same basic ingredients, namely a breakdown of the employees explaining what jobs they do, how old they are etc, and charts showing length of service, the growth of employment in the various sections over the years. But they should also include information on safety, training and pensions, none of which, admittedly, are of great interest to employees, in spite of the efforts of unions to stir up enthusiasm, but which are important none the less.

This section can then be rounded off with a few statistics showing the capital employed per man, the sales per employee, the profit per employee and the amount reinvested for the future.

The forecast of future developments

This is where all the pressures coincide — the pressure for clues on wages, on profits, on product performance, on every single thing in the employee report. Anyone can reveal historic information. When it comes to the crunch, the forecast will make or break the report. Back, briefly, to *The Corporate Report* to see what it said on the subject:

"It is important to recall that forecasts are projections rather than predictions. They do not so much predict the future as set out, in a logical and systematic manner, the future implications of past and present known facts adjusted by reference to estimates of likely future developments. Such projections may be judged to have different degrees of probability attached to them; but rarely is their probability so sure that they could be termed predictions. It is the certainty of uncertainty that makes entities unwilling to make public projections, though all those acquainted with such exercises are perfectly familiar with the limits on reliability which are inherent in them. The fear is that those less instructed will misunderstand and be misled. Many users are more concerned with the future prospects of entities than with past results. Investors, employees and creditors are examples of such user groups. And yet published financial reports, other than prospectuses and takeover circulars, rarely contain precisely qualified forecasts. Our recommendation is that corporate reports, as a minimum, include a statement of future prospects for the year following the balance sheet date. Such a statement should include information concerning:

(*a*) Future profit levels
(*b*) Future employment levels and prospects
(*c*) Future investment levels.

It should also include a note of the major assumptions on which the statement has been based."

Others have said that forecasts should specifically cover profits, sales, employment prospects, new products, expansion plans, mergers and takeovers, and research and development. Of course forecasts cause problems, and of course forecasts are difficult. But forecasts are what management is all about. If you are in command of your job and in command of your business then you ought to be able to forecast — and justify what happens to the employees.

The statement of objectives

Finally comes something we have touched on elsewhere, which is the statement of corporate objectives. Here is how Derek Boothman and his colleagues explained the philosophy.

"Users need to assess the effectiveness of the reporting entity in achieving objectives established previously by its management. If such judgements are to be made, and if users are to be able to judge how management objectives differ from their own, it follows that corporate objectives should be published.

"We believe there are two distinct components to such objectives. These comprise general management philosophy or policy and medium term strategic targets set as steps towards implementing management philosophy or policy.

"We recommend that corporate reports of entities falling within our tests of significance should include a statement of corporate objectives including a statement of general philosophy or policy and information concerning strategic targets in the following policy areas:

(*a*) sales;
(*b*) added value;
(*c*) profitability;
(*d*) investment and finance;
(*e*) dividends;
(*f*) employment;
(*g*) consumer issues;

(*h*) environmental;
(*i*) other relevant social issues.

As with forecasts, the more specific the statement the more useful it is likely to be. We recommend that strategic targets should be quantified wherever possible."

It would not suit every company, but it is something for every company to consider.

Miscellaneous extras

And lastly, a few gimmicks. One company, Oyez, brought in Bob Mellish, Labour Cabinet Minister, and its local MP in Bermondsey, and gave him half a page in which to make a statement. He did, and what it said, more or less, was that he was pleased to see the company making the effort to communicate with the employees and he was pleased that it had had a successful year, as success meant growth, and growth meant more investment, jobs and prosperity. Whether or not this endorsement meant much to the employee is debatable. He probably feels as far detached — indeed further — from his MP as he does from his board. But it is an idea to investigate. British Oxygen included a statement by a national trade union official — chosen because his had most members in their factories. But they dropped the idea two years later because, for one thing, the union official again seemed fairly remote from the employees and was therefore not sure what to say. Then, when it came to the second year he had nothing new to add, and basically the same message had to be repeated. Obviously it was an experiment of only limited success.

On the same lines the local shop stewards could be given a page in which they could present their report for the year. This could work, but most managements are against it. For one thing, it is getting away from the concept of communicating strictly financial information. They claim the proper place for such shop steward statements would be in a lively house journal though it may not happen there — one can understand management's reluctance to produce and pay for something in which they are going to be criticised. A second reservation is that a shop steward's page brings this report back into the world of "them and us", when in fact the attraction of this document is that it is above the day-to-day battle. It is something which must be considered in a lot of factories though, because if the unions are not consulted in the project, and if they do not agree to participate in its preparation, you run the risk that they will resist it and try to undermine it. But by the same token, if management tries to get union participation and the unions still refuse to offer any assistance, then at the end of the day management has no choice but to go it alone, and hope that in future years attitudes will mellow.

Next, an idea developed by a small West of England company, Mardon Flexible Packaging. It hit on the idea of compressing all the relevant financial data on to one sheet of card. They then printed a calendar on the reverse. So the package folded into one of those triangular desk top calendars and it was clearly hoped that the employee would keep it with him for the whole twelve months. Presumably in those twelve months he would have at least a few moments to browse through the financial information on the other side.

And finally, a novel idea from National Westminster Bank — who, incidentally, publish their financial report in the house journal. In the issue following the publication of the results they produced an imaginative quiz, based on the report, and offering a prize of a weekend in Paris for two for the first correct answer.

CHAPTER TWELVE

CONTENT — DESIGN CONSIDERATIONS

Harold Macmillan, when he was Prime Minister, once said that you should never underestimate the intelligence of the working man but always under-estimate his knowledge. The distinction when it is spelt out is obvious, but it is a distinction which is often overlooked in preparing reports to emp-loyees. Nowhere does judgement falter so consis-tently as in the field of design, when illustrations which are used in the hope that they will make something clear, go badly wrong either because they are far too simple and insulting in their comic strip format, or because they are so misconceived that they turn a simple concept into one quite unfathomable.

In newspapers there is an adage that a picture is worth a thousand words. Sometimes it is, but it depends on the picture, and on the subject. It may seem paradoxical, but in employee reporting the reverse is more often true — content is usually more important than design. However, the two cannot really be separated. A report may have the most marvellous content but no impact, because it is presented in dense, closely packed type which looks like a tombstone. At the other extreme, a report which is short on information can still create a good impression by presenting what it has got in a clear, uncluttered way.

So where does that leave us? As everywhere else, with something of a compromise. The content comes first because at the end of the day the "meat" must be there. But design exerts the most powerful negative influence even if it cannot exert a powerful positive force. Good design cannot be sabotaged by bad content, but good content most certainly can be ruined by bad design.

It is perhaps necessary to attempt a definition of a good illustration but it was something which proved elusive until one day I looked at some reports prepared for a Swedish company. My speaking not one word of Swedish meant that the text was meaningless. But what emerged was that you could follow the gist of the report and its explanations from the illustrations. This then would seem to be the definition of a good illustration — that it conveys the desired message without the use of words. The purpose of this chapter is to comment on some of the ideas which have been used to illustrate employee reports. It is not intended that these be put together and rolled into one to provide the all-purpose report, but rather that if you are looking for ideas to illustrate cash flow or the balance sheet once you have decided on the content, then these ideas may help.

The cover design

Let us start where the readers start — with the cover. No-one puts enough thought into the cover. Most reports have a blank front page with the name of the company, and a statement that this is a report for employees. In general they look similar to the annual report to shareholders. There is nothing in such an approach to grab the employee's attention and persuade him to read further. But some companies have tried harder. At an early stage in the evolution is a cover like Dowty's [Fig. 16], which illustrates products like the advanced passenger train and Concorde which rely on Dowty components. It is an advance on a blank front page, but it is still dry and it still has the weakness that it gives little indication of what is inside, or what relevance the report has for employees. The next stage in cover design comes when companies make a clear effort to tell the reader what the report is about. Automotive Products made this point with a compelling head-line [Fig. 17]. This is an obvious advance because it sets a theme for the report. If the employee wants to know the answer to the question then he will obviously read on. He knows what the report is about. The only criticism, and it is perhaps frivolous, is that a picture of a 10p piece is understating the company's profitability some-what. But again it does add to the impact of the cover, and inside the report — when the coin becomes the "cake" for a profit and loss diagram — it provides useful continuity.

Coubro and Scrutton [Fig. 18] also tried to tell the employees what the report is about, but less successfully. The cover is down-market, and it is a question of taste whether it goes too far or not. But given that the cartoonist is well-known to *Daily Express* readers and therefore entrenched in the middle-brow mind, then perhaps this is the right level to strike. The complaint against the cover is not so much the illustration, which is eye-catching, but the text that goes with it. In trying to explain what the document is and why it is of interest to employees, the company says that it is the accounts "presented in readily digestible form as figures are not always easy to follow". The statement seems patronising. But the question is whether or not the employee would find it so. Although I don't particularly like the cover, it may well have succeeded in its objective and encouraged the reader — which is all to the good, because this was a good report, especially considering Coubro is a private company. This example report shows the danger of illustrations, and cartoons. They very easily degenerate into a comic strip, and to assume that your employees can only read comic strips really is patronising. There are no hard and fast rules for this difficult area. The Thorn cover [Fig. 19] was one extensive cartoon which had concealed in it considerable numbers of the Thorn products, and the idea was that the employee spent many happy hours seeing how many he could spot. But there was a flaw. You had to read the report to find out that that was the point of the cover. It gets the report off on the wrong foot. The Thorn report was unambitious certainly, but it was still worth reading. But the cover forgot even to state what the document was, or at whom it was directed. So anyone turning the page to read the rest of the comic would have been surprised and disappointed. By the same token those who disliked the cover would never have found out that things were different inside. So it is important for the cover not to jar with the contents. It must reflect the tone of the report.

Another example of a cover which has gone wrong belongs to Metal Box [Fig. 20]. Its positive point is that it states what it is — namely a report for employees. But it goes wrong in several ways by trying to be too clever. First, it makes use of the Metal Box logo on its £524,000,000 headlined sales figure. But this does not work. Most people on whom the cover was tried failed to understand and thought the figure was only £524. It is a fine example of a good idea that was not quite good enough. Second, the drawing round the outside of the report actually represents a till, but again it is

not quite well enough done. If the message on the cover is not immediately apparent it is an unsuccessful cover. A third complaint against the report is its message from the chairman. It does not look easy to read, yet on reading it you find it is bland rather than hard-hitting. As such, it fails to do justice to the rest of the contents.

The next cover goes for the newspaper approach, complete with a compelling headline. Tarmac [Fig. 21] lays the message on the line: "How we fared in a tough year when one in twenty of the UK workforce had no job." Apart from the power of the statement itself and its obvious effect, it sets an unmistakable theme for the rest of the report which then follows logically on. Turn the page and you know exactly what you are going to find. EMI [Fig. 22] does this too, but adopts a different approach. In a way it harks back to telling the employee what the document is about — namely money and people. But it then summarises the salient points on jobs, sales, wages, taxes, exports and the future. This is the only report where even if the employee got no further than the front cover, he would still have got something of management's message. It is almost crude in its bluntness, but it is effective.

And finally, the joker in the pack, produced by Electronic Rentals [Fig. 23]. The holding company is a tree, and each of the roots is a different subsidiary channelling into the whole. It is one of the best graphical illustrations of the strength and interdependence of a group. But again it does not explain what the report is about. It does not arrest the reader and force him to read on — unless it appeals in a whimsical way.

So these are the lessons of cover design:

be imaginative;
be positive;
bear in mind the theme of the report as a whole;
be dramatic and create impact;
keep it simple and uncluttered;
remember to tell the reader what the report is
    about;
don't try to be too clever;
don't lose touch with the rest of the report.

Sales information

Next to the cover, the information most commonly presented by companies concerns sales. Most companies take the turnover for granted, and just try to illustrate how it is divided between wages, fuel and raw materials, etc, to arrive at profit, but a few give specific emphasis to the sales, and where they came from, recognising that judging from reports prepared in collaboration with unions and employee representatives, it is an area of prime employee interest.

The habit of companies merely to give the sales figures without breakdown is perhaps mistaken. However, having said that, one is not too happy either with the way some companies try to illustrate where their sales come from, where perhaps it is better to tabulate the information, or superimpose the figures on a map of the world. Take the effort by Macarthy Pharmaceuticals [Fig. 24]. Each container has a different degree of "fullness" representing a certain level of sales by different divisions in different markets in different years. The information could be of interest but the diagram fails to put it across. Indeed it positively obscures the message. The mistake made is that there is too much competing for the reader's attention and no one fact emerges strongly. It is doubly unfortunate because the information is really very simple and did not need this graphic overkill.

The same is partly true of Gestetner's diagram of the world [Fig. 25]. The idea of linking parts of the world to a block of sales was good. Where it went wrong was trying to talk away those inter-company sales in a casual way which to a sceptical employee might smack of cooking the books. Better to have dropped the chart altogether than to take a chance like that, because the diagram was not so successful that the report would have been severely weakened by its non-appearance.

Perhaps the only justification for taking the trouble to illustrate your sales income is if you want to do it the EMI way [Fig. 26], and push in a bit of management philosophy as well. This diagram is not simply talking about sales volumes. If you look closely at the EMI table, what it is in fact saying is that sales did not result solely from the efforts and skill of the employees, but that there was a vital earlier stage during which the assets for today's manufacture were built up. The customers, satisfied in previous periods, decided to come back for more and the raw material suppliers continued to keep the group stocked up with prompt deliveries. Only when it has made this point, does EMI show where the sales were made, and how much they were worth by value. The sales message here actually benefits from being given a visual treatment.

The lesson which emerges strongly from the last three examples is that it is wrong to over-embellish, and that there is no point in putting something in visual rather than written form just for the sake of it. Visuals should only be used when

they help to clarify the message or make a point which can only inefficiently be expressed in words.

The profit and loss account

One of the main purposes of employee accounts in most companies is to explain to employees the role of profit. How visual techniques can help put this message across is therefore of prime importance. In this section are a series of examples, each of which has made certain basic design mistakes. The idea is that one can see which are the most effective presentations and understand why they are effective. The examples chosen have been selected simply because they illustrate specific points, not because they are the best or worst examples of their kind. With a good visual the message comes across the moment you glance at it. If this does not happen then there is something wrong.

There are several things wrong with the J. Lyons illustration [Fig. 27]. First, it is not apparent what is being measured. The heading refers to receipts and spending. But the diagram is concerned only with spending. The parts of the diagram are poorly labelled, in a typeface which is far too small, so you jump immediately to the wrong conclusion, that the largest block is income and the other blocks are expenditures. You seem to see, at a glance, that income quite dwarfs expenditures, an entirely wrong conclusion. The parts of a diagram must be clearly and succinctly labelled. People are not going to read the small print — if they were then you would not need the diagram in the first place. The second weakness of this diagram is that it does not convey anything. It is drawn to scale to put across the relative sizes of the different proportions of expenditure. But it is not apparent that it is drawn to scale — unlike a pie chart — so it fails on that score. The third weakness is that there is no logical progression from income through expenses to profit so that the page appears as a collection of unrelated blobs. If the eye moves horizontally from left to right, which is logical, it expects the last vertical column to be the residual — the profit. But, on the contrary, it is depreciation. To find the profit figure you have to drop down to the horizontal bars below. But again there is a problem. The figure for profit appears in two different places (again, showing the lack of structure in the diagram), and it is defined differently both times — once as profit before tax, and once as profit from operations. Look, too, at the distribution of profit. Tax is deducted, then dividends. But the residual (which is profit retained in the business) is left hanging in the air as "Leaving us with £2,276,000." "Leaving who with

£2,276,000?'' one might well ask. The diagram is full of loose ends like that. Contribution is another item not defined and the unsophisticated reader would be quite bewildered by it all; by the different figures for profit, by the lack of cohesion in the diagram, by the ambiguity. It is a pity for there is a lot of good information lost on that page.

How could this diagram be improved? First, the amount of information needs to be reduced so that there is less to squeeze in. Second, management should decide what key figure it wants to convey, what figure it wants to implant in the mind of the reader. Then it should work progressively towards it, by rearranging the blocks in a logical form, and relating one to the other. This is not an easy job with these kinds of blocks — so perhaps there is a good case for adopting a different kind of treatment.

Our next example comes again from an EMI report [Fig. 28]. This has been reproduced to make three points. The first is to show that cake diagrams divided horizontally do not convey an impression of the actual size of different items. Perhaps if the labels were directly on the layers it could be clearer. But it is still a misconceived idea — cakes are sliced in wedges, not in layers, so why fly in the face of realism? It is hard to relate the proportion of one layer to the whole, as you can see by looking at the diagram and then checking with the figures. The second criticism is that the page gives two numbers for everything — and the two seem to have no relation to each other. One, of course, is the cash value of sales, tax or whatever, and the other is the proportion it represents in earnings per share terms, but nowhere on the page is that explained. And for that matter even if it was explained, what relevance would these figures have for employees? All the extra columns of figures serve to do is create ambiguity and cause confusion. If a reader does not know which of two figures is the "right one", he will end up believing neither. The third criticism of this page is that it suffers from having three diagrams on the same item. The fact that one cake comes into the foreground creates the illusion of growth and bigness. The big cake relates to the distribution of profits. The two smaller cakes relate to the contributions to profits of different products and different markets. But the impression — and remember it is impressions which are all-important — is that profits are much bigger and more important than sales.

It is an impression which is reinforced by figures given for the percentage increase in profits, most of which look extremely large. The implication of these figures therefore is that the profit itself is unreasonably large — which is unlikely to be the impression it was intended to give. Finally it puts too much information on one page.

So does Molins [Fig. 29]. This chart is simple and has considerable success in putting across the flow of cash into the company and out the other side. Where it fails is in the follow-through — in explaining what happened next. You get the idea that £82 million went in and only £77 million came out. What you don't get a picture of is what happened to the balance. That is the question you ask after seeing the diagram, but the text does not answer this. It digresses instead into a breakdown of the expenditure. By the time you get down to the "balance" of £5.3 million you no longer relate it to the diagram. You are no longer sure if it is talking about the same thing. Diagram and text must complement each other. In this page they tend to pull the reader different ways. Again, there is too much information on the page. Try putting a piece of paper over the two tables — one of sales percentages, the other the breakdown of every pound spent. What is left has far more impact and clarity with the surplus concealed. The final thing about this page is that it does not make its point. The idea presumably was to show how small retained profit was relative to the needs of the business and to the sales volume. But it is not spelled out — the point does not come through. It is clear therefore that one of the tricks in this business is knowing what to leave out so that the main message is not obscured.

The page produced by M.K. Electric [Fig. 30] partially succeeds. But the designer should have chosen one concept and stuck to it — was he going to illustrate the figures diagrammatically, or was he going to use a table? The mixture of diagram and table does not bring more enlightenment — it just dilutes the impact that either treatment would have had on its own. What the designer was trying to do was use the diagram to get attention, and use the tables of figures to supply the facts. But it does not work in practice, because the diagram is too effective. You concentrate on it and ignore the columns of figures. The weakness which then becomes apparent is that the diagram by itself does not properly convey anything because it is not properly explained. Each chart has a £ sign, and it has lines of coins. But the reader who has not seen one of these reports before is not going to realise that the lines of coins added together make up one pound, so all he will get from the diagram is an impression of the relative proportions spent on materials and services, or how much sales income comes from electrical wiring accessories, but it will be no more than a general impression. The answer is to concentrate on doing one thing and doing it well and clearly. The breakdown of every pound earned is a powerful technique. This diagram therefore only needed a bit more effort in that direction and it would have worked.

On then to the successful reports, Norcros, Smiths Industries, Dowty and Ransome Hoffmann Pollard. Each of these is successful visually in a different way. But they all make the same point. You know immediately the page is about money, and you know immediately that it is about how the money is divided up. Yet each uses a different artistic concept to put this across, and a few detailed comments are in order.

Norcros [Fig. 31] wants to show employees how small the surplus is and the reader is led logically from left to right across the page. Then the marginal nature of that surplus is hammered home by a black band running vertically down the page. This adds tremendously to the impact because the reader just glancing at the page and not really reading it still absorbs that the surplus is only a tiny proportion of the total page area. Full marks to Norcros!

Smiths Industries [Fig. 32] achieves the same effect with its carefully constructed pile of money, though perhaps not quite as well. It is only fair to say, however, that the emphasis was more on explaining the breakdown of expenditure rather than on showing how small the profit is. The company has reproduced the relevant page from its official report and accounts alongside the diagram to show that the two are compatible. The danger of this is that it can look messy. but in this case the extract is sufficiently small and low-key for it not to compete. It therefore is successful and in fact serves to offset the strident, almost brash, picture of the money pile. And it has the added advantage that it has established the authenticity of the figures.

Dowty's chart [Fig. 33] is the only one to make the point strongly that income from sales is exactly absorbed by expenses and profits and that there is an unbreakable connection between the two. It ties the two sides of the business together better than the alternative approach of taking the turn-over figure as given and simply dividing it up. The weakness of the Dowty page is not a weakness of the diagram, but only that its labelling leads you to the wrong conclusion. You think the bottom drawer, the trading surplus, is the profit. You have to read the small print to find that there are a whole string of items still to be deducted. Better to have

made the diagram bigger and incorporated the information in the table, because how many people read the small print? But at least the print does answer the question which flows from the diagram — the question of what happens to the surplus. Drawing and text are complementary.

The page from Ransome Hoffmann Pollard [Fig. 34] shows what can be done with "breakdown of £" diagrams provided they are done clearly. The sacrifice management has had to make for this simplicity is the omission of actual sales figures. But they have made the sacrifice in order to get the message across and the result is a fine example of concentrating on one thing and doing it well.

Now to losses. Many managements draw back from telling employees about losses. Indeed there are senior people in industry who maintain that it would be positively unwise to do so. But this is unjust to the employee, for if his company is making losses he surely has a right to know. It has a definite bearing on his prospects and security. One can see the point however of bringing out the first segmental report when the company is making money. If the segment subsequently moves into losses it should not cause too much alarm and despondency. For by then most employees have seen the good times and are aware enough to know that business activity fluctuates, so they can put the losses into context. One can see too from the competitive point of view how companies may be reluctant to reveal divisional losses. But the competitive argument can be overdone, for it is a soggy competitor who needs to rely on your employee report to find out how you are doing. J. Lyons [Fig. 35] illustrates this point in this page from its report where it can be seen on the graph in the middle of the page how it is possible to show segments making losses and still also make the point that within the context of the group as a whole, it does not spell disaster. What is missing in the Lyons case is a detailed follow-up for each of the divisions mentioned.

Avon's explanation of a loss [Fig. 36] is perhaps the best-ever explanation of a loss. The page explains itself but what gives it the impact are the two telling quotes, one from Mr Micawber, the other which is the title to the page: "How a fraction of a penny multiplied 72 million times becomes a £½ million loss." It really makes the point to the employee that every penny counts. It is sad but true that most of us at one time or another will have to try to explain a loss, so the Avon page may well be one of the most widely copied of the examples in this book.

The next illustration is taken from the Nuffield

Nursing Home Trust [Fig. 37] — an unlikely source — and the interest of this is that it has tied together the profit and loss account and the balance sheet so that the reader can see the link between the two. If this is something that a company wants to do then this illustration shows how it can be done. And so we move from profit and loss account to balance sheet with Nuffield providing the bridge.

The balance sheet

There are many who say there is no place for the balance sheet in employee accounts on the grounds that it is difficult to understand and of no direct interest to the employee. One of the most progressive accountants in the country insisted more persuasively that the balance sheet was the only thing the employee should be interested in because this was the statement of risk. If the employee could understand the balance sheet then he could get the answers to all the questions which were uppermost in his mind — like how secure was his job; how well was the company doing; what were its prospects; how long could it keep going in a recession, and so on. So when looking at the illustrations of balance sheets what one was looking for was something which brought out the fundamentals, something which drove to the heart of what the balance sheet was about. Yet there were only two which even came close.

One of them was Grand Metropolitan [Fig. 38]. It made the point first by taking the "What we owe" and "What we own" approach which is how most companies get round the jargon of assets and liabilities, and turning it on its head. Then the main point of the balance sheet came to the fore in the heading for its table which was, "This is our backing". Thus it explained in four words everything that the balance sheet was about. The other skilled touch about the illustration was that it made its point about the balance sheet by not making it balance. It had three sections, "What we own", "What we owe", and the "balance". And it spelled out that Grand Met owned £345 million more than it owed. No balance there! A statement like that means something to the employee. It gives him a measure of his security. It brings home to him the size and power of the group for which he works, even if the accountant goes grey at the liberties taken with presentation. Such liberties are worth taking if they get the message across. This is a very effective piece of communication.

Balance sheets are a measure of strength and most illustrations of the balance sheet do not bring this out, so they fail. Dowty [Fig. 39] comes nearer

than most however, by showing the assets and liabilities as balancing in the pans of scales. It is a literal interpretation of balance but it has strengths which the more conventional diagrams lack. For a start it hammers home the point about the balance. It is obvious immediately that changes in the size of one item will immediately make the system unstable. Thus if stocks shoot upwards the business will be "off balance" and the only way it can be restored to equilibrium is by piling in something on the other side — like bigger bank loans — or cutting back. The diagram brings home to employees that the different parts of the system are all interlinked — and that management's job is to keep the business on an even keel even as the different items in each scale pan rise and fall in size.

Contrast this with the dryness of the Babcock and Wilcox pie chart [Fig. 40]. The best thing about this chart is that it gives half the pie to assets and half to liabilities thereby avoiding the frequent problems of needing two separate cakes — one for assets and one for liabilities, side by side with no link between them. But it is pretty dull stuff.

The Smiths diagram [Fig. 41] has more information than either Dowty or Grand Metropolitan. But volume of information is not enough. The reader sees piles of building blocks but the relevance of the figures does not emerge.

At this point let us bring in Gestetner, and its balance sheet treatment. It is not reproduced here, partly because it relies on colour and partly because it takes the form of a gatefold. But what the finance director tried to do in his 1976 report was relate the opening balance sheet there to the closing balance sheet of 1975. To do this, Gestetner first explained the impact of changing currency rates in dollars, francs, yen, Deutsche Marks and Danish kroner, and then worked these changes through across the gatefold. It took the equivalent of three pages. It was a superb effort. But it was quite unfathomable — even to chartered accountants. So what chance had the employees? It seems the company had not thought through what it was trying to do. It wanted to make it possible for the employees to tie in the opening position in the 1976 report with the closing position in the 1975 report — which is itself quite commendable. But surely this should have been done in words with a brief statement of the effects of currency changes. Restating the balance sheets was not the purpose of the employee report. The purpose was to give a picture of the year's performance, sales and profit — or at least it should have been. So this restatement was an irrelevance which if it could not have been accommodated in a few short lines should have been done away with. Instead, by persisting with the attempt, a major section of the report was given over to a largely unproductive exercise, and the document as a whole was made quite bewildering. I doubt, as a result, whether the other very good pages in the report had anything like the impact they deserved.

And so, finally, to the joker in the balance sheet pack, which comes from the UK subsidiary of Nissen [Fig. 42]. It takes a totally individualistic approach, by first printing the balance sheet, and then writing in explanations of what the different items mean. The strength of this approach is dependent on the skill of the person explaining the items and his ability to capture the essence of an accounting term in a handful of words. This report scores some notable successes there. But it is not an easy thing to do; where it goes wrong is that the employee could read it through to the end, but then will wonder why he bothered, because the point of the exercise is to try to capture the spirit of the balance sheet, and that is where this treatment fails. This actually seems to have dawned on the Nissen author, because at the end of his balance sheet he tried to relate the balance sheet totals to the selling price of the business as if it were up for auction.

So what is the main lesson? It is that the balance sheet does not have opinions, and does not form conclusions. People do that. The person who knows his way round accounts can look at the balance sheet and draw conclusions from the figures presented there. But the figures themselves are dry. So if you are going to use a balance sheet in employee accounts you have to make it positive, you have to turn it round so that the conclusions emerge. The reader is not sophisticated enough to do this for himself. You have to do it for him.

The value added statement

Considering the amount of publicity given to value added statements there are surprisingly few of them in employee reports. However, it is likely that they will become more common because the preoccupation of industry at the moment is with the "division of the cake" rather than with its absolute size. Nothing shows better than a value added statement how the cake is divided. Where most reports fall down is not in the pictorial representation of the value added, but in explaining clearly what value added is in the first place. They therefore tend not to be accepted by employees. The same kind of mistakes we have seen

companies make in the profit and loss account and balance sheet are repeated in value added statements. Comment here is on four specific examples.

First, the statement from H. P. Bulmer [Fig. 43]. It is quite ungimmicky and simply sets out the facts and figures, in this case for a six-month period with the corresponding period of the previous year alongside for comparison. This has clarity. You can see where the value added comes from because the diagram explains that it is turnover less materials. If this is not established at the beginning — and a surprising number of reports don't explain it clearly — then the exercise is a waste of time. The division of something which the employee does not accept or understand is obviously of no interest. So this report has got the first priority right. It makes it clear what it is talking about. And the second strength is the inclusion of overheads. Most employees know that overheads exist, but they look in vain in most value added statements to see any mention of them, as they are sliced up between materials (for fuel etc) and wages. The result, of course, is to make it seem as if employees take most of the added value. Even if they do, there is no need to overkill the point by making them bear the brunt of overheads as well. Such mild dishonesties serve only to undermine the credibility of the document.

The most effective statement visually, once again, is the Smiths Industries division of a pound [Fig. 44], where, apart from their not taking enough space to explain what value added is, it is hard to find fault. Contrast it for example with the Metal Box approach [Fig. 45]. True, the Metal Box page is only one half of a spread, which accounts for the fact that only part of the pie appears across the page. But the information should still have been better presented. The simple test is to cover up the illustration and see how the page looks without it. The result is a clear improvement, which does not say much for the illustration. The mistake is a straightforward one — the eye does not relate the segments of the pie to the amounts listed in the column so that the two parts of the page compete instead of work together to help the reader.

Finally to Tate and Lyle Refineries, a subsidiary of the sugar giant [Fig. 46]. This page does three things — it shows how value added has increased over the year; it shows how the money this year is being spent in different ways and it gives, at a glance, a percentage breakdown of the slice each interest group gets of total value created. So this is the most ambitious treatment of value added information.

The cash flow statement

Cash flow, and the related, though not identical, sources and application of funds statements, come next. Quite a few companies do not try to illustrate cash flow, but simply produce a table showing cash in and cash out. Others rely heavily on the pie chart, with one half the sources of cash and the other half the uses of it. If you are going to do a cash flow diagram, the message once again is to link it into the employee perspective. Cash flowing in and out is unexciting. Cash being used to run the business, or cash being used for investment, is quite different. It is a concept which means something. It smacks of purpose.

A most imaginative explanation of how cash flow worked was from Macarthy Pharmaceuticals. Again it used the balance motif, and showed, at a glance, how additional cash was needed to correct a tilt on the scales one year. Then in the next twelve months period a slice of the borrowing was paid back to correct the tilt the other way.

Another to capture the dynamism of cash movement was Johnson Group Cleaners [Fig. 47], and it went one better than Macarthys in spelling out where the money came from and where it flowed to. It paints a most successful picture of how the company used its cash. And though the information given is virtually identical to the information in the Macarthys statement, it comes more alive.

Against both these the Turner and Newall diagram [Fig. 48] with its building blocks is pretty dull stuff. It looks solid and boring. It *is* solid and boring. The illustration fails to convey the dynamism of cash flowing through a business and being channelled into different ends, and as such, though it is obviously better than nothing, it fails to capture the imagination. It is worth bearing in mind that one purpose of these reports is to convey the flavour and personality of the company. If the company is exciting it should come through in the report. If it is pedestrian then it is uncanny how this will show through too. An important part of what you are trying to do is to capture the imagination of the employee and one of the best ways of doing this is to give him a taste of the pace of business life. If you can do this even in a small way through cash flow statements then you have opened his mind to possibilities and created an awareness which he probably did not have before.

Investment information

It is a short step from talking about cash flow to talking about investment. Indeed, Dowty [Fig. 49] combines the two into one effective diagram — those scales again — which brings home as a written statement never would just how vital ploughed-back profits are for future investments and growth.

It is one of the weaknesses of most illustrations of investment that they do not establish the link between investment and profits strongly enough — even when they adopt the "piles of money" approach like Smiths Industries [Fig. 50]. Smiths' figures seem impressive, but you have nothing to relate them to so you do not really know whether to be impressed or not. Of course, the comparative figures are there in the small print, but that is not strong enough. A further point about the Smiths report is that its definition of investment may not be what the employee thinks of as investment. Research and development for example, and even increased working capital requirements, are not investment in the sense that most people think of it. It does no harm to spell out the facts, but beware of the dangers of being vague.

Employees will also be interested in where the money goes within the company — as Macarthys realised in its page [Fig. 51] which gives just those details with graphics directly related to the company's activity. The weakness of the Macarthys approach is that the figures for investment are not related to the rest of the accounts. So looking at the drops of investment in those bottles you get a distinct impression that there is not much money being spent. Visuals can be very two-edged in that way.

Tate and Lyle [Fig. 52] earns a mention because it was one of the few actually to explain what investment was about whereas most reports which talked about investment forgot to explain why it was a subject worthy of the employee's interest. Once again, knowledge was assumed when it should not have been. Visually, the Tate and Lyle approach has little to recommend it. The content, though good, breaks down the allocation of investment between direct investment and acquisitions.

Conclusions

What lessons can one draw from the examples in this chapter?

The first is that an illustration must have impact. It must dominate a page. An illustration which does not have impact is plain dull. Second, it must be able to stand on its own, tell the story by itself. It must be well constructed and say all you want to say because if it is good it will steal all the reader's attention and leave him unaware of or uninterested in the accompanying text. Third, it should be simple. Always resist the temptation to over-embellish. Fourth, it need not be multi-coloured. Good illustrations work equally well in black and white.

Illustrations are difficult, but more than any-thing else, they can convey the flavour of your report and your company to the reader. If you do get it right then you bring an added dimension to your report — and you will achieve clarity and a level of communication which is quite impossible with words alone.

CHAPTER THIRTEEN

THE FOLLOW-THROUGH

Following the production of an employee report, the final message for everyone connected with it is not to spoil the whole effect by failing to follow it through, thereby not reaping the maximum benefits for your efforts. There are three aspects to the follow-through which will be dealt with in turn — distribution, presentation and research. All are interconnected and the right approach to each can make a big difference to the impact achieved by the report.

Distribution

Remember at all times that you are trying to get the employee to read the report and to absorb its contents. Therefore, you need to give it to him at a time and a place where he is likely to read it. This effectively means that you have two choices which are efficient — to post it to his house, along with a personalised letter explaining what it is, or to give it to him personally, via front line management.

Posting it to the employee's home is the best approach because it reaches him when he has time on his hands and it also partly involves his family so that they too will join in any debate and put pressure on him to read it. Inside the factory, on the other hand, the pressure is frequently on him not to read the "boss's propaganda". Some companies say it is too costly to post the report, but this is difficult reasoning to follow. The postage cost is minimal compared to the weekly wage bill of the average employee, but even that is not the point. It seems absurd not to make every possible effort to get the report read when you have gone to all the trouble of publishing it.

Failing this, the only acceptable alternative is for the front line manager to give the report to the employee and explain what its purpose is. But the weakness of this approach is that the average foreman will be as much in the dark as the average employee and the blind informing the blind is hardly the best way to launch an ambitious communications exercise.

Presentation

Distribution is the thin end of a much bigger wedge. Having generated interest with the mere production of the report the next point is to drive the wedge home by holding meetings of employees and management using the report as the theme for the meeting. There are several basic rules for such meetings. The first is to keep them small — certainly no more than 100 people at a time, and if possible, to hold them in working hours. At these, management makes a presentation loosely based on the report, but providing more localised information and more detailed forecasts and plans. But this should last no more than twenty minutes and after that the session should be thrown open for questions. There is no doubt that the impact of these reports, and the understanding of the employees, is increased out of all measure by this kind of presentation. It really does hammer the message home.

The problem is one of management time and there is no one answer to it. For one thing, it needs a member of senior management to make the presentation to give it credibility, but there are obvious limits on the number of times one man can do this kind of presentation. Cascade meetings are often recommended as the way to overcome this problem. Under this system the top tier of management briefs the tier below, which in turn passes the message on to the one below it so that ultimately it reaches the shopfloor. But the weakness is obviously that the message and its presentation are at their weakest where the need is greatest — where foreman meets the shopfloor. There must therefore be grave doubts that this system is at all effective. There is therefore no short-term solution. In the medium term though, management has to re-align its thinking so that communication is recognised as the vital area it is, and given the priority in the allocation of management time which it deserves. When management begins to take these reports seriously then the employees will begin to do likewise.

Research

Finally, there is the question of research. Most companies push out a report and listen in vain for some indication from the employee as to whether they liked it. And, of course, they hear nothing. But it is a simple matter to devise a questionnaire which will give you an indication of employee response. It may not be statistically perfect but if you test how much of the information in the report has been remembered, what bits were found to be difficult and what additional information has been requested for the future, it will help in the preparation of the following year's report. And most people want and need as much help as they can get.

PART FOUR

SPECIAL PROBLEMS IN EMPLOYEE REPORTING

CHAPTER FOURTEEN

THE PROBLEM OF INFLATION ACCOUNTING

One weakness of simply supplying financial information without any education programme is that it presupposes that the employees trust the management and will therefore believe and accept what they are given. But does this trust really exist? If it does not then it throws a considerable element of doubt on the worth of any "simplified" statements like value added, where wages and raw material costs are generally shown to dwarf profits, and even more where inflation accounting is explained. If the facts that the employee is given are too much at odds with his preconceived ideas he will simply reject the facts. And this is a particularly difficult problem when the facts themselves are, as is the case with finance and accounting, more a matter of opinion. This is particularly relevant when dealing with inflation.

The lack of credibility

It is difficult to explain the eroding effect on company finances caused by inflation because it works in such a mysterious way. Outwardly, it has meant higher profits for many companies, and to show that these higher profits are illusory in real terms means falling back on working capital and other similar concepts which mean little or nothing to the employee. It is debatable really whether inflation has a place in employee reports. Most show already that wages cannot be increased at the expense of profits. Most show, too, that the increased demand for working capital is far in excess of the profit required to meet it. It is hard, however, to imagine a time when employees would temper a wage demand because they felt the company needed greater profits so it could top up its working capital. The business system does not work in such a clear-sighted way.

Most reports attempt to show how the effect of inflation accounting on company finances leads to a major drop in profit. It is inevitable therefore that they be treated with total scepticism and suspicion by employees. It is ironic from the employees' perspective that when, for the first time, managements have begun to provide detailed financial information, they have also come up with ways to manipulate the profit figures.

It has been shown, however, that employees have little difficulty in accepting the logic of replacement cost depreciation, or a last-in first-out stock valuation policy. To them it frequently seems rational and sensible. What they cannot understand is why business should persist with such an irrational historical cost-based system. However, having said that, few creatures are more conservative than the British employee and while he would readily accept replacement cost if it was the traditional and generally accepted way of calculating profit he knows it is not and nothing is going to make him believe that inflation accounting is anything other than a trick.

Some attempts to explain the effects of inflation

The most successful attempts at explaining inflation therefore have been those which simply illustrated how the costs of goods purchased by the company had spiralled, and which showed that the company, just like an individual, had great difficulty making ends meet. Avon did this by making the following six bold statements on a page. They were that in the previous twelve months:

1. The cost of telephone calls made by the Group had increased by 60% and the cost of postage by 45%.
2. The cost of natural rubber bought by the Group had increased by 47%.
3. The cost of stationery had increased by 35%.
4. The cost of chemicals and carbon black had increased by 25%.
5. The cost of fuel oil had increased by 25%.
6. The cost of freight had increased by 12%.

"These basic commodities", the report adds, "now cost an average of 35% more than a year ago. Nothing could demonstrate more clearly the need for increased productivity to enable the company to offset the costs of inflation — let alone achieve growth in real terms." This would seem to be the most effective way of tackling the problem. The company has laid out the facts — and chosen non-controversial ones at that (studiously avoiding the mention of wages) and left it to the employee to draw the obvious conclusion. It showed too what could be done to overcome inflation, thereby putting the responsibility on to the employee. But at the same time, it resisted the temptation to plead poverty — which was a wise decision. As one seasoned trade unionist once remarked, "I have yet to meet a boss who wasn't going broke when it came to the annual wage round."

Grand Metropolitan [Fig. 53] also links inflation to everyday events but takes the argument a stage further by showing how inflation makes investment more costly and therefore threatens the security of everyone in the group. It shows how the cost of various products central to its business — everyday products with which people are familiar, like a bed, or a milk float — have gone up. So the employee will understand and accept the facts of the case and probably also go some way towards accepting why inflation is dangerous — which presumably is the point of the exercise. Contrast the clarity of this approach with the effort made by M.K. Electric [Fig. 54]. It devoted two pages to the topic, the first showing how depreciation was inadequate, the second showing how the cost of stock rose also, year by year. What is interesting about these two pages is that the diagrams actually make the concept harder to follow. We have seen in the Grand Metropolitan example how easy it is to convey the rising price problem. What the M.K. charts show is that it is almost as easy to get carried away and put in too much information, so that the message no longer comes across clearly. This confusion means that the explanation of inflation accounting again lacks credibility.

Continuing this theme was Ransome Hoffmann Pollard [Fig. 55], which told the story of inflation accounting. The strength of this approach is that it treats the employee as an intelligent person capable of understanding the facts clearly presented. The weakness is that it dwells far too long on the techniques and technicalities of inflation accounting and does not press hard enough the reasons why it is of relevance to the employee. Basically, it is too long and fails to spell out as Avon did how the employee can help overcome the problem.

An example of how the specific company problem can be related to the general debate came from Mardon. Here, a specific case of the increased cost of an item of capital equipment was shown graphically and pictorially and this was backed up again by an explanation of inflation accounting. Again, however, even in this very straightforward treatment one is left with the feeling that it assumes too much accounting knowledge, and it is still too remote from the reader. "What if inflation accounting does cut 'profits' from £3 million to £2 million?" one can hear the employee ask. "What difference does it make to me? They have already told me that I can't get a wage increase by squeezing profits, so the fact that inflation cuts profits is of little importance."

In short, it is not inflation accounting which is important, nor is it the effect on profits, it is the effect of inflation on the fabric of the business which matters. This is where diagrams like the Gestetner explanation [Fig. 56] also go wrong. What the company has tried to show is that inflation gradually increases the need for working capital. As a diagram it is not particularly easy to follow but that is not its real failing, which is that, at the end of the period, the company borrows from the bank. The assumption has to be that thereafter life continues as before.

This weakness is shared by the other "working capital approach" from Smiths (not illustrated). The problem is that as the employee will have no idea what working capital is, he is not going to get very disturbed when he is told it has increased. After all, everything else is going up these days too, and the employee has other more pressing things to worry about than working capital. So the Smiths approach, which consisted of a series of piles of money for each year, and further piles representing the increase needed because of inflation, was fairly useless. True, it illustrated the five-year trend of working capital, but what good is that when no one understands what working capital is? (Smiths, incidentally, explained it only as "stocks and debtors, less creditors".)

Working capital is, of course, only one aspect of the inflationary problem. But very few companies mentioned the other major factor — wages. Carpets International (not illustrated here) did. It showed how cost inflation hit the company in three important areas:

people;
fixed assets;
working capital.

For each of the areas it gave specific examples of how prices had risen. It then also admitted that companies put up prices too, and showed how much the selling price of Axminster had gone up over the preceding three years. The figures were quite startling and helped to confirm the company's claim that, though putting up prices was one way to offset inflation, there was a limit to what the public would stand. This is a point companies have to make if they want to win over the employees. Like it or not, most employees think that companies simply pass on rising prices to the purchaser of their own products.

Finally, two quite different approaches. The first, from EMI [Fig. 57], actually gives figures which the shareholder did not get and it shows with remarkable candour how the growth in both sales and profits over the previous three years had been virtually all due to inflation. It is unusual for any company to spell this out to its shareholders. Second, we have the UBM chart [Fig. 58], explaining how the company has failed to keep pace with inflation. In a way one admires the company's courage, for in spelling out this message they make a dismal profit performance look absolutely atrocious. And they fail to lay all the blame at the door of inflation — one is left with a distinct feeling that management has put up a pretty poor performance too — though nowhere is this either acknowledged or hinted at. Employee reports are supposed to be building bridges between shopfloor and management but one doubts if this report did much in that direction.

Conclusions

The first point which emerges is that employees understand inflation as it affects them very well indeed — it means ever-rising prices. If you want to put over the effect it has on a company then it has to be done in this same way, by taking individual items as examples and showing how they have gone up. The second conclusion is that it is a waste of time explaining inflation accounting to employees. Few enough directors and accountants believe in it (or understand it). There is not the remotest chance that employees will accept it. Indeed, all it will serve to do is undermine the value of the information you have already given them and cause them to distrust everything in the accounts. It hardly seems worth taking that chance.

CHAPTER FIFTEEN

DIFFICULTIES FACED BY LARGE COMPANIES

The basic problem

The special problem the big company faces is, of course, its size. The typical industrial group is so large that its units are scattered widely over the country; it makes a diverse and sometimes totally unconnected range of products; its workforce runs into many thousands, few of whom know each other, identify with each other or understand the group; and it frequently has far-flung trading interests overseas. The perspective of senior management surveying the business from the top is therefore quite different from the perspective of the employee. The employee is interested almost exclusively in the detail of what has happened and what will happen in the local unit where he works — though this might be so small in the total group scheme of things as to be not even a separate profit centre.

The problem, therefore, is that the overall group employee report will mean little to the employees. The solution to be discussed here is to produce segmental reports — separate employee reports for each operating unit, to be prepared by local management for the local workforce, within general guidelines laid down by head office to avoid contradictory statements between companies.

The DoT is unhappy at the way in which companies avoid giving the detailed information on divisional performance required by the Companies Act 1967. The United States accounting profession has taken major steps to introduce segmental reporting in US companies, and the UK profession is also trying to put together an accounting standard on the same subject. So it is only a matter of time before companies are forced one way or the other to provide this sort of information. The enlightened approach, surely, is to move before you are kicked, and to steal what credit there is going for making the disclosure voluntarily. It must pay to be positive.

Current approaches to the problem

A big company currently has one of five different approaches to employee reports. First, and simplest, it can produce an employee report based on the annual accounts and distribute it to all employees. Second, it can produce an employee report, but distribute supplementary reports pitched at different grades of management to reflect the different interests of different groups. Third, it can produce an employee report for the group as a whole, and follow this up with presentations by management at plant level where local problems will be raised and discussed. Fourth, it could produce an overall employee report, and supply in addition to this, individual reports for each of its locations, divisions or subsidiaries. Finally, it could ignore the concept of the group altogether and just produce a report for each subsidiary as if it were an individual company.

The group approach

The simplest course is one report, based on the group annual results, and distributed to all employees. It is important to recognise that such an approach means that you are more or less obliged to restate what was in the annual report whether or not you think it is relevant to employees. Once you accept that what you are restating may not be wholly relevant you then have to accept that you are merely making a gesture to the employee, an indication of good faith, but no more than that. What you produce is not going to have sensational results, either in terms of employee relations or in terms of feedback and interest from employees.

Smiths Industries employs 20,000 people round the world, the bulk of whom are in the United Kingdom, and though diversified, it mainly operates in light engineering. The report it produces runs to 12 pages and consists of a value added statement; five year trends for the different segments; a balance sheet breakdown; cash flow statements; the effect of inflation on working capital; statistics on the number, age and distribution of employees; a breakdown of shareholders and the role of institutions; and a worldwide indication of where Smiths operates and where it makes its sales. What emerges from the report, and from talking to the man who compiled it, Bill Mallinson, the managing director, is that the document is not so much a report to employees as a statement of management's philosophy. Mallinson started his employee report by trying to put over one basic message. This was that in business the generation of wealth should come first, and that the distribution of the wealth should come second. He sees no problem at all in persuading employees to accept the need for profit. The difficulty is persuading them how low profits are, and what is a minimum acceptable level. Mallinson accepts that his employee report is only going to scratch the surface, if it does even that. But he regards this effort as one small step in the massive re-educative process which is now needed to try to foster a better business climate.

Smiths, says Mallinson, has 33 operating divisions, all of which are marketing oriented and all of which have their own general manager. He says that almost all the real communication which takes place in the company takes place at plant level. So if the nitty-gritty talking is reserved for plant level the employee report must be confined to a discussion of the information in the report and accounts. The report is straightforward, but even so it made him think clearly about the annual accounts in simple terms and reappraise his own methods of reporting. It helped clarify in his own mind what were the important trends in the business in a way that preparing the annual report never did. Second, the contact with trade unionists following his first report brought home to him the need to supply information on trends. The performance of one year is fairly academic in isolation and the union insistence on trend information helped focus management's ideas on longer term progression. Smiths' employee report is, however, only one small part of the total communications programme. The company has a house journal, indeed it has several. It has consultative committees, briefing groups, works councils — call them what you will — at which much more pertinent financial information will be passed on than will ever see the light of day in a historically based employee report. So what we are talking about here is public relations. We are talking about a one-off annual gesture from the management to the employees in which management simply takes the trouble to tell the employee what sort of year it has had, and how well the firm has done. It won't cut much ice with the employees but it might make them melt a little.

It seems to me, however, that if a company is going to make an effort like this it ought to aim higher than a vague PR gesture. And that to me means that it must provide detailed segmental information — it must provide a separate report for each division or subsidiary. The question is, how much emphasis to give to the group and how much to the individual segment.

In the Tate and Lyle approach, the group position was spelt out quite clearly in its own report. You could not, however, see from the overall report where each division slotted in. Management tends to be more in favour of a group than the rank and file employees are. As a result management thinks that employees should be informed about its advantages and Tate and Lyle in the first year of employee reporting included a long discussion in one segmental report on the benefits of group membership. It was, however, dropped the following year. And it was not picked up by any of the other subsidiaries, which suggests, though it is only surmise, that it was an unsuccessful exercise. For the record, it stressed first the benefit to salesmen round the world of being part of a large group. Then it touched on the problem of financing international trade, the problems of bad debts, and how the bigger you were the easier it was to insure and arrange export credits. Internally too, the group provides finance. The cash-rich companies lend to the cash-starved — the group as a whole provides a shield in lean years.

Elsewhere, GKN talks of head office as banker to the operating companies. Lyons did a similar exercise when it posed the question in its main report — why must we be so big today? It answered thus:

"To survive we must be strong enough to compete with big European and international companies. This is why we had to expand both inside and outside the UK and there are other advantages. It is because we are such a diverse organisation that our more profitable operations can help to tide over any which suffer temporary setbacks and lose money."

But perhaps it is being less than frank. Without wishing to be unkind to Lyons it was a precipitate dash for growth financed with overseas loans which brought the business to its knees in 1976, and to get off the floor it had to sell off a string of assets, so desperate was it to raise cash. Being a member of the group did not really help the employees in those companies which were sold off to pay for mistakes elsewhere.

Far from responding with favour to the concept

of a group the individual employee is likely to respond negatively in three ways:

(a) If his company is doing well he will resent its profits being taken away and pumped into a less successful venture elsewhere.

(b) If he is doing badly, or rather his company is, he will still continually be told by the management that individual companies in the group must be self-sufficient, and should stand on their own two feet.

(c) Thirdly, if he is a member of a group he will look at the group organisation chart, and if it is a company like GKN, the chart is quite vast. Somewhere way down the bottom he may (if he is lucky) find his company. Will his chest swell with pride at being a member of a worldwide organisation? Or will it make him realise just how tiny and insignificant he and his own factory are?

But the main case against promoting the group too heavily is that the advantages are ultimately a matter of opinion, not fact. One of the most stirring advocates of the group concept was later on the wrong end of a takeover bid. It produced the typical defence, stating that there were no benefits to be gained from the increase in size, the extra diversity of products or the pooling of talents. In short, it happily demolished all the arguments in favour of a group, which a few months before it had been selling hard to the employees. It would be a brave man who bet that the employees don't notice such things. They do not help the management's credibility.

A word about the Stock Exchange is perhaps also in order here, because there are so many misconceptions about a company's obligations under the listing agreement. Time and again companies are asked for information by employees, which the management in principle want to give but have drawn back because the information was not available to shareholders. But the point to remember is that the Stock Exchange is worried only about price-sensitive information. What it never wants is for a group of people to be in possession of information and able to deal in the shares, when that information would affect the share price. The Stock Exchange rules should never be used as an excuse for holding back information. The Exchange wants as much information about a company as possible — its only reservation is that this information should be available freely to everybody at the same time. So the fact that certain information had not been made available to shareholders but is made availa-

ble to employees is not necessarily a problem in Stock Exchange eyes — provided the information is not price-sensitive. And the profit figures of one subsidiary out of a hundred are not going to move the share price — particularly as they will probably be on file at Companies House anyway. Indeed at the end of the day very little information is price-sensitive. Company chairmen talk to bankers, brokers, analysts and financial journalists all the time, so why not to the employees? The stock market is very rarely caught on the wrong foot by profit figures. It may overestimate, it may underestimate, but it is rarely hopelessly wrong. And when it is, it is usually because the company got it wrong itself.

The segmental approach

It is the simplest of matters either to include segmental information in the annual report, as will be obligatory in the United States, or produce separate segmental reports. Just how much can be done in this area is shown by Tate and Lyle and GKN. At the time of writing Tate and Lyle has had two attempts at producing local information. In the first year it produced rather glossy tabloid-style news sheets. The news sheets were sent to employees and shareholders at the time of the announcement of the profit figures — that is, well before the annual report came out. It was timed to coincide with the bulk of the press comment and to show all concerned how the company had performed. But as John Lyle wrote, it was also to compensate for the growth and diversity of Tate and Lyle which "can sometimes make the company and its problems difficult to follow". It was, too, a reflection of the greater problems round the world faced by multinationals, and an attempt to foster understanding between shareholder, employee, customer and government. This report was posted to all employees and shareholders the day the results were announced. Then, in addition, a report was prepared for the major manufacturing subsidiary, Tate and Lyle Refineries. This came out a few days after the first report and was intended to follow it up. It had the specific object of explaining Refineries' financial position and how this division related to the group as a whole. A third report went out to employees of A. and W. Smith — a subsidiary with problems peculiar to itself, as the managing director candidly wrote. Then a videotape presentation featuring John Lyle and Saxon Tate, two of the most senior board members, was produced. This explained the financial results for the year and was shown at all the major locations of the company the day following the announcement of the results.

This seems like a major effort. But if anyone has any doubts about how fast progress is in this field, they should compare this with what Tate and Lyle did the next year. The tentativeness of the 1975 report had gone in 1976. The tabloid presentation was abandoned for a conventional report format and the use of colour and diagrams was bold, if not always original. But it was in the proliferation of segmental reports that the group really scored. Where in the first year there had been two, in the second year there were six main divisional reports and on top of these some divisions were broken down still further. Most notably, Tate and Lyle Transport produced additional reports separately for four sub-divisions — distribution, contracts, Silver Roadways and truck services. These were not lavish. In most cases they amounted only to a single sheet of paper. But one sheet of paper which is read is worth a hundred which are disregarded.

Two of these reports are shown [Figs. 59, 60]. The first is from one of the sub-divisions — selected because it is the smallest — and the second is its divisional report. Taking first the sub-division, Tate and Lyle Truck Services, the first thing to note is how small it is in the overall context of Tate and Lyle — sales are only £2.8 million, value added is £367,000. The Tate and Lyle group as a whole that year had value added of £146.1 million and pretax profits of £52.5 million. The content of this report is little more than a letter from the local managing director to his employees. It explains the four main developments of the past twelve months and the redundancies which were necessary, and it gives vague forecasts of better times in the current year. Then it shows the local sales and value created. Incidentally, neither of these terms is explained because they have been dealt with in the main company documents also circulated to employees. The main segmental report was for Tate and Lyle Transport. Though it ran to only two pages it gave a wealth of information, mainly in the value added statement. It broke down the wages bill, the interest costs, the tax charge, the depreciation, and the amount ploughed back — in other words you got the profit of that division. The other segmental reports were in some cases even more forthcoming and in most of them you could work out the profit figure, though it was not always spelt out.

So here we have a company which has given detailed value added statements for several major subsidiaries, though not all of them. Out of Tate and Lyle's total value created of £146.1 million roughly half was separately accounted for. There were no separate reports for segments making losses, though some parts of the empire most certainly must have been, and you also must note that the report was aimed primarily at the UK employees and information about overseas operations was limited. But on balance, Tate and Lyle has supplied detailed information for the bulk of its UK companies. And if Tate and Lyle can do it, why can't everybody else?

Guest Keen Nettlefolds, our next case study and one of the largest engineering companies in Europe, is a pioneer in reporting to its employees. It first produced a simplified version of the annual accounts in 1971 when a Roneo sheet was issued and from the following year onwards a printed version has been prepared and distributed to its 72,000 employees. Cost of this project is currently running at around £15,000 per year. Then late in 1975 the board decided that the group report was inadequate and if communication with employees was to be effective, then all the employees would have to receive additional information about their own companies. As a result, in 1976, as a pilot effort, the first subsidiary company reports were produced and distributed down to foreman level in 30 to 40 companies. Then the following year, based on the 1976 accounts, 125 of GKN's operating units in the UK produced their own reports to employees. Some of these were printed, four-colour and sophisticated. Others, in the smaller units, tended to be cheaper, mainly typewritten and duplicated. It was obviously a major effort and one which was not launched without a degree of heart-searching at the centre, and downright hostility in some of the units. But GKN thought it was worth it, and it had reached the conclusion because it recognised that responsibility for human relations should be the joint concern of management and employee. If both were to accept this responsibility then they had to be given as much information as would be useful to them, to give them a better understanding of the operation of the company and of the group as a whole. It was from there recognised that if employees (including managers) are to make their full contribution to the success of the enterprise then they need to understand much more about what is going on around them. Obviously, the provision of information plays a major part in this.

The GKN ideas recognised that the tide of legislation would increase disclosure anyway. But from the outset it was decided that irrespective of legislation the time had come for employees to be told more. Legal requirements therefore played only a small part in deciding what should go into the package. There is no great mystery in producing a segmental report — it follows exactly the same principles as a normal independent company report with the addition of some group information (probably a family tree) and some checks to make sure that it does not contradict group policy. So what is worth concentrating on in the GKN context is the effort the company put in to educate its employees and managers before it gave them any information. GKN believed that the education had to come first, but in the end it was forced to compromise because education took such a long time and it was vital to get the programme started. This, in fact, accounted for a year's delay in the programme. But the company could still claim that by the time it issued its 125 subsidiary company reports in summer 1977 80% of the company representatives down to foreman level had had some training in understanding company accounts in the previous 18 months. The syllabus for this programme was laid down by head office though the actual training was carried on at company level. The courses covered the elements of balance sheets, profit and loss accounts, cash flow, and its relation to profits, accounting principles, accounting terms, the relationship between subsidiary companies and the group and the impact of inflation on both real profits and working capital.

To get the training programme off the ground the group made sure that senior people were committed to it and would give it their full support — something which in a three tier company like GKN, with head office, sub-groups and operating companies, was no easy matter. The agreement to the programme was secured by running two personnel conferences attended by all the senior management and it then became possible to:

(a) make the issuing of the training syllabus the responsibility of the directors of personnel and finance;
(b) enlist and pay for competent teachers from inside and outside the organisation;
(c) secure through the commitment of the company chairman the corresponding commitment of the line chief executives to the programme.

Developing from this, one senior director in each sub-group (the middle tier) and one director of each subsidiary company was designated "Mr Information" and given the responsibility for organising and ensuring the continuance and development of the programme. These directors were not chosen by any specific process — rather, those who had the facility to explain finance in

simple terms and were interested in the topic tended to choose themselves. The group then launched further conferences to train the trainers in the companies and supply them with data on ticklish problems to come up in discussion. When that was done the programme moved into top gear. At the same time as the education programme was taking place among management the group actively encouraged the setting up of employee councils throughout the subsidiaries. These employee councils were seen as developing in parallel with the written employee reports as a means of disseminating information from the top downwards. GKN already had well developed channels of communication with various trade unions throughout the group but the employee councils were a new departure — and one which, though regarded at first with suspicion by the unions, are now quite well accepted.

The need for the councils arose from the basic management belief that it should be the source of information and that it should communicate direct with employees and not through union channels. The provision of information was seen as a management exercise. Therefore, the infrastructure for the spreading of information had to be developed. They were democratically elected from a cross-section of the entire workforce and were not union-based. But the pace of their development has depended on the state of relations in each of the individual companies. In the best of them the representatives on the employee councils have been sent on outside training courses run by non-GKN people to give them a grounding in the economic facts of life. In the worst, the councils have still to come into existence. The information members of the councils are given varies but the intention once the conditions are right is that the employees should be supplied with monthly reports on how the business is doing. These will then be the focus for discussion in the council.

Nothing is distributed in writing, to assist confidentiality and encourage frankness in the discussion, and the results tend to be discussed in production rather than in financial terms. Trends in volume and sales are talked about and probably some touch on capital expenditure plans. Other firms apart from GKN have found that in written reports long-term plans for a subsidiary cannot be made available in every single case, but most recognise that efforts should be made to inform employees of short-term objectives and targets up to twelve months ahead. Again this raises the problem of security once you divulge plans on investment, credit or anything affecting the general commercial position of the company. But if the employees are to be involved you need to give them meaningful information. The 100 Group says that, for instance, "capital investment both short- and medium-term could be provided on a plant departmental or merely local basis". But they go on to say that such information is best disseminated by means of a local discussion at plant level, echoing the GKN approach, and that the annual report can provide a focus for the meeting — a briefing which is out of the ordinary so it is essential that the manager in the unit brings the workforce up to date and stimulates discussion.

The employee councils along the lines of GKN should, when fully developed, help counter the widespread belief that the employee report — one piece of paper, issued in isolation once a year — is a waste of time. They should help to ensure a continuing dialogue between management and employee and the provision of more regular and more relevant information so that when the annual employee report comes out, it can be put into context.

Overseas subsidiaries

Next, how much attention should be paid to overseas interests, and should overseas representatives get the British documents? Some firms — Allied Breweries for example — translate their UK employee report into Dutch, the home language of their principal overseas interest. Other companies like Metal Box shunt copies of the English-language report to its various outposts round the world. And some, British Oxygen being perhaps the prime example, prepare a special employee-style report aimed solely at their management staff round the world.

Overseas investment, and the worldwide strength of companies, may mean a lot to management, and a fair amount to shareholders, but it is not going to appeal to employees. For the moment, when there is quite enough to be written about and dealt with in the United Kingdom, it is as well therefore for companies to tread carefully — and only trumpet the successes of the overseas companies if they have also had such a splendid year back home that the employees will not mind.

GKN found that by devolving responsibility to the subsidiary, which was purely home-based, the overseas problem solved itself. Some of the overseas companies in Australia are now likely to follow the UK lead, but if they do it will be purely their own internal affair. There has been no central directive from head office to the overseas com-

panies, and indeed given the different legal frameworks and union structures abroad, it would have been singularly unwise to do so. The GKN employee learns about the overseas operations in general terms from the GKN group employee report, but the key document for him is the subsidiary report — which confines itself to local information.

There are three aspects of overseas activities where the employee might be interested — though each is strewn with political hazards. And the usefulness of the information to the employee is doubtful. The first, as we have just seen, is when the British company is investing overseas. Far from responding warmly to this and interpreting it as a sign that the company is expanding globally and is therefore bigger and more secure, the employee is far more likely to react against overseas investment because he sees it as creating jobs and capacity abroad which will ultimately hit exports from the UK — and thereby put his job in jeopardy. Second, there may be interest in the labour conditions overseas — particularly in terms of wage rates and hours worked. This can again cause problems if, say, the wage rates in Germany are far higher than the rates in Britain for roughly the same number of hours worked. There is not much you can do to solve that problem other than include a comparison of the relative productivity of the two workers, and an adjustment for the differences in the cost of living. But once you produce a chart explaining how productivity is higher in Germany you may well be asked why, and it will probably be at least partly because the German worker is better equipped. The third area where you may have trouble is what can loosely be termed involvements with politically sensitive countries and the wage rates paid there: South Africa and Rhodesia, or some of the poorer developing countries. If there is a demand for the information it might as well be shown — these things have a habit of coming out anyway — but it is unlikely that a majority of the employees will be interested.

On another tack GKN also endorses the line taken earlier, that the Stock Exchange repercussions of reports by individual units are not such as to cause any problems. GKN is so large that no one segment's results will influence the whole, and the unit reports come out after the group results have been published, so there is no leakage of information that way. The pressure of its huge overseas interests, which are not covered under this reporting programme, mean that the information will always be, to some degree, incomplete.

GKN comes out against separate reports for different grades of management, partly because, so far, the reports as published have been more helpful to middle management than they have to the employees, and partly because such reports would immediately serve to make worse the us and them attitude which the present reports, to some extent, are hoping to break down. Others take a different line. British Oxygen's 24-page journal *Headway* provides its managers around the world with a forum for the exchange of ideas and experiences. Its special "employee reports edition" attempts to abridge the annual accounts in some respects, and to expand them in others. To do this it reviews the operations of the group on a world-wide basis and goes into some detail about the economic prospects for the following year. It is probably very widely read; certainly, it deserves to be, and it would probably be of interest right through the company.

The role of the group in subsidiary reporting

The case for segmental reporting has been made. It suffices now, in conclusion, to make one or two general observations about the relationship between the group head office and the reporting subsidiary.

Everybody has to accept from the beginning that some of the information supplied will be used to strengthen the arguments of union negotiators — all the more reason, therefore, to bypass union channels and talk direct to employees — and it will also become available to competitors. Secondly, at any one time part of the group will be doing well and another part will be doing badly. So some subsidiaries and their employees will feel they are putting too much into the group and getting little in return. Efforts will have to be made to explain that membership of the group is a long-term exercise.

For both these reasons, however, it makes sense for the head office to control the timing of the subsidiary company reports, and to lay down guidelines for minimum content. There will therefore be some information controlled centrally but in all other respects what goes into the reports should be up to local management — provided always that they retain the commitment to disclose as much as possible. If in doubt, they should put it in.

There is next the problem of deciding at what level to report. Basically, the answer must be to make the reporting unit as small as possible. Remember that the weakness of groups is that they destroy team spirit, frustrate initiative and kill off the sense of identification of the individual with the business. Therefore, you want to make your reporting unit small enough to have a human scale, and to be capable of being understood by the employee. But having said this, it is not really feasible to go smaller than a limited company or its equivalent if the company is divisionalised. Departmental figures can rarely be given without arbitrary cost allocations, so normally the operating unit will have to have its own separate management accounts on which the report can be based. It may, or may not, be on a single site — obviously, if it is, then the task is that much easier. But in other cases, production may flow from one site to another and it is therefore impossible to separate one unit from the other. The other side of the coin is where one site embraces several different units. Here each unit should be encouraged to report separately — again with figures culled from management accounts.

There is one further problem which will arise from the free use of management accounts, and that is that the profit figures so derived may not square with the profit figure in the financial accounts filed at Companies House (and no doubt inspected by the union officials). As a rule of thumb, therefore, the profit figure used should be the "official" one filed at Companies House. This should always be the starting point, even if it does mean extra work reconciling it with the management accounting figure. If, on the other hand, the management accounting profit figure is used, it will probably relate to the trading profit only and therefore take no account of finance costs or tax. In other words, it will be twice as high as the real profit figure — and the employees will probably not appreciate the distinction. So, all in all, this will entail a lot of extra work. But management is about getting people to work for, as well as with, each other. And if segmental reports make that job any easier, then they will be worth all the time spent on their preparation.

There is one other problem in the area of segmental reporting. What information does the head office supply, and what does it leave to the discretion of the local units? The list of topics in Table 7 is not original — it was prepared by one company which was looking at segmental reporting. It is a valuable guide, first in the way that it splits the information into four categories and second in its split between "controlled" and "discretionary" items — even if it could be regarded as ultra-cautious in some areas. The first part of the list deals with items described as discretionary, the provision of which and the form and content of which should be at the discretion of local management. The second part shows those items of financial information and associated matters described as controlled. The definition of controlled items and the timing of their provision should be co-ordinated centrally.

Table 7. *Breakdown of topics for segmental reporting*

SUBJECTS	SUGGESTED CONTENTS, etc
Discretionary items Many of the discretionary items may already be published to employees; in particular, several of those under the headings of "general information" and "personnel matters" will be incorporated in works and staff rules, conditions of employment and induction documents.	
General information Organisational and management structure.	A description of operating unit activities and structure and its relationship with other units within a company or group of companies. A chart showing directors, senior managers and line/functional responsibilities.
Products, important customers and competitors. Major contracts.	End use of products. Markets.
Capacity and demand.	Volume of orders received related to capacity. Arrears, supply position, surplus capacity.
Technical developments.	Internal and external factors affecting the operating unit.
Personnel matters Numbers and categories of employees.	Degree of analysis appropriate to circumstances, e.g. direct employees, indirect employees and staff, or to classification by job description.
Grading structures.	Job evaluation and merit formulae.
Wages and salary policy.	Pay structure, incentives, premium payments, promotion policy.
Trade unions.	Representation, procedure agreements for the settlement of grievances. Redundancy procedures.
Hours worked.	Overtime and short-time related to total hours worked.
Employee turnover, sickness and absenteeism.	Hours lost, comparative figures: % to hours worked. Bar charts or graphs.
Accidents and safety record.	Number of reportable accidents, percentages and comparisons.
Disabled persons.	Numbers of registered disabled persons employed related to total workforce.
Effects of strikes.	Man-hours lost as a result of both internal and external strikes.
Training arrangements.	Apprentice intake and other training schemes.
Personal achievements.	Scholarships, long-service awards, promotion obtained, etc.
Suggestion schemes.	Effects of suggestions adopted.
Financial information Sales.	As a total figure in £ and quantities where appropriate. Main activities and home and export by %. Comparisons with previous years or periods by bar chart or similar diagram and adjusted for inflation.

SUBJECTS	SUGGESTED CONTENTS, etc
Discretionary items	
Financial information (cont'd)	
Order intake.	Relationship to sales in monetary and physical terms.
Cost information.	Major movements of costs in total categorised into headings such as materials, labour, employee-related costs, energy, etc.
Performance statistics.	Output per man, preferably in units other than money.
Capital expenditure.	Major items and total for minor items. Details of significant items.
Prospects and plans	
General international, national and local economic situation and outlook.	Demand, inflation, exports, imports, relevant industry statistics, etc. Changes in market, new products, declining products. Effects of legislation.
Current investment plans.	Explanation in general terms of impending extensions to productive capacity, replacement of existing plant and effects on employment.
Environmental issues.	Noise and pollution problems, etc., requirements of legislation, plans for improvements.
Controlled items	
Financial information	
Cost structure.	Cost structure diagrams should be given but the depth of analysis should be restricted so that cost levels and changes in cost levels for products or narrow product groupings are not made available to competitors.
Assets employed.	Composition of assets employed, e.g. buildings, plant, working capital.
Annual accounts.	As part of operating unit. Annual report to employees. Information equivalent to that contained in statutory accounts.
Flow of funds statement (annual).	Based on audited statement.
Interim accounts.	Profit and loss account in same form as for annual accounts.
Annual accounts adjusted for inflation.	Issue to be deferred until such time as annual accounts are understood.
Pension funds.	Provision of information on pension funds.
Prospects and plans	
Review of business prospects for the operating unit.	Extracts from business plans.
Review of future investment plans including long-term prospects. Intended changes, extensions and contractions in capacity.	Review could include an account of research and development plans (but information useful to competitors would have to be excluded).

One final comment on segmental or unit reporting is perhaps in order. In many ways this is the major test of management's commitment to information disclosure because the key to unit profitability is transfer pricing — the cost at which the product of one unit is sold as the raw material to another unit in the same group. If management wanted to (for employee reports if not for the tax authorities) it could arrange whatever profit figures it wanted by adjusting the transfer prices and thereby the profit margins till it got the desired result. It could do it. But one hopes it would not feel it worthwhile.

CHAPTER SIXTEEN

EMPLOYEE REPORTING IN A SMALL COMPANY

The benefits

In a large company, a company with, say, 27,000 employees, a single employee report will make its impact mainly as a gesture — as an indication that the management does care, and is willing to make an effort. But in a smaller company, one with 1000 employees or less, the employee report can be a significant force for better industrial relations. Among the examples which prove this is Fluidrive — the case study which forms the basis of this chapter. Equally, in small-to-medium companies there are reasons why management might never consider an employee report, nor ever think it is necessary. So, in looking at the case study, it is hoped that most of the reservations held by management in such companies can be overcome.

A case study

Fluidrive is a quoted engineering company with two main factories — one in Isleworth in West London and a more modern factory some 40 miles away in Bracknell. Both units are roughly the same size and the total workforce of 680 employees divides evenly between them. When the present non-executive chairman, David Donne, became involved in the early 1970s, he was disagreeably struck by how poor the labour relations were, given the size of the units. In particular, there was high absenteeism, go-slows, and days lost in general turmoil. A new managing director, Richard Miles, who took up his post in late 1973, brought with him a belief in the need for effective communications, and since the implementation of his communications programme, he claims, there has been a major shift in attitude of the employees. In particular, he claims that employees no longer resist the introduction of new plant. They now accept the need for mobility in the factory and they allow management to move them round — to build up one function and run down another. This willingness to be mobile means management can be much more flexible in how it tackles problems on the factory floor. And in general, says Miles, he

has found that the more employees become interested in the financial condition of the company, even if they do not identify with it, the easier it is to enlist their help in solving the problems.

When asked why he bothered to produce an employee report for the first time Miles said that he very nearly did not. But on reflection he decided that such a document was a necessary part of his overall communications programme. What actually convinced him was the feeling that the employee should receive a document at the same time as the annual report went to shareholders. It was wrong, he felt, that employees should find out how the company was doing at secondhand, through press comment. Miles could, in principle, have overcome this problem by distributing the annual report to shareholders among the employees. Indeed, the report had always been made available. But he took the view that the annual report was not only full of jargon and getting worse with each successive year, but that its relevance to the employee was limited because reports do not say clearly what it is the company is doing. Nor do the legal requirements with which the report has to comply have much bearing on the life and work of the employee.

However, and this is important, Miles did not start straightaway by producing a report. He considered that to jump in at the deep end and to bring out a report "cold" was dissipation of effort, because even simplified accounts would make little impression on the employee who was unprepared for them. The first priority as he saw it was to build an educational base in the workforce. Once this had been established, the employee report would have a chance of being accepted and understood.

What he did, as a first step, was to form a communications group which consisted of himself, the sales manager, works manager, foremen, representatives of the office staff and shop stewards. This met once every two months, and for the first year the input was totally educational. Donne himself took one meeting where he explained the role of the non-executive chairman. Other sessions dealt in turn with the problems the company faced, and talked about inflation, cash flow, prepayments and so on — all matters at the heart of business life, but a total mystery to anyone on the outside. Simply setting up the communications group took months and was a major success in itself. At first the unions would not agree to take part and to allow shop stewards to attend. But in three months of continual talking Miles persuaded them to overcome their objections to sitting at a table with non-unionists — which was the root of their resistance. Initially, they came in for a trial period. But they stayed. If they had not agreed after three, or even six months, Miles claims he would just have had to carry on trying to persuade them, because without union involvement the communications group was a non-starter. It would be failing in its prime purpose before it began.

After twelve months Miles felt there was enough understanding and the beginnings of a rapport between management and employees for the first accounts to be distributed. The minutes of the communications meeting had been circulated round the factory and put on notice boards, so there was a higher degree of understanding among employees at large than there had been in the early days.

When the report was published there was a meeting of the communications group, at which the finance director went through the report with the employee representatives, amplified certain points and gave more information where it was wanted. He also reconciled the employee report with the annual report so that employees accepted that they were being told the same story as the shareholders, and that there was nothing underhand going on. By this time the company had set up a lower tier of communications groups on departmental lines, and each of these departmental committees had a representative on the main group. So the representatives from the central committee passed the message on to their own committees and thus to the shopfloor, or design office. The report itself was distributed by the front line management or foremen to each employee. Each person's copy was personally addressed; Miles thinks that is very important.

He has not implemented any formal monitoring programme, but he does say that he thinks the report has been successful. Most employees have said they thought it was interesting — and perhaps a better guide, none were left around in the factory or hung up on notice boards with rude comments attached. So, all in all, he avoided giving the impression that it was a piece of propaganda.

It all sounds a bit too good to be true. But Miles insists that there were few real difficulties though readily admits to problems in the consultative group where the shop stewards approached the company from such a totally different perspective that it was often difficult for him to put his line across. Even now there are several shop stewards who will never change their attitudes — they are too firmly entrenched. But this does not particularly bother him because, he says, they have got a much better understanding of what is going on in the company, and while they might not like an idea themselves, they are much happier than before to be voted down by their colleagues, and accept rather than resist the resultant decision. But for every traditionalist shop steward, Miles claims, there are two who have really benefited from the course — who now make an active contribution, whereas under previous management policies, they had felt frustrated.

Overcoming resistance was one problem. Another was finding the time and sustaining the interest of the group once it was established. Miles was determined that he, as managing director, should be present at all the consultative group meetings, because it was important that he be personally identified with the project and be seen to be giving it his wholehearted support. His main problem was to keep the momentum of the group going, because having got everyone involved and wanting information it would have been disastrous not to feed this appetite — so he tried to have burning topics on the agenda all the time. One technique was for each of the different interest groups on the committee — the shop steward, the drawing office, the commercial director and so on — to give a talk explaining their role in the company and problems to the others in the group so that each could understand the other's function. Then, at results time, the group dissected what the company was, and where it was going.

Consultative committees operating company-wide have led to a considerable increase in employee participation in decision making. Holiday dates, to take a simple example, are never fixed without consultation and, on a more important level, no item of capital expenditure over £10,000 is passed by the board without first going through the production director's joint committee with his shop stewards. The shop stewards have to look at the proposed expenditure and, in the case of a new machine, they have to sign a statement saying that this is the machine they want. If the shop stewards decline to endorse the selection, then management will think again — if only because there is obviously something wrong. Shop stewards from the relevant departments have also accompanied buyers when they have gone abroad to look at foreign machine tools. This too has been successful, for not only does the steward have first hand experience in doing the job and using the tool, and so can provide good advice, but if he is involved in its selection then he is much more likely to support the management's efforts when the time comes for the tool to be installed. By the same token, not only are stewards consulted about these manning levels, but when employees are to be transferred from one part of the plant to another, they take part in the selection process, deciding who will be moved. They then help to persuade those involved to agree. So, obviously, the company has come a long way in a few years. What is equally to the point, it is now growing really fast and clocking up record profits.

There is a danger in all this that the foreman, the manager in closest contact with the shop stewards, will feel undermined and therefore resent the changes. The Miles approach does not, however, take away the responsibility of a foreman to manage, simply because he has more alert employees working with him. Indeed, Miles claims that any resistance to his approach stems from the fact that it is more difficult to be a participative manager. He believes that those who do not like participation, in general, tend to be those who are unsure of their ability to do the job and take refuge in the maintenance of their authority, mystique and position — rather than in their effectiveness.

The communications background has been dealt with at some length because it is important that employee reports are not seen as an end in themselves but should be recognised as just part, albeit a valuable part, of a company-wide communications programme and integrated into it.

Turning to the report itself, it is not particularly inspiring to look at, but it does have several distinctive features, as Miles points out. First, he says, the report has a theme. If you tell the same thing to the employees year after year they will lose interest. He means by theme that while the report's primary function is to be an explanation of the published accounts, there are parts of those accounts which can usefully be amplified. There is a limit, of course, and Miles is against putting in too much extraneous material because it is all too easy for the message to get fudged. Also, he believes that it is inefficient to try to use the accounts to push management philosophy; if you have something like that to say you should do it by personal

contact through the consultative committees.

The theme of the first report was who owns the shares and why do the institutions invest in Fluidrive. This took up two pages of the eight-page document. The breakdown of shareholdings quantified those held by individuals, by employees (including directors) and by institutions. And on the facing page a three-way diagram illustrated a point that few, if any, employees realise, which is that they, through pension funds and insurance policies, have a major stake in industry.

The following year's report was slightly larger and took as its theme the banks — why they lend money, what they have lent to Fluidrive, why, and how much that will cost the company. Again, it was simple, straightforward and lucid. The remainder of the information in these reports consisted of a guide to where the company made its sales around the world, in cash and percentage terms, a profit and loss account and a chart showing the distribution of every pound of income between wages, raw materials, tax, retentions and dividends. A page was also devoted to explaining where the profit had gone and making the distinction between profits and cash. It also took a stab at showing how working capital requirements increase in times of inflation. Then the final spread was devoted to the balance sheet, pie chart form, with a fairly comprehensive explanation of the terms.

The report was very straightforward. There was no colour, and little illustration, and the text was unpretentious. Perhaps this avoidance of gimmicks is what helped make it successful. Keeping it free from gimmicks also helped keep the cost down. Copies of the report went to shareholders so on a print run of 2000, the total cost was roughly £575, which worked out at 28.75 pence per employee. The amount of time involved in the production of the report, which was done by Miles himself, he estimated at three man-days.

The timing of the report, when it is to be published, is another area where Miles' thoughts are of interest. He was adamant that the report should go out at least no later than the report to shareholders, for the reason stated earlier, that employees should learn at first hand the results of the company. He recognised, however, that most interest is generated at the time of the preliminary statement, which can precede the report by several weeks. Because his employee report is based on the annual accounts it cannot therefore come out any earlier than the annual accounts which means, in turn, that it cannot come out at the time of maximum outside interest in the company. Miles deals with this problem in two ways. First, the preliminary profit figures are released and distributed internally at the same time as the announcement to the Stock Exchange. Second, he arranges for a montage of the press cuttings which result to be photocopied and circulated to all notice boards and departments the morning after the announcement. The combination of these two measures, he feels, bridges the time gap.

There is, as has been mentioned earlier, no specific monitoring procedure to see what employees think of the report, nor to ask whether it is giving them what they want. But there is an intensive briefing based on the document which takes place through the consultative committees, and if individual employees subsequently have queries, which happens most years, then they can, and do, go to the finance director to have their questions answered.

Some companies these days have an annual meeting for the employees. The advantages are that the employees like it — if it takes place during working hours — and respond to the fact that the chairman or managing director has taken the trouble to come and talk to them. Miles does not agree with this approach, however. He says with some justification that the employees see enough of him already. More to the point, he feels that such an approach smacks of force-feeding the employees. To give the employee report the heavy treatment of an annual meeting gives it too much importance in his view. Far better for the report to slip in and be accepted as part of the normal programme of communication. He dislikes the personality cult. He much prefers to keep his communication low-key.

General principles

It is possible therefore to sum up the Fluidrive approach under four headings. First, they place great emphasis on the singleness of purpose of the document. It is there, as Miles explains, on the cover of the report, "to explain the Company's financial report in non-financial terms". Second, the employee report is part, but only part, of the overall communications system. Third, the content of the report is confined to the content of the annual report — as this is the logical approach to be adopted if one accepts the first two points. And, finally, a point we have not touched on so far, these reports must be continuous, they must appear every year. Once you have stimulated your employees to take an interest, then you must make the management commitment to ensure that that interest is fed and indeed further stimulated. The reaction if you let them down, and the frustration

which will result, will be very disruptive otherwise.

Having said all this, however, there is probably a cut-off point below which it is not worth producing an employee report. Small companies, which can be defined as having only one tier of management between board and shopfloor and employing up to 100 people in one location, are probably not going to get much out of it. They are probably private family businesses, and the owner, if he works full-time on the premises, has probably got ideal informal relationships with the employees anyway. He will also probably be quite reluctant to disclose financial information because it will be possible for employees in such a small unit to identify individuals, and, for example, they could put names to salary figures. Furthermore, small companies are much more susceptible to competition, and it is much more important for them to operate on a confidential basis, than it is for the medium and large companies. So the small company might well feel constrained not to give much away. There is also, in really small companies, a shortage of information to be worth communicating. Employees have a much clearer idea what the company makes, and how sales are going, simply because they do not have a large group to cushion them from the swings in the market.

So at what level does it become worthwhile? One obvious stage is where the company has outside shareholders and has to report in a formalised way to them. At that stage the employee report could be considered. A second possible point would be where the lines of management extend so that the board is no longer in direct day-to-day contact with the employees, but has, instead, to work through intermediary management.

The Fluidrive case suggests that it is communication which is the important thing, and the form which that communication takes is secondary. So in a lot of medium-to-small companies, the first priority is to establish a forum for talks. In this way the performance of the company, and the progress it is making and the problems it faces, can be discussed, without necessarily disclosing detailed financial information. This will then provide the education base on which an employee report, when one is considered necessary, can be founded. So in a small company, even when resources are limited, when most people know each other personally, and where there is a shortage of information to be communicated, it is perhaps still worth making the effort. There are few companies where performance could not be improved if the employee can be made to identify more with the business, and the lesson to be remembered is that the report need not be glossy, it need not be expensively designed, and it need not shine a light into all corners of the business. The lesson is that every little helps.

CONCLUSION

We have come a long way since the beginning of this book. We have plotted the different strands in legislation which have come together in the production of the employee report. We have observed and commented on the changes in society which have created a climate in which disclosure of financial information to employees — a most unlikely subject at first sight — has become a live issue.

We have seen that different groups of people have different opinions as to the function and content of the employee report — in particular, the accountant will see it one way, the personnel director another. The TUC puts emphasis on one point, the CBI puts its weight behind something else. But as important as the differences, though often obscured by them, are the similarities in their approaches. The areas of agreement are far greater than the areas of dispute.

This in itself is remarkable. But it does not actually solve many problems. For what can make or break an employee report are the small things — the profit figures which seem inconsistent, an illustration which goes too far and becomes patronising, a genuine effort at explanation which founders on the rock of jargon. Sometimes it seems amazing that anyone should try to put together a package in the first place. And it is even more surprising that so many should succeed.

There is a body of opinion which says that industry in this country will never do anything innovative or reforming unless and until it is forced to by legislation. But there is no legislation in the United Kingdom which says specifically that you should produce an employee report, and even if there were some in the pipeline, it would not appear for years yet. So this voluntary move to disclose information — often at considerable expense and inconvenience to the managements involved — is something of which industry can be justifiably proud. It is also an area in which this country is setting the pace. Other European nations may have more formalised structures for passing on information to employees, but few, apart from Sweden (and it has quite different problems), have made such a major and wide-ranging effort to try to present all the employees with basic financial information.

Many firms are, of course, disappointed with their early results. It is particularly hard, when you have put in considerable time and effort, to feel that your efforts have gone unnoticed, and have caused no visible reaction from the employees. But here at least one can offer some hope, for it appears that even if there is no outward reaction from the workforce, there can be a positively favourable attitude below the surface. This is not just wishful thinking — an increasing number of companies are following up their employee reports with market research aimed at finding out how much of the financial message was absorbed by the employees, and which parts of the report caused difficulty. Interestingly enough, none of the surveys so far have uncovered a hostile reaction from employees. Some, it is true, are sceptical; others are nervous, reflecting the fact that in the past management has only tried to communicate with them when times are bad. But no significant part of any workforce has been alienated by an employee report. Almost without exception employees are prepared to give the management some marks for the effort — whilst perhaps feeling that the exercise was excessively costly. And that, in turn, means that in almost all companies there is a foundation on which employees and management can build a system of genuine communication of financial information.

One is forced to conclude, however, that an effective system of financial communication will involve as many, if not more, changes in management attitudes as on the part of the employees. In many companies line management is as lost with the financial figures as is the man on the shopfloor. In other companies front-line management already feels alienated from its superiors and the sign that the latter are trying to communicate direct with the employee can leave the junior manager disenchanted and isolated. That is a problem which, though dangerous, can be avoided. Harder to change is the feeling that in many cases senior management is paying lip service to an ideal, without really thinking through the implications of a communications programme, and what it needs in order to be made effective. In other words, they recognise a moral obligation to inform all who are interested in finance about the state of the company, but they are not always prepared to build on that new awareness and encourage communication back up the line.

This then ought to be the final thought. Employee reports are just a stage in the evolution of communication and participation programmes in industry. They are worthwhile, but on their own they will not solve many problems. In the long term, if the benefits of greater financial literacy are to pay off throughout British industry management must foster a climate where communication becomes genuine — where both sides talk to each other, instead of the present typical case where one side (the management) talks, and the other side (the employees) listens. For effective communication is like effective conversation — to have meaning and relevance to both parties, both must take part. No-one wants to listen to one person talking all the time, even if they are talking about money.

INDEX